Two Good Dea...

WORKBOOK PRESS
RECOMMENDED
LITERARY BOOK COMPETITION 2020

KEN DEAL & SHIRLEY DEA...

WORKBOOK PRESS LLC
187 E Warm Springs Rd,
Suite B285, Las Vegas, NV 89119, USA

Website: https://workbookpress.com/
Hotline: 1-888-818-4856
Email: admin@workbookpress.com

Ordering Information:
Quantity sales. Special discounts are available on quantity purchases by corporations, associations, and others. For details, contact the publisher at the address above.

ISBN-13:   978-1-954753-61-7 (Paperback Version)
                      978-1-954753-62-4 (Digital Version)

REV. DATE: 17.03.2021

"May 2017 photo of Ken 91, and Shirley 92, last look at the Patuxent river in Solomons, Maryland just prior to driving 7,167 miles in May and June on a 20 state tour of the US to visit family, friends, Lions Clubs and Gideon's and old Veterans."

Dedication

It has been our greatest desire to find some written word, journal, or other documentary summary written by family members on either side of our families. As we grow older, family and friends often ask us many questions about growing up during the great depression and living through World War 11, Korea, Vietnam and the Cold War periods. We decided to start such a record by recounting our lives of two farm kids who grew up thousands of miles apart. Our seventy (70) years together, living in several states and foreign countries, raising a family who has produced grand and great grandchildren has been an interesting adventure. Many who have read our book, only wish that they had the desire to put into words their life experiences. We hope the ease of reading the accounts of our lives, separately and together will stimulate others to put in writing a history for their children, grandchildren and those to follow. It is easier than you think and a great legacy to leave behind.

CONTENTS

SECTION ONE

SECTION TWO

SECTION THREE

SECTION FOUR

Preface

"If the job is ever going to get finished, it has to have a beginning."

—John Newton "JN" Deal, Jr. (July 3, 1877–February 1943)

"If anyone can do the job, Kenneth can."

—Annie Elizabeth Ruble Deal (May 29, 1879–September 1953)

I've heard the above quotations many times, but somehow, today they seem clear and more pronounced than I can ever remember. The last of ten, and now in my late eighties, it occurs to me that if there is to be any history of the Deal family—of which I am a part—it should better begin with Shirley and me. I don't expect it to ever end. As new and fresh information, and yes, even corrections, become available, we hope the record will continue.

Acts 5:38–39 (NRSV) tells us, "If this plan or the undertaking is of human origin, it will fail; but if it is of God, you will not be able to overthrow it." If God did not inspire us, we would never tackle this project. Both Shirley and I are old enough now to see in our children and in our grandchildren and great-grandchildren the many traits that are similar to both of our parents and our grandparents. Perhaps a more detailed description of our lives will assist them to better understand some of their own traits, and this includes nephews and nieces.

It has been our greatest desire to find some written word, journal, or other documentary summary written by or told by or parents or grandparents. In my case, what led their ancestors from Somewhere in Europe to Lancaster County, Pennsylvania; to Augusta County Waynesboro, and Staunton in Shenandoah Valley, Virginia; to Marshall in Saline County, Missouri; and finally to Parker and Lucas in Collin County, Texas. In Shirley's case, we know even less of the Taylor/Dennison background.

We have sequestered ourselves in the mountains of New Mexico in our daughter Linda's mountain house on six and one-third acres in a 1,500-square-foot, two-bedroom, and two-bath home with all the luxuries found in a modern subdivision. We may finish this in another mountain house on similar acreage in the mountains of West Virginia near Berkeley Springs where our son Larry along with his wife, Virginia, his son, Bryan, and a few of his employees built a modern log home. Yes, we are here in the spring of 2015 in this lovely mountain home following the Seventieth Delmardic (Delaware, Maryland, Washington DC, Northern Virginia) Gideons State Convention in Frederick, Maryland.

Final submission will no doubt be at our current home, 11450 Asbury Circle, Unit 217, Solomons, Maryland 20688, a waterfront continuing care facility (AsburySolomons.org.) located at the junction of where the Patuxent River flows into Chesapeake Bay. We moved here from 2688 Amber Way, Grand Junction in Mesa County, Colorado, where we lived from June 1997 until March 2013. We moved to Colorado from the home we had built in 1956 at 10,000 Old Fort Road in Prince George's County, Maryland, on June 1997. Both of us were active in our local Grand Junction, Colorado church, Crossroads United Methodist, with continued ties to our home church, Providence-Fort Washington United Methodist Church, Friendly, Maryland, where we transferred back our membership in April 2013. We are also lifetime members of the Lions Clubs International and Christian Business Men's and Women's Committees and longtime members of Gideons International, Masonic Fraternity, and Freedom House Ministries. We held active roles and leadership positions in each of these community organizations. Shirley is a longtime volunteer with the Veterans Affairs (VA) Hospital, and Ken has been classified by Grit Magazine as eight among the top fifty community volunteers in America.

We will be recording highlights, some photos, and a few memories in the chapters ahead.

1. Each of us will search our memory from our earliest recollections up until our marriage on December 2, 1949, at the Base Chapel, Offutt Air Force Base in Omaha, Nebraska.

2. Shirley will capture events that deal with our lives together to include our children, different places we have lived, some of the good times as well as a few that may have been difficult, and some of the relationships we developed along the way.

3. I will cover the low points and highlights of my careers. This would include the period from being a farm boy in Texas to my time as the custodian while attending Plano High School, Plano, Texas; to my first job after high school followed by a military career in the army, Army Air Force, and United States Air Force, including my second career in real estate from which I retired on December 31, 1990.

We will include only as much genealogy as we know to be reasonably true. My dad, JN, was somewhat of a legendary figure and since I came along late in his life, some data I record will be what I learned and heard from others, not necessarily from him. We sincerely hope the coverage of other family members will in no way be offensive. Please forgive us for what we have left out that you wish we would have included. Deuteronomy 4:9 reminds us; "...Do not let these memories escaped from your mind as long as you live! And be sure to pass them on to your children and grandchildren."(NLT) This book is divided into sections so the reader may be selective.

Section 1 covers Shirley's birth to marriage.
Section 2 covers Shirley's bio, 1949–1997.
Section 3 covers 1997–2013 in Grand Junction, CO.
Section 4 covers Ken's bio from 1926–2015.
Section 5 covers photos.

SECTION ONE

CHAPTER ONE

Shirley's Birth to Marriage

Shirley Lee Taylor was born on October 14, 1925, to Pauline Dennison Taylor and Reginald C. Taylor at Columbia Hospital for Women in Washington DC. After the ten days that mothers and babies were kept in the hospital, I came home to Friendly, Maryland. My dad, Uncle Harold Denyer, and possibly others had built the home down the lane that eventually became known as Oldbury Drive. At that time, it was the only house, and the lane continued past the house and down into the meadow where vegetables were grown. My grandparents William Francis and Sarah Ellen Taylor, lived in the Taylor "home place" at the intersection of Old Fort Road and Allentown Road. My grandfather owned about 350 acres, partly in pasture and partly in truck farming. The home place consisted of the house, barn, cowshed, garage, corn crib, two- seater outhouse, and woodshed.

There was an orchard out back and a well on the side. The house actually faced Allentown Road, but the side kitchen door was the most often used as entrance.

There was a porch across the front of the house. I barely remember my great-grandma, known as Little Grandma, Celestia Taylor. My father had many brothers and sisters—Clara, Percy, Beulah, Bernice, Raleigh, Edith, May, Calvin, and Irma. His sister Alma had died in early teens from appendicitis or pneumonia.

I remember the cook stove in the kitchen and big kitchen table. Grandma made good biscuits and good rice pudding. I am sure she made other good things, but those are the two that I remember most. There was a summer kitchen attached that had a kerosene stove. When the main house was torn down, my dad moved the summer kitchen to his house on Oldbury Drive as a tool shed. My cousin Marian Thomas (Saunders), who was about a year older than me, lived with my grandparents for several years while her mother, Aunt May, worked in DC. Marian was a leader, and I was a follower. One time she and I went to Aunt Aggies's (Roland) which was just down Old Fort Road (across from Ken's and my home at 10,000). We hadn't let anyone know where we were going. When my father found us, he switched us all the way home! When I was even littler, I walked in the woods and by our house. Everyone in the neighborhood searched for me, and it was getting late in the day. My folks were frantic. A man who was cutting wood recognized the dog that was with me and brought me home. My mother said that she was so mad because I danced on the front porch and was not a bit disturbed at being lost.

My cousin Lois Havens Jamison tells of the time she was visiting me. Mother had put us both in a chicken wire enclosure to play. I climbed out and left Lois in there even though she was a few years older. Lois grew up in Hyattsville, Maryland, and didn't know how to climb. Think she learned after that.

My other grandparents, Millard and Emma Dennison, lived on top of a hill in Oxon Hill near the "district line." There was a winding, rough dirt road up to their house. When I was young, the family all came to Grandma's for Sunday dinner. At first, it was the Havens, the McConkeys, and us. Then later, we were joined by Aunt Eunice and her daughter Fay, Uncle Irmon and Aunt Hilda with Jean, and Uncle Millard and Aunt Juanita with Kay. Grandma cooked the best fried chicken and baked sliced sweet potatoes. I remember that she loved corn on the cob, hard rolls, and hot coffee. My grandfather, called Papa by his children and some of us older grandchildren, would thump you on the head if you misbehaved. Uncle Maurice was still living at home, and we grandchildren gave him a hard time, I'm afraid. Once when Lois, Betty, and I were visiting for a week in the summer, Lois said, "Sling me a piece of chicken, Shirley Lee." I picked a piece up and slung it to her, much to the horror of Maurice! We had lots of good times there on Sundays and also when we came for a week's vacation after school was out. My grandmother loved flowers, and she would pick a bunch to give to a visitor. There was a summer kitchen there too, but it was down a little pathway from the house. Next to the summer kitchen was a bois d'arc tree or mock orange. It had nasty thorns on it and milky green orange-sized fruit that you couldn't eat. There was a lawn swing, and we swung many happy hours there. There were several cherry trees. We learned to climb them and ate cherries until we were nearly sick.

My dad was anxious to teach me everything. He wanted to teach me to drive when I was ten, but I was too scared. I was scared to try new things, I guess, because my mother fell from a tree teaching me to climb. The branch she held and the one she was standing on both broke. Fortunately, she wasn't hurt, and I learned to climb. Dad wanted me to know how to shoot the shotgun, and I did learn. I never particularly liked handling a gun.

Halloween was a big thing when I was a kid. My grandmother Taylor always walked with all the kids up Allentown Road, through Old Fort Place, to Old Fort Road. The bigger boys would be ahead somewhere and would try to frighten us all the way. We squealed and laughed all the way. Oh yes, it was black as pitch because there were no street lights, and there were very few homes that would have an inside lamp burning. We had lots of scavenger hunts at Grandma's. On a farm, there were always so many things that could be included on the list. Marian, other neighbor children, and I played tag, hide-and-seek, etc.

I started first grade at Oxon Hill Consolidated School on Livingston Road in Oxon Hill, and I graduated from the same school in 1942. Mr. George Moore was our bus driver most of those years. (Ken's note: She never told me that she was the valedictorian of her class. I found that out at her fiftieth high school reunion.) The bus stop was at Taylor's Store across the home place. My dad was quite a tease. Everyone took a lunch in a paper bag in those days. He liked nothing better than to put a pig's tail (after slaughter-time) into a girl's lunch. I took tap dance lessons after school. That is, I took two lessons, and the teacher committed suicide. I missed quite a few days in my early years because of childhood diseases, colds, and tummy aches. From seventh grade on I had perfect attendance. My grades were above average except for those in Music and Art. I took a Business course in High School and ended up with the highest grades for the four years.

At graduation, I was awarded the Reader's Digest award and a one-year subscription. Somehow, I never thought it was a fair evaluation as the Academic course seemed so much harder. When I entered high school, I was still very shy, and I didn't like to speak in front of the class. I joined a club called Churchill Literary Society. There was Van Dyke Literary Society too, and competitions were held at the end of the year. Whoever was in charge of the weekly programs seemed to realize I needed help in speaking, so I was put on the program quite often. It helped because in later years, I was asked to make many announcements in the assembly and to give speeches in various programs. I was honored to be made a member of the National Honor Society, and I later served as president.

I worked on the school newspaper and yearbook. I wasn't very good at basketball or softball, but I did belong to the school's volleyball team. Our class elected not to have a guest speaker at our graduation ceremony but to select a subject and have several members of the class give a speech. I gave one of the speeches. I was so thrilled to have Grandma Dennison attend my graduation that when I saw her in the audience, I nearly stopped my speech. My dad was in the hospital that night with a cataract operation, so my grandma took his place.

I grew up in the Depression years. Although we didn't have much, I never felt the impact as some folks did. It helped to be living on a farm. My dad tried to sell cars and vacuum cleaners, but he soon returned to the Taylor Store and the farm. In 1936, he built a store in Broad Creek, in addition to the one in Friendly. These were the typical groceries, Hay, Feed, and Grain stores built in each community. Dad joined Nationwide Grocers. I always liked to go with him on Eleventh Street SE, Washington DC, to get the groceries as we often went to the restaurant next door for a hot roast beef sandwiches while the order was being filled. He would go over on Seventh Street NW to buy notions. Usually we would have to double park, and I had to stay in the truck. I was always scared if a policeman would come along. One never did. The Taylors still farmed and took the vegetables into the Farmers' Market in DC. They would pick the produce, wash some of it in the branch by the meadow, load the truck, and leave about 4:00 a.m. to go to the market. The Taylors raised hogs and slaughtered them to sell in the Store. They salted some to be sold later. All my life, there were vegetables and animals being raised on the farm to be sold.

We attended Providence United Methodist Church. The Taylor and Thorne ancestors had helped start the church in the late 1800s. The original church was about a mile further down Old Fort Road. It probably burned down, and then a replacement was built in its present location on Old Fort Road in 1903. There's a cemetery at the old location and one at the present site. My parents and sister are buried there as well as many other relatives.

My sister, Beverly, was born on June 10, 1936, my parents'

twelfth anniversary. She was later diagnosed as having microcephaly, a neurological condition, possibly a birth defect as my mother experienced a long and hard labor. My parents took care of Beverly, and because of their dedication, she lived until 1983. Attached to the store in Broad Creek was a two-story apartment building that my dad also built. He had hopes of living there, but my mother had other ideas. She said that there were no trees and no lawn, and the building was right beside the road. She preferred the house in the woods on Oldbury Drive in Friendly, Maryland.

In 1940, my dad had his first cataract operation at the VA hospital in DC. It was successful, but in those days, the recovery took weeks. He had to have sandbags placed beside his head for days at a time. Because he was declared legally blind, he collected a small amount of money from the Veterans administration. This was important to us at the time because the store was not doing too well. My uncle Calvin Taylor now had the Friendly store. An employee of Dad's had to take over the Broad Creek store, but it was a little over his head. People brought groceries "on the book," and many times monies collected were never credited nor given to Mother. My folks nearly went bankrupt, but Mother persisted until all debts were paid. The business was sold to W. R. and Sadie Davis. When Dad had his second cataract operation, and his sight was restored, he went to work at Ft. Washington, Maryland, as an operator in a water pumping station. He wrote the Veterans administration that he now could work and no longer needed the pension. He worked at Ft. Washington until the facility closed. He then started to raise cattle and pigs. He hauled slop from DC to help feed the pigs. Uncle Raleigh's sons, Ronnie and Buddy, helped when they got older, as well as any other boys he could find when necessary. He always welcomed Thanksgiving—not so much for the holiday but because he could get help when the kids were not in school and any others who were not working.

When Ken and I lived in Maryland from 1956 to 1959, he put Ken to work, helping to build a pigpen. Often, Thanksgiving would be the day to slaughter hogs. My dad went with a friend to the Maryland State Fair in Timonium in a Jeep; and possibly because of the rough ride, he suffered a detached retina. He went into the VA hospital to have it repaired. They did repair it even though a successful retina reattachment after cataract surgery had not been reported before. This time, sandbags were placed beside his head for three weeks. So when the retina detached on the other eye several years later, he would not have the reattachment operation as long as he could see out of one eye.

My dad was a teaser. He would steal the heart of Mother's watermelon, and she'd never catch him. He would tell her a fib just to get a rise out of her. Sometimes, he'd forget to tell her the truth. Even though they were married for fifty years, she never caught on to his teasing. She said that she hoped to live long enough that she didn't have to smell the pigpen. She did. When my dad died in 1974, the pigs were sold. The cattle were kept for several years. It was necessary to sell them when the kids in the subdivision built beside our part of the Taylor property kept cutting the fences to ride their motorbikes in the meadow. After getting out so many times in Underwood's corn field, the cows were hard to catch, so we sold them.

During the years 1917–1925, Mother had worked as secretary in an office that dealt closely with Capitol Hill. In fact, they were involved with Robert LaFollette's presidential bid. She would go to LaFollette's office, ride the Capitol subway, and return to her office. She was always interested in politics, and she always knew why she voted for someone, whether Republican or Democrat. She was proud of her grandchildren when they voted as soon as they were of age.

She had some interesting and sometimes frightening experiences. Her brothers, Irmon and Millard, had to meet her at the end of the streetcar line in Congress Heights. Sometimes she'd work so late, they tired of waiting and walked home, leaving the horse and buggy behind for her. Sometimes she stayed with her aunt Nanny in Northwest Washington. One night A man kept following her, but she managed to get home by crossing the street, crossing the street again, and running part of the way. Another time she was crossing Pennsylvania Avenue when the elastic in her petticoat broke. She just stepped out of it, picked it up and stuffed it under her arm, and kept going. She also got motion sick on the streetcar sometimes. Often she had to get off and take the next car when she felt better. Mother had a remarkable memory. She could recall poems she had memorized in elementary school word for word. It used to upset me when she was helping me memorize a poem that she would know it before I had hardly started. She was a kind and compassionate person, often writing a note of encouragement to others.

My teenage years and early working years were during WWII. My cousin Betty McConkey (Dye), of the same age and same shoe size, used to shoe shop with me sometimes. We would each try on the shoes because we wouldn't buy if they didn't fit both of us. Because of the gas shortage, I rode my bicycle lots of miles. I often went to see my cousin Jean Dennison (Smart). I would ride to Fort Foote to see classmate and second cousin Margaret Thorne (Gates). The requirement was that I get home before dark, and boy, did I ever have to pedal fast to make it before dark. Lilymae Conley (Wilroy) and Beulah Lewey (Wyatt) both lived in Broad Creek near Daddy's store.

Sometimes I would work in the store a while and then go see them. I remember once when I was sweeping the floor (about age ten or eleven), my dad had to teach me how to do it the right way. I fell off Uncle Maurice's pony once; and then later when I was working, I fell off a horse. The riding stable said that it was a gentle horse but neglected to tell me that he was a jumper. When we came to a little ditch, he jumped. I went up, but when

I came down, the horse was not there. Boy, did I hit the ground hard! I couldn't get out of bed for two days. No wonder I admire horses from afar! I was always riding my bike down Friendly Hill, no hands. It could have thrown me just like the horse, but I was fortunate! Sledding was a fun time in the winter. I used to sled down the front pasture in front of our house, but the best place was Roland Lane. I'd get so tired and so cold that I could hardly walk home. I always regretted that I didn't get to sled down Friendly Hill. When Uncle Maurice lived at our house and worked for my dad, he would go over on the hill at night and sled with other teens and young adults. I could see from the front bedroom the bonfire at the top of the hill and wishing I was old enough to sled too. When I was old enough, the traffic on Old Fort Road was too heavy to close down the hill.

I began to work eight days after I graduated—June 13, 1942—at the Adjutant General's School, Fort Washington, Maryland. I worked for the Editorial Division that put out pamphlets to help with administration of the army. Even though I was hired as a clerk stenographer, I did very little shorthand. Many of the officers were accomplished writers, and they used their own hunt-and- peck system. One of my jobs was to fix lunch for Colonel John Kenderdine, the division chief. He wanted Corn Flakes, canned peaches, and hot tea. He never left his desk. Later, I was secretary to the battalion commander of the Student Officers' Battalion. Again, I seldom took shorthand. In August 1944, the Adjutant General's School was moved to Fort Sam Houston in San Antonio, Texas. Major Julian Beakley was the commander of Student Officers' Battalion at that time and was very helpful when I agreed to transfer to Texas.

When I arrived in San Antonio at the train station, I didn't know where I would live. I called a friend who was living in a rooming house near Ft. Sam. The landlady found a bed for me on the screened-in porch. Soon after, I moved into a four-bed room. There were over twenty girls living there, and there were two bathrooms. It was wartime, and we made do. I lived there until the Adjutant General's School moved to Fort Lee, Petersburg, Virginia, in May 1945. The buildings we were occupying were needed by Brooke General Hospital for wards for the wounded. In May 1945, I moved to Petersburg. Mary Vanzant and I shared a room in a tourist home, Blue Heaven. The first room we had was so small that one of us had to get on the bed so the other could go to the one chest of drawers.

The second room was a little bigger but was not exceptional. We had to eat all our meals out. I ate a lot of bacon, lettuce, and tomato sandwiches at the local Peoples Drug store. The buildings that we were so hastily assigned at Ft. Lee were tar paper shacks, so a few months later, we received orders to move to Fort Oglethorpe, Georgia. I contacted Bolling Air Force Base in DC to see whether I could be transferred to that base.

In August 1945, I began working in the personnel section of Continental Air Forces. That headquarters became the Strategic Air Command (SAC). It moved from Bolling Air Force Base to Andrews Air Force Base, Camp Springs, Maryland. I lived at home during that time, and one base was as close as the other. We moved into the pentagon-shaped building on Andrews when it was brand new. I had worked for Colonel Gilbert Erb in the personnel section, and after about a year I moved to the civilian personnel section.

The training section needed someone to teach military correspondence to both civilians and military. Since I had had a ten-hour course on "How to Instruct" when I worked for the army, I got the job. It was at Andrews that I had to instruct every typist in the headquarters on how to use a stencil. Since these type stencils are no longer in use, better take a moment and explain that stencils were used to make copies of orders, pamphlets, etc. A typewriter— maybe that needs an explanation too—contained metal keys which made an impression on a wax-type material known as a stencil. The stencil was then fastened to a circular metal drum, and the ink was fed into the impressions, resulting in copies printed. Copying machines and computers were years away, at least in the military. It seems that someone had typed over a hundred stencils that had dried out to a point they would not reproduce copies in a legible manner which upset the vice commander, Major General Montgomery, so he requested that every person who could type, go to a class and learn how to cut stencils.

SSgt. Virgle Kenneth Deal and his coworkers from the base's finance office could type, although they never cut stencils. So as typists they were required to attend. My class was only an hour long and was scheduled throughout the day. When Ken and his crew arrived a little late, I asked if they could come back to another class. Ken began to partially obey on our first encounter. He and his crew had signed in as having taken the class, so they never came back. Even today, when asked how we met, he embellishes the story and says, "She ran me out of the classroom."

In the fall of 1948, the Strategic Air Command headquarters moved from Andrews AFB, Maryland, to Offutt Air Force Base in Omaha, Nebraska. I decided to transfer with the job, but I couldn't go right away. My dad was to have the retina surgery. I stayed at home and worked temporarily at the local civilian personnel office until he was home.

I left Washington DC by train on January 1, 1949, for Omaha. Again, I arrived in town with no place to live. I contacted Lois Clevan (Turner) from my old office and learned that Kitty Brown (Owen) needed a roommate. Her roommate had gotten married and had moved with her husband. I moved in with Kitty in the Logan Hotel in Omaha. It was a completely furnished apartment with maid service once a week. I had never cooked a full meal, and Kitty taught me a lot. The first apartment had a Murphy bed that closed into the wall; it was quite small. We moved to a larger one which was hard on our budgets. We looked for an apartment in Bellevue, Nebraska, which was nearer to the base. We found a new basement apartment in a new home at 2526 Van Buren Street. Kitty worked for Ken in finance, so Ken took her to look at the apartment. When we moved in, the Bradys were confused. I had started to date Ken when we were in the Logan Hotel, and Kitty was dating Ken's roommate, Delbert Owen, who also worked for Ken. They finally got the two couples straight. Beth and Jack Hargons lived on the next block, and Jack also worked for Ken. Kitty and Delbert got married September 2, 1949. I needed a roommate. So on December 2, 1949, Ken and I married at the base chapel. We lived in the apartment until May 1950. The Bradys treated us like relatives. Our rent was $80 a month for the furnished apartment, including utilities. We visited them several times later as we traveled across the country. It was like a homecoming. The people I worked with in the civilian personnel office were great people. The division chief, Bob Groover, stood in for my dad when I got married.

When Ken received orders for the Philippines in the spring of 1950, I transferred to Andrews Air Force Base, Camp Springs, Maryland, and moved back home with my parents until I could join him. I worked for the base surgeon, Colonel John Norton. I really had to brush up on my shorthand as it had been years since I had taken much dictation. Medical terms were foreign to me. When I wasn't busy, I studied shorthand and the medical dictionary. I survived, but I recall I made a few boo-boos along the way. I resigned from government civil service after nine years in the summer of 1951 when I went to join Ken in the Philippines. Later, I drew out my retirement to help buy a car when we were at McChord Air Force Base, Tacoma, Washington.

I met some very nice people in my working life. Some I have lost contact with, but some I still write or see from time to time. At the Adjutant General's School were Dennie Sue James (Read), who now lives in St. Petersburg, Florida; Corporal Betty McLaughlin (Henson) of the Women's Army Corps, who died after raising three children in Illinois; Betty Crane (Landreville) who died from Lou Gehring's disease; and Kitty Brown, whose husband, Delbert, died suddenly of cancer, leaving her three young boys to raise. She later married a man named Rogers, but unfortunately, we have lost contact. She is probably in Smyrna, Georgia, or thereabouts.

In Section Two, Shirley's Autobiography, 1949 and Counting, readers will find a few slight duplications in the very beginning. Then in Section Three where Ken's autobiography begins, there will be a little repetition also but from the reader's point of view. We tried to put this book together in a manner that permits the reader from each family to pick and choose parts they consider most applicable.

SECTION TWO

CHAPTER TWO

Shirley's Autobiography 1949 and Counting

O ur wedding was on December 2, 1949, at 8:30 p.m. at the base chapel in Offutt Air Force Base, Bellevue, Nebraska. Delbert and Kitty Owen were our attendants. This was appropriate as Kitty had been my roommate, and Delbert had been Ken's roommate. Although none of our relatives were present, the chapel was nearly full with friends and coworkers. The wedding reception for a small group of friends was held at the home of Erma and Paul Brady, our landlords. After the reception, we drove to Hotel Fontanel in Omaha, Nebraska. Don and Ann German, Don and Norma Keller, and Delbert and Kitty Owen followed us and tried to go up in the elevator with us. Ken had the idea to go up an extra floor from our assigned room then quickly walk back down to the sixth floor to fool them. It worked, although we waited for a while to see if they were going to find us.

The next morning we drove to Kansas City for a short honeymoon. We stayed in Kansas and then moved to Missouri. The Christmas lights prevented Ken from seeing a divider as we came off the bridge. We often laughed that we nearly knocked the dividing line out between those two states. Yes, we think about it each time we drive through Kansas City.

Ken moved in with me in the basement apartment at the

home of Paul and Erma Brady at 2526 Van Buren St., Bellevue, Nebraska. After Kitty married Delbert in September, I needed a roommate. So we laughed that Ken felt sorry for me and married me so I didn't have to look for another roommate! Erma and Paul Brady treated us like family—we were fortunate. They had two young sons, Tom and Dick. Tom was in kindergarten, so Dick would be at home when the mailman arrived. He loved to come see what the mailman delivered to us in the packages. One time, he went upstairs to his mother to say, "It's just another wug." Ken was a staff sergeant at the time we were married, but he had a lot of responsibility. He was division chief of military pay, civilian pay, and travel pay and commercial accounts in the base finance office. Delbert Owen was his travel pay chief, Kitty Owen was his officers' pay chief, and Jack Hargons was enlisted military pay chief. Bob Brown, a brand new airman, had just reported in, and Ken put him in the travel section. Bob attended our wedding, and he is the only contact we have with whom we are still in touch sixty years later. You will read more about him and his family in later chapters.

I was a military correspondence instructor and was secretary in the civilian personnel office at Strategic Air Command headquarters, later referred to as SAC. Ken received overseas orders in May 1950. We left Omaha to drive to Texas to see Ken's mother and other relatives. We also saw Ken's sister, Corda Hardaway, mother of Helen Etter and Anne who died later in 1950. I never met her as they lived in Crystal City, Texas. Ken was always sorry that we did not drive there to see her when we came to Texas. She had liver cancer. Then it was on to Maryland to meet my folks and other relatives. As we approached Washington DC, we were faced with the dilemma as to which bridge to take over the Potomac River. We decided on the Lincoln Memorial Bridge, down Pennsylvania Avenue around the Capitol, to Eleventh Street SE where we took the Eleventh Street Bridge across the Anacostia River, Nichols

Avenue to South Capitol Street, and into Southern Maryland. I transferred to Andrews Air Force Base and worked as secretary to the base surgeon. The hospital was very small at that time.

Ken left for the Philippines in early June 1950. We had been told that housing on Clark Air Force Base would be available in about four months. However, the Korean War started two days after Ken arrived at Clark Air Force Base, so all dependent travel was canceled. It was May 1951 when dependent travel was restored and I got orders to travel. Beth Hargons had returned home to Mississippi while Jack was in the Philippines. She received orders for the same ship. She came to Washington DC to drive with me to San Francisco. We left DC in the latter part of April. The first thing that made us chuckle was a sign in Pennsylvania that said, "Hill, 3000 ft." We thought that should have said Mountain.

The trip went very well until we hit some potholes in Ohio that caused a flat tire. We were fortunate that it was noticed as we were in the evening traffic right by a gas station. One night in a motel, I was taking a shower. Every time my elbow hit the tile on the shower stall a tile would fall off. Apparently, the motel hadn't been used much over the winter. Soon the water was seeping under the wall and into the bedroom. Beth and I almost became hysterical. That was the first day! We stopped in Bellevue, Nebraska, to see Kitty, Delbert, and their young son, Jimmy. As we drove through Wyoming, the snow began to fall ever so softly. We didn't get too excited as we didn't expect a blizzard in late April! Little did we know what was in store for us down the road! The night we stayed in Winnemucca, Nevada, we knew what it felt like to be a minority. I think we were the only non-Indians in town.

We left Winnemucca early as we were anticipating our arrival in San Francisco that day. We needed gas in Reno, and we had to wait for the station to open. We were really surprised when we approached Donner Pass to find a sudden heavy snowfall closed the pass. We had to rent chains and wait in a long line to go over the pass after the snow ploughs opened the pass. It was beautiful and sunshiny where we were. My mother had given us tomato juice and crackers to eat, if needed, when crossing Salt Lake Desert. We ate them at Donner Pass! When the pass finally opened, I was so nervous driving as there was some snow on the highway, snow piled high on the sides of the road, and snow covering the fir trees. As soon as we were over, we turned in the chains, getting back our deposit. Then we headed for the first motel. San Francisco would have to wait for the next day!

I forgot to mention, Beth had never driven a stick shift, so I drove the cities and left the open spaces for her. Beth and I made record time coming cross-country. Jack and Ken couldn't believe the mileage we were making when they received the postcards we mailed along the way. This was before the Interstate Highways went into effect. San Francisco was a delight, but it was scary driving straight up and down hills. I truly left my heart there! We turned the car—a 1950 Silver Streak Pontiac—in for shipment to the Philippines and reported to Fort Mason, CA for our passage. We met Ethel Fay Kirby there at Fort Mason. Her husband, Henry, worked in the finance office with Ken and Jack. It was only after meeting in the Philippines that Ken and Henry found they were from the same county (Collin) in Texas.

We embarked on the USS Butner for an eighteen- to twenty-one-day trip which took us to Yokohama, Japan. We were on a troop transport, and troops disembarked there for the war in Korea. It was a sad time because we knew some of the guys would not make it back. On the way to the Philippines, the captain announced that we could see Okinawa on the starboard side. The island looked so small while we went past it that my hope was that we would never be stationed there. Oh, but we were from 1958–61. We met another finance wife, Louisa Miller, whose husband, Harlan, worked with Ken, Jack, and Henry. In addition, we met Kay Isberg whom Beth called Ma as she was a few years older than the rest of us. We have remained friends with all these people.

The husbands met the ship at Manila, and we all rode back in GI (Government Issue) buses to Clark Air Force Base. The Communist Huks were fighting the Philippine Constabulary at that time, so travel to barrios off the main Manila–Baguio Road was prohibited. Fighter planes from Clark flew as our escort for the sixty miles back to the air base. As we passed by homes resting on long stilts made of thatch, Ken would point out that our quarters were much like those so the water could run under the dwelling. When we arrived at Clark and I found that we had a regular house instead of what he described, I was much relieved.

Although we could observe houses, rice fields, animals, and sugarcane fields as we rode by, we couldn't get to know the people. We did have a maid, named Noty, two days a week and a yard boy, named Ansing, once a week. They had to converse in English because they couldn't understand each other's dialect. Tagalog was designated as the official language when we were there to correct the problem of having eighty-seven different dialects. Jack Hargons had a GI driver's license, so he could check out a vehicle to drive up to Baguio where there was a recreation center for service families. The trip up was along Zigzag Road, where you could see up to seven switchbacks. It was quite an experience! We could stop at a local store to purchase soda. The little children always tried to sell us baluts, which were considered a delicacy to the Filipinos. However, a partially rotten egg with an embryo inside did not appeal to the taste or smell of the Americans. It was delightful in Baguio with cool mountain breezes blowing through the fir trees. The Igorot tribe lived in the mountains there and came to town to sell their produce and carvings. The women carried the stuff on their heads.

Kay Isberg's husband, Olan, immediately became Pa. We—the Hargons, Millers, and Kirby's—met often at Isberg's. One time that particularly stands out was Halloween. Louisa was pregnant, and she loaned her maternity dresses to Jack and Ken. Beth and I dressed as GIs. Ma and Pa nearly died laughing when we showed up for trick or treat. At Christmas, Pa also made a tree out of aluminum, and Ma put green crepe paper on it. We shared Christmas dinner. What a joy to have such good friends when away from home. Beth was expecting when it was time to return to the States, so they stayed until Rick was born. Louisa, Harlan, and baby Janet returned on the same ship as we did. Airline tickets were scarce when a large ship docked in San Francisco. Ken and I were in line for the last tickets, but we let the Millers have them instead. We took the train—three nights and two days—to Pontiac, Michigan. We stayed in an old hotel that Abraham Lincoln stayed in. Ken had sent a wire to Delbert and Kitty, so they met us at the train station in Omaha as we had a brief delay there. We had ordered a 1952 Pontiac from the factory at Pontiac, Michigan. After picking it up and making sure to put our check in the mail to the insurance company, we headed toward Warren, Ohio. We spent the night there with Louisa's parents and the Millers.

Then, it was on to Washington DC to see Mother and Daddy. After a short visit, we drove to the Dallas area to see Ken's mother, his brother Jack, and her sisters Leona (Tony) and her husband, Berle Poteete; Bea and her husband, Jake Moore; and Ruth and her husband, Pike Ross. We also went on to Hale Center, Texas to see Ken's sister Edna and her husband, Dennis Chandler. For some reason, Ken's nephew Eugene drove us down to Lubbock, and he drove so fast I could hardly stand it. We left there to go by Denver to see Fay and Henry Kirby at their new duty station, Lowry Air Force Base in Denver, Colorado. Then we had our first glimpse of Ole Faithful at Yellowstone National Park. We drove through Montana and Idaho, and we arrived at Moses Lake Air Force Base in Moses Lake, Washington.

When Ken reported in, he found his unit had been

transferred elsewhere. He was a technical sergeant without an assignment! So we stayed at the El Rancho Motel for about three weeks until he was assigned to McChord Air Force Base, Tacoma, Washington. Our hold baggage from the Philippines was on a rail siding somewhere. It finally caught up with us several weeks later. We reported into McChord and found that no base housing was available for us and a newspaper strike was in effect. Ken stopped in a little store near McChord, and the owner happened to know of a vacant duplex on Olson's chicken ranch. We lived there from July 1952 to March 1956. Grandma and Grandpa Olson treated us like kinfolks, and it was a happy three and a half years. The five-acre chicken ranch was located at 2111 South 116th Street and was used for production of eggs. Ken, being from Texas, found it amusing that five acres was considered a ranch! In addition to fresh eggs, another advantage was the beautiful view of Mt. Rainier from the window of the duplex. Weather in Tacoma was fairly mild with about nine months of mostly drizzly and cloudy days.

The flowers and lawns were beautiful. It was the only place I ever lived in where diapers would dry outside even though the air felt damp. Several times a year the fog would be bad—so bad that Ken knew exactly how many tenths of a mile from the gate to the ranch. Otherwise, he didn't know when to turn off the street into the lane! Yes, we needed diapers as Linda Lee weighed in at five pounds and fifteen ounces on February 19, 1953. She was a good baby, and I considered we were blessed with a no-colicky baby. We soon made new friends—Dick and Betty Houk, Jim and Adeline Ford, Bill and Nell Denney, Sherman and Colleen Bryant, Dick and Carol Smith, Ned and Ruth Huff, Sherrill and Bonnie Martin, etc. The one disadvantage in Tacoma was that summer was short. It was difficult with a young baby to picnic in the beautiful mountains or sightsee as much as we would have liked.

We were anxious to show off our baby to the relatives in

Texas and Maryland. So in September 1953 we drove to Texas where Ken's mother saw Linda for the first and last time. She took Linda in her arms and never even acknowledged that we were there for a long time. She died of liver cancer about two months later in November at the age of seventy-four. We drove on to Maryland so my parents could see their first grandchild. Linda got so excited that we had to take her for a short ride to get her to sleep that first night. We drove back to Tacoma in four and half days—a feat I never want to do again. One reason for the long days was lack of motels in the West. The motel chains had not come into being. We allowed $20 a day for traveling in those days. I recall the first time we had to pay as much as $9.00 for a motel, and gas was about $0.16 a gallon. One day we traveled over seven hundred miles, and when we stopped, we felt like we were still riding! We spent the night with the Bradys, our old landlords in Bellevue, Nebraska. We left early in the morning. I was driving, and we stopped at Grand Island for breakfast. Ken had been sleeping before breakfast, and he began to drive after we left Grand Island. Several miles out, he noticed the sun was coming up and wondered why it was rising from the west when he discovered we were headed back toward Omaha—just one of the times we took the wrong road or made a wrong turn.

We had several picnics on the chicken farm with our friends. We even introduced homemade ice cream to many of them for the first time. We were saddened when Bill and Nell Denny lost their first child and gladdened when they had Debbie a year later. Janet Houk was about two when Sister Brenda was born. Dick and Carol Smith married, and Rick was born before Dick left the air force. Sherman married Colleen, who already had Cathy, about three years old. One time Dick Houk was away, Janet pulled a table over on her fingers. I stayed with Brenda and our Linda while Ken took Betty and Janet to the base hospital and then on to Madigan General Hospital. Janet had red hair, and so did Ken. It was hard convincing the corpsman that Janet wasn't Ken's daughter.

Ken had his first cup of hot tea (Texans drink iced tea) at Dick and Carol's when her English grandmother was visiting. When Debbie Denney was born, she had to have her eyes flushed ever so often day and night. Several of us ladies took turns so Nell and Bill could get some rest.

Our Larry was born August 14, 1955, weighing in at seven pounds and eight ounces. He was a good baby too, but he didn't want to go to bed as early as Linda had. Guess that was my first experience with day and night people. In addition to our air force friends, Edna Kelley, who attended Oxon Hill High School with me, married Chester Kipisz. They lived in Seattle, where their son, Patrick, was born. Linda and Patrick enjoyed playing together. Ken knew his next assignment would be overseas, so when his enlistment expired in March 1956, he took his discharge. We left McChord to fill an opening in the base finance office at Andrews Air Force Base, Maryland, where he reenlisted. We wanted my parents to enjoy their grandchildren for a while.

We decided to have a house built on the Taylor land so if Ken got a remote assignment, we would have some place to live close to my parents. We took all the savings bonds we'd accumulated during World War II and after we got married to have the house built. First, we had to have a well dug as public water was not available in Friendly. Larry and Linda helped break ground for our new home. We lived in a rented home nearby and watched construction carefully. We signed a contract with a local builder and paid $2,000 to him at various stages until the home was completed for a total contract price of $14,950. Since we did not obtain a loan, we never went to settlement. We didn't know anything about settlements at that time. The tax assessor finally came by, and we began paying taxes on that portion of the property. They were $176 per year compared to $4,200 as we write this in 2015.

We moved in on my mother's birthday, October 10, 1956. There were so many incidental expenses connected with owning a home that we literally lived from payday to payday for the first time in our married life. We even had to borrow money from my folks in order to put in our lawn. We all raked and carried rocks to get the ground ready to sow seed. The land had a natural drainage because of the rocky soil. That was an advantage because we also had to put in a septic tank, and the grade permitted us to have a walkout basement at ground level in the back. My first cousin Geneva Skinner and her husband, John, had just moved into a new house in Temple Hills. When we visited, lo and behold, they had the exact floor plan as ours. Since our children were the same age as theirs we spent lots of happy days with them. Ken worked with Art Withers in the finance office, and we became friends with his wife, Beryl, and boys, Alan, Dale, and Gary. Neal Hesselton, a civilian who was the deputy finance officer, and his wife, Elizabeth, also became longtime friends. Years later, we attended their fiftieth anniversary party. Both are now deceased.

Ken joined the Masonic Lodge at Camp Springs, Maryland. My dad was so pleased. Just like my dad, Ken's fifty-year pin was presented to him by the Grand Master of Masons in Colorado dated in 2008.

In the summer of 1958, Ken got orders for assignment to Kadena Air Base, Okinawa. Remember how I hoped never to go to that island? We were expecting to join him in a few months, but available housing was taken by the transfer of a group from Japan. Ken put a year's rent in advance to have a house built, as many Americans did. Every letter from Ken spoke of the problems associated with getting the house finished before our arrival. My first cousin Bob McConkey drove with me to New York City so I could turn in the 1955 Pontiac at the Brooklyn port for shipment to Okinawa. Finally, we left in June from

National Airport in Washington DC. Geneva Skinner and her two children, Jeanne and Tom, drove us over and saw us off. This was my first flight. Linda and Larry enjoyed the flight. We stayed overnight in a hotel in San Francisco before taking the bus the next night to Travis Air Force Base for our flight to Okinawa. We took a streetcar ride to the zoo the next day before going to the bus station. I was frantic about the bus because the early one didn't show up. We had to take the next one that got us there just before flight time. I called base operations at Travis to explain our situation, and I asked them not to give our seats away. Larry experienced an earache when landing in Honolulu, but it soon cleared. Dramamine kept him from air sickness. We also landed at Tachikawa Air Force Base in Tokyo, Japan, where Harlan and Louisa Miller visited with us during our short layover. Louisa had her leg in a cast. I appreciated her effort to come see us!

We were glad to arrive at Kadena early in the morning after a thirty-three-hour flight. Ken met us in an old car he'd bought for $75. Larry couldn't get over seeing the road below and the front tires as we drove along—the bottom was so rusted out! Ken named that 1950 Ford Beetle Bomb as he didn't know if it'd bite him or blow up! We went to the noncommissioned officers (NCO) club for breakfast and then to our house off base at Kadena Circle. We met our neighbors, all air force enlisted men and families. One of these was Allan and Marjorie Dill and their three children, Linda, Steve, and Glenn. Allan and Marj became part of a Pinochle Club to which we belonged. The house at Kadena Circle was beside a wall that separated a graveyard from the housing area. These were unique in that the graves were built like giant turtle shells. The bodies were placed inside at death, and months or years later the family returned to scrape the bones. The bones were then placed in very large jars. There was a huge rock in the ocean just off shore. The kids liked to go to the shore and look for hermit crabs. We had been in that house only a few weeks when base housing became available. We sublet our house and moved on base. Ken was told that our car had not arrived yet, so he had to make the move in Beetle Bomb. You couldn't drive it too fast or the hood would fall off, so it took a while to get moved. Then we learned the Pontiac was in port all the time! We sold Beetle Bomb pronto—no problem, as old cars were in demand.

We were in our North Terrace home by Larry's fourth birthday. We had a little family party. That was the nicest home with a large screened-in porch. Water from typhoons would somehow come in the windows even though the house was considered typhoon-proof. It was never damaged, but Ken and I had to take turns all night several times mopping up water to keep too much from getting on the floor. We "inherited" the maid of the former occupants, and Fusako was a jewel. She lived with her mother in a village not too far but far enough that she rode a bus to the base.

She would stay overnight if we needed a sitter. She helped Larry get ready for kindergarten. More than once, she said, "Boy-san, hurry up, you'll miss bus!"

We also inherited a dog named Joto. He was a nice dog, but a dog in the neighborhood kept jumping on him. Joto could whip him, but I got tired of separating them with the water hose. We gave Joto to someone off base who needed a dog for protection. Joto would search out the corners in every room when he came in the house. Years later, daughter-in-law, Ginger, gave us a robot vacuum cleaner. We noticed that it also searched out the corners, so we called it Joto.

Ken worked in the Base Finance office with several fellows who became good friends over the years. One was Tom Kelly with his wife, Dorothy, and his sons, Michael and Andrew. They later moved to Maryland and lived within a few miles of us. Another fellow one was Jim Valk with his wife, Margaret, children, Jimmy and Cheryl. And another was Vern Archey with his wife, Dot, and his children, Patrick and Nancy. We had lots of good times as families and as couples. We usually had Thanksgiving dinner together. We teased Margaret about picking the turkey bones, and she teased me about wiggling to stir the gravy. She also called me Grandma since I was quite a few years older.

I belonged to the Chapel Guild. One of the projects was inviting Okinawa students from Ryukyu University to visit American homes. We participated in several such visiting days. The students would be brought by bus to the base chapel, and the families would pick them up. We would serve them dinner, and they would become acquainted with our customs and us with theirs. In appreciation, we were invited to the Christian Student Union at the university. We were served sukiyaki which was delicious. In addition to our work with the students, Ken and I visited a missionary family working with Okinawa Christian Missions, and we continued to support their mission effort for a number of years. A notice came out asking for volunteers to teach English pronunciation at Maehara High School. I thought that would be interesting, so I volunteered. I guess they learned to pronounce the Maryland way!

I taught for a year, and it was quite a pleasant experience. The teachers and students treated me quite well. They invited me to their games day and gave me a nice framed plaque when I returned to the States. Life on Okinawa, an eight-mile-wide and sixty-four- mile-long island that I dreaded to go to, was good. The people were friendly. I learned enough Japanese to be able to buy something at the local market, and I neglected to learn the Japanese answer. So I had to go back to English which most of the shop owners could understand fairly well. The weather was pretty nice most of the year except when typhoons came through. I remember distinctly the typhoon eye that appeared directly over Kadena. It was beautiful and sunny.

We were allowed to go to the club to eat dinner and to church but were told to return to our homes at a certain time. The eye passed over, and the other side of the typhoon came through with more wind and water. The island did not seem so small. In fact, we had a thirty-day leave and didn't get to do or see all that we wanted, but it was fun to travel and come home each night.

When time to leave Kadena Air Force Base came, Ken received his requested assignment to the Air Force Accounting and Finance Center in Denver, Colorado. Jim and Margaret Valk, their children, and our maid Sako saw us off. In a way, it was both a glad and a sad occasion because we had made good friends, enjoyed our extracurricular activities, and hated to leave Sako. We had a brief layover in Honolulu. Bill and Nell Denney met us at the terminal, drove us to their house for lunch, and whisked us back just in time for takeoff. We had driven no more than 30 mph on Okinawa for over two years, so going 50 mph seemed like flying! Our plane was on a Constellation four-engine prop, and we made a fuel stop on Wake Island in addition to the one at Hickam Air Base, Hawaii.

We landed at Travis Air Force Base, California, and as was true after each overseas assignment, it was good to be back in the USA. Our 1955 Pontiac was at the port in San Francisco but was delivered to Travis the following morning.

We had shipped the car in advance of our departure to be sure it would be there when we arrived. We stayed overnight in transient quarters. I remember Ken went looking for breakfast to bring to us and came back with hamburgers. That was all he could find! We drove south and east to Needles, California, where we enjoyed the frostiest root beer, and we thought it absolutely divine. We were very hot from the drive through the desert. We saw campers on pickup trucks for the first time as we traveled through California and wondered what they were. Also, car air conditioners were becoming the thing. How hot our car became with the windows open when a car drove by with its windows rolled up! The motel we stayed in had a window air condition unit, but it froze up at about 4:00 a.m. and cut off, so we got up and left early that morning. We stopped to see Ken's sister Edna and Dennis Chandler at Lubbock, Texas. They had recently moved from the farm at Hale Center because Dennis' health was failing from arthritis and from many years of working that irrigated cotton farm. We left there for McKinney and Dallas to see the rest of the relatives and friends. Then, it was on to Maryland to visit my folks and relatives. I brought my dad an Okinawa gourd hat to wear in the field. He thought it funny but saved it as a souvenir. Mother and Daddy were glad to see us, especially Linda (age 8½) and Larry (age 6). It was soon time to hit the road for Denver.

When we arrived in Denver, we went to Henry and Fay Kirby's home in Westminster, Colorado. Henry was stationed at the Air Force Accounting and Finance Center, 3800 York St., Denver, Colorado, the same place Ken had been assigned. We set out looking for housing, and there was hardly anything except broken- down houses. So we looked at new construction and bought a house to be built at 9270 Julian Way in Westminster. Combines were cutting wheat two blocks north. Now in 2015 the number of streets have been extended another hundred or so blocks north. Our home was brick; it had three bedrooms, one bath, a full basement, and one car garage. We obtained a VA loan, no down payment at 4 percent on a $15,900 home with payments of $118 per month.

We stayed in a nearby motel and finally the builder, who was from Texas, let us live in an unfinished and unsold house across the street from our house that was under construction. The builder, Mr. Thompson, was a nice guy. He charged us only for utilities, and he loaned us his truck to move across the street when our house was complete. Ken said that was one of the hardest moves despite the fact he had a borrowed truck! Our subdivision was at the end of a huge wheat field that has long since been developed. We became friends with all the neighbors as we're almost the first family to move into the block. These neighbors were Leonard and Dorothy Olson with Lynn and Denny; Jack and Bobbie Oliver with Tami, Karen, and Jeff; Bob and Helen Reierson with Paul, Dave, Jimmy, Ronnie, and Ann; Bill and Lois Ferguson with Paul, David, Laurie, Wayne, Susan, and Sandi; Guy and Bea Humphrey with Donna, Terri, Glenda, and Tommy; and Bob and Frances Holbrook with Frances, Kathy, and Pat. Our backdoor neighbors were Harold and Betty Brauer with Nancy and David. On Irvin Street across from the Brauers were Warren and Elaine Barnhard with Ted and Debbie. When school started, Larry went to first grade at one school and Linda in third grade at another.

The area had grown so fast that schools had not been built to accommodate the influx of new students. Each year they moved around as space permitted. Larry went to five different schools in five years. Sunset Ridge Elementary was built the last year we were there, so he got to walk to school for the first time. Linda went to Shaw Heights Junior High that year. The area from Denver south for about a hundred miles was known as the Strep Belt. We certainly could attest to that! Larry had strep throat many, many times. He would start with low-grade temp. I would take him to Fitzsimmons Army Hospital, about twenty miles away. The throat culture would show strep, so he had to take penicillin for ten days. That resulted in three or four trips each time he contacted strep. In those days the culture had to be read; if it was positive, there's another trip for the medicine and a final trip to be tested after the medicine had been taken. Linda also had strep a few times but not nearly as often as Larry. We were so careful to prevent it from going to rheumatic fever if he were not treated. Ken remembers that as a kid, he had an untreated illness that went into typhoid fever and could have possibly resulted in his left eye becoming blind due to high fever. We will never know the exact reason, but doctors indicate that is one possibility.

I was den mother for Larry's Cub Scout Den for several years, and I enjoyed it very much. Linda took accordion lessons for a number of years. Ken remembers taking her to a function held for the students, and she won the top honor. He felt sorry for her sitting there while all the awards were being given out to the end, and then it was her turn to receive the top honor. She sang in the children's choir at church and the chorus at school for one or two years. I worked with Sunday school and Vacation Bible School at Westminster United Methodist Church, and I also was active in the United Methodist Women. Ken led one of the adult Sunday school classes and invited his commanding general, Tom Corwin, to be a guest speaker one snowy Sunday morning.

We made many friends at church. Two in particular were Mary Ellen Bradley with Dan, Duane, and Linda; and Jim and Eva Van Arsdale with Kim, Scott, and Duane. The kids on our block were a compatible bunch. Larry and his friends had staged a scare show in our basement, put ketchup and cooked spaghetti on a plate, etc. They charged a small fee, but everyone received free lemonade, courtesy of the mothers. Linda and her friends played games, had slumber parties, and played four square on the driveway. We drove to a ski area the first winter we were there, but we soon decided it was too expensive for a master sergeant's family. So we bought ice skates and went to a local frozen pond. Loved it! (Ken's note: Speak for yourself.)

During the five years Ken was at the Accounting and Finance Center (AFAFC), we made two trips home to Maryland and two to Texas. In 1965, we went from DC to New York to see the World's Fair. We stayed with Bob and Anne Brown and their two sons in New Jersey. We drove through the Holland Tunnel into New York City, parked, and rode the subway to the fair. We stopped one day at the United Nations. (Ken's note: We should have closed it down while we were there.) On the way home to Denver, we stopped by West Point and also Niagara Falls. One of those trips we went through the Black Hills of South Dakota, Wind Cave, and Mt. Rushmore. We went to Texas for Christmas in 1965 in our new Pontiac station wagon. Ken hid a BB gun for Larry in the compartment underneath. He was some kind of surprised at Jake and Bea's when a BB gun showed up! We stopped to visit overnight with Jim and Margaret Valk at Shepherd Air Force Base in Wichita Falls, Texas. On the other trip to Texas, we visited Verne and Dot Archey at Shepherd AFB. One thing about finance personnel in the air force, they keep showing up, and we can renew our friendships. Henry Kirby retired from the air force and civil service; he, Fay, and Billienell moved back to Texas. We visited them in Mesquite, Texas, several times later while in the Dallas area.

Ken was promoted to Chief Master Sergeant on April 1, 1966 (he made Senior Master Sergeant on April 1, 1963). The minimum time in grade from E-8 to E-9 was three years; he made it right on the day. Only 1 percent of the enlisted force can be chief master sergeants, and he was fortunate to be one of only sixteen who were made in 1966. Orders were received for Chateauroux Air Force Base in France. I was pregnant with Vikki, but we all decided we'd like a tour in Europe. We put our house on the market, and it sold immediately. That was surprising because by then there was an overabundance of houses on the market. The hitch was the buyer wanted immediate possession. We had our household goods picked up for shipment to France, and we moved into a furnished apartment. I had to transport the children to and from school until the end of the school year. We left soon afterward for Washington DC. The adult Sunday school class where Ken was the leader gave us a going-away picnic and presented us with several little mementos to remember them, like Colorado dirt, Colorado water, Colorado air, etc. We stopped on the way at Fort Knox, Kentucky, to see Dick and Betty Houk. Dick had taken a warrant officer position with the army. We stayed in the transient quarters at the fort that night. When taps sounded, Larry came right out of bed, stood at attention, and saluted. Before leaving, we went down to the gate at Fort Knox where the gold bars were kept. We were startled when a voice over the speaker system said, "Halt." We were a long ways away from the gate, but he halted immediately.

Soon after we arrived at my parents in Maryland, Ken took the Pontiac station wagon to Bayonne, New Jersey, for shipment to France. After a short visit, we left Friendly, Maryland, on July 5, 1966, in a rented car for McGuire Air Force Base, New Jersey, to fly to Paris. Upon arrival at Orly, Ken was informed that those with school-age children would be assigned elsewhere as Chateauroux was going to be closed along with all other bases in France. While still in the terminal at Orly Ken was told that we would be going to Lakenheath Air Base, England, and a plane was scheduled to leave in about twenty minutes. I took the children to get something to eat after the all-night flight over the Atlantic.

When we returned, the assignment had been changed to Ramstein Air Base in Germany. After the orders were cut, we found the next train to Germany did not leave until the next morning, so we took a taxi to the train station. The driver seemed to speak no English, but he did turn around to me in the backseat as we drove along and said, "OK, lady?" That was a wild ride as we have five bags tied all over the taxi. Cars on the right side have the right away in France. It didn't matter if they were leaving from a parking place or coming through an intersection. It seemed we were always coming to an abrupt stop. When we arrived at the train station, we learned that the next train to Landstuhl, Germany, would get us there in the middle of the night. We elected to go to a hotel close by, have a French meal, and take a train the next morning. Our hotel room was a couple stories above a busy intersection, and we learned that traffic never ceases all night in Paris! Larry and Linda were amused at some of the furnishings in the room, especially in the bathroom, where there were things we had never seen before. The train trip took four or five hours. We were amazed that all the stops were exactly on the minute they were scheduled. The trip and scenery through France and Germany was quite nice.

We piled all our stuff (five bags) into a taxi to go to Ramstein AFB, only to learn on arrival that there were no vacancies in the transient housing. After Ken reported in, we took a taxi back to Landstuhl to a German Gasthaus where arrangements had been made at the base for us to stay. One of the sergeants in the finance office, Paul Krisik, loaned us a car. We lived on the economy for a month until quarters were available. We usually ate breakfast and lunch at the Gasthaus but ate at several different restaurants for dinner. We tried all of them that were in the town of Landstuhl. The employees at the Gasthaus could speak some English, so we managed there. It was amusing to see an employee dash out the back door and over to the market to buy what we had ordered to eat. There were several foosball machines there, and that was new to the kids. Also, the Gasthaus had a TV set that broadcast the soccer games. Many Germans came to have beer and watch the games. Sometimes, they could be quite exuberant long into the night. We enjoyed walking around Landstuhl and getting to know something about the culture. Some of the houses had beautiful flower and vegetable gardens. The streets were so clean. The shopkeepers cleaned the sidewalks daily and washed the windows even when it was raining. Saturday was cleanup day; all streets and sidewalks were swept and washed down. Sunday was dress up and walk day. Everyone who could walk put on nice clothes and walked. Some went to church as the bells began to ring on Saturday evening all over town. We played lots of board games and read lots of books that month when we lived in the Gasthaus. We were still living out of suitcases, so we went to the base to do laundry. Paul and Evelyn Krisik invited us to their apartment on the economy for dinner one night. Paul was a master sergeant in charge of military pay; he worked for Ken who was in charge of military, travel, and civilian pay at the base finance office.

Chief Master Sergeants were entitled to base housing without having to be on the waiting list, so as soon as a set of quarters were vacated, Ken was assigned to the second floor of a twenty-four-unit family apartment house at Ramstein AFB. It was like a third floor because there were so many steps up to the first floor. Ken was immediately made the house commander as he was the ranking member in the unit. Our household goods were delivered but our hold baggage was lost somewhere in the shuffle. Hold baggage was always shipped first so it would be there while we waited for our household goods to arrive. Not this time, as it was somewhere in France anticipating our arrival. This had been canceled, like our car which was also on the way to France. As the Germans unloaded our household goods, there was a real estate sale sign that the packers included when we left Colorado. The Germans stuck it in the ground and tried to sell the big twenty-four-unit building all day. They had a lot of fun doing that. Ken had purchased a case of cold beer and set it out for the workers. He was surprised that they let it set out in the sun until it warmed up before they would drink it. We had shipped everything since furniture was in short supply at Chateauroux. This included a twenty-one-square-foot upright freezer. Those German men carried it up three flights of stairs on their backs. I stood in amazement. Our hold baggage had gone to Spain and then back to Denver to wait further instructions. It was late September before it arrived. I had bought Larry a game for his birthday. So when August 14 came, we had to look for something else at the last minute.

Ken had put in a request that our car be diverted from shipment to LaHarve, France, to Bremerhaven, Germany, but it was already on the way to LaHarve. He had to take a train from Landstuhl to get it. He couldn't read the menu in French, so he just pointed to something. The waiter kept bringing him course after course—he ate almost all the way! On the return trip to Germany, he had a funny experience with a runaway tractor. As he tried to dodge it, the wheels would suddenly turn. He finally got by it. The French take vacations in August, so he found little activity in towns he passed through. Many homes and businesses were boarded up, and sheep and cows were in the streets. He stopped overnight at the base where we were originally scheduled and spent the night in the transient quarters. He even visited the finance office where he would be assigned and met the sergeant who was his sponsor. He had our on-base quarters ready to go, even a limited supply of groceries, all of which had to be removed when we didn't show up.

Vikki Kay was born early on October 1, 1966, weighing in at six pounds and eight ounces. We had left Linda and Larry asleep when Ken took me to the hospital, and they were still asleep when he returned. When they awoke, they couldn't believe they had a baby sister. She was born at the military hospital located in Landstuhl. (This is the same hospital where those wounded from the war in Iraq were sent.) I was thankful to have a German maid who came once a week. Vikki had her days and nights mixed, so I spent lots of time trying to quiet her in the wee hours when everyone was asleep. She straightened out at about three months. We would leave her with Linda and Larry so we could go to the NCO club or see a movie occasionally. The building had a central laundry room in the basement. Each apartment was assigned a time and day to do laundry, and each had a short unassigned period. That's when I would rush down to put the baby clothes in. Linda had joined the Rainbow Girls in Denver, and she was pleased there was a chapter in Kaiserslautern about ten to fifteen miles away. Ken and I joined the Eastern Star there so we could help with the Rainbow Girls. Larry was in the Boy Scouts. I had a time finding a sleeping bag for his overnight stays. I finally bought a colored one in a German store. Larry and his friend Bart enjoyed walking or riding bikes to the old lady's store just off the base. They could get all kinds of goodies—gummy bears, stink bombs, firecrackers, etc. Those were big deals for an eleven-year-old. Bart happened to be the son of the base commander, a brigadier general, and occasionally Bart would get the general's driver to take them places. He thought that was great.

Since we were close to the French border we drove to Verdun. The white crosses in the Cemetery were sobering and reminded Ken and me of the crosses in Punchbowl Crater in Honolulu. We walked among the bunkers on the Maginot Line.

Ken was reassigned to US Air Force (USAFE) located at Lindsay Air Station in Wiesbaden in the summer of 1967. We lived at 23A Washington Strata, an eight-family apartment building— four families to a stairwell. Once again, Ken was the building commander. It was in the city of Wiesbaden, close enough to walk to the Base Exchange. The commissary, school, and chapel were nearby. One of our neighbors was Phil, with his wife, Vera Phillips, and sons, Dan and Brett. Phil and Larry played water tricks on each other from time to time as the Phillipses' apartment was above ours. Phil retired as a master sergeant, and they moved to a farm in Tennessee. We visit them as we travel between Maryland and Texas. Vera, originally from England, is a delight, and on a couple occasions her sister is visiting from England when we stop by. Larry and his friends practiced a rock-and-roll band in the basement, and there were two sets of maid's quarters also in the basement. We were visited by Dot and Vern Archey and the Dorseys stationed in Norway, and we put them in the maid's quarters when they were in Germany.

Linda transferred to the Rainbow chapter that met in downtown Wiesbaden, and Ken and I transferred to the Eastern Star (OES) Chapter 1 in Frankfurt. Linda advanced to be Worthy Advisor, and I was on the OES Advisory Board; Ken became the Rainbow Dad when Linda was Worthy Advisor. The girls engaged in charitable endeavors, such as visiting German hospital wards, bringing them cookies, and singing them American songs. They held fund-raisers such as chili suppers, bake sales, dad weigh-ins, and clothes hanger collections.

We missed our friends at Ramstein. The Krisiks and their family and another family—Don and Vivian Younts with Dave, Dan, Nancy, and Doug—were all back at Ramstein Air Base about seventy-five miles south. Ken was the Division Chief of all the military and civilian pay and travel pay in all of Europe at a time when Europe was the test command for centralized pay. Ken had the background of developing the system while in Denver, so his responsibilities were great and time consuming. However, we took a trip to the Netherlands, Belgium, and Luxemburg the spring after we moved to Wiesbaden. We happened to be in Amsterdam for the Tulip Parade. Our room in a bed and breakfast was up the steepest stairway we'd ever seen. It was almost intimidating to go down—thought we might have to leave Linda there! The owner of the house was very nice, serving us a delicious continental breakfast the next morning. In addition to the parade, we rode a streetcar to the Rembrandt Museum to see the famous paintings. We saw fields of beautiful tulips and hundreds of bicycles on the street. We drifted over the Belgium border to see General Patton's statue and grave site and had dinner in Luxemburg. Linda and Larry were fascinated watching a couple eat artichokes. The pile of discarded leaves was immense. We seldom have artichokes that we don't recall the event. While we were in Wiesbaden for two years, we had several visitors. As mentioned earlier, Dot and Verne Archey and the Dorseys came from Norway a couple of times. Jim and Margaret Valk were stationed in England, and they stopped by on their way to Bavaria in southern Germany. Captain Kathleen Wilkowskie who had been in the finance office at Ramstein and now in USAFE headquarters brought her mother, Norma, by to meet us. It was always good to see old friends and make new ones.

We visited Garmisch and stayed at the American Military Hotel when Vikki was little. We thoroughly enjoyed the scenery and Hotel Linderhof. Then, when Vikki was a little older, we went to Berchesgarten. She was so fussy that it was almost a disaster. Thought afterward that she must have had a type of car sickness that just made her hyper. We did manage to go down (slide) the Salt Mines. The road to Hitler's Eagle's Nest was closed. As we were driving home and were near Nuremburg, we heard on the radio that the Russians were marching into Czechoslovakia. We realized why we were stationed in Germany, and we were glad to leave the area and get back to Wiesbaden.

We decided to try traveling without Vikki. So Linda and I took a tour to London on a four-day Thanksgiving weekend. Colonel Coon's wife, Gerry, and daughter Norma went on the same trip. Norma was in Rainbow Girls with Linda. It was so foggy in Frankfurt, the airplane from London could not land. We were taken by bus to Bonn to catch the flight. We were late arriving in London, but we only slept a few hours. We didn't want to miss anything! We were at the Regent Hotel at Piccadilly Circus, a main subway stop.

We could go all over London. In addition, we took a tour to the countryside to see Shakespeare Theatre and Anne Hathaway's cottage. We stopped at Banbury Cross for tea and crumpets. The fog was heavy the whole weekend, but we enjoyed England just the same. On Thanksgiving, we ate a Wimpy's hamburger in London. Ken and Larry took a tour to the Italian Riviera and Monaco. Then, they accompanied Linda and the Rainbow Girls to Berlin to see the Wall. That was quiet an experience because the train stopped at stations in Russian held area of Germany. There were Russian soldiers on guard. Seeing the Wall had a lasting effect on everyone. Larry was the only boy on the trip, and he was a big hit with all those Rainbow Girls. We took many day trips to see the many castles dotting the German countryside. After a few trips, Larry said that when you had seen one, you had seen them all, so he stopped going. I loved driving beside the Rhine River, seeing the tugboats with their barges loaded with goods, and seeing the castles and vineyards. In the city of Trier, we saw aqueducts that the Romans built when that area was part of the Roman Empire.

It was amazing to realize castles, aqueducts, Roman baths, etc., had been there so many hundreds of years. We became friends with one of the secretaries in Ken's office—Ann Wust, with her husband, Gerhard, and son, Martin, who was born just before we left Germany. Anne spoke excellent English, and they were going to teach Martin to be bilingual. We had the pleasure of having them visit us in Maryland during one of their trips to the US to show Martin some history of the Civil War that he was interested in seeing. He was a history buff.

While we were in Germany, my dad fell off a ladder, hit his head on a tree root, and cracked his back. Although he recovered eventually, his mind never seemed as clear. I flew home on emergency once because the doctors thought he was dying. So when it was time to come to the States, Ken requested the Washington DC area. He was assigned to the Air Force Data Systems Design Center in Suitland, Maryland, near Andrews AFB. We vacated our quarters and stayed at a hotel one night before leaving Wiesbaden. The next day we drove to Bremerhaven, turned in our 1965 Pontiac station wagon to go on the same ship, and spent the night in transient quarters.

On July 26, we boarded SS United States for the trip home. This was a luxury liner on its next-to-last trip on the ocean. We had several courses at dinner. Vikki, not quite three, ate all the rolls or crackers before the food came. She was finished. We each took turns taking her outside on the deck. Seas were calm the first couple of days, but it got a little rough when we were about mid-Atlantic. Vikki got a little seasick, and I did too. It was good to see the Statue of Liberty as we sailed in to New York on August 1, 1969. We went through customs, rented a car, and drove straight to Bolling Air Base, DC, where our sponsor had reserved transient quarters for us. Ken and Larry went to McDonald's for the first time in three years and brought dinner home for us. Vikki said, "Will whobody tell me which bed is mine!" We still tease Vikki about the term whobody that she used when she didn't know who did something or who hid her toys. We all gave a big sigh and thanks when we went to bed that night back in the good ole USA.

On to Friendly the next morning to see Grandma and Grandpa Taylor who also gave out a big sigh and saw their newest grandbaby for the first time. Then, it was time to check out our house on Old Fort Road. It had been rented for ten years while we were in Okinawa, Denver, and Germany. The folks looked good, and my sister Beverly was the same.

We went to our house which would be home for the next twenty- nine years until our move to Grand Junction, Colorado, in June of 1997. We had given notice to the tenants who moved out a couple months prior to our return. My dad had boarded up the windows, etc., to avoid break-ins which were occurring in the area as a result of the Watts burning in Washington DC. Things were not the same as when I left with the kids to go to Okinawa back in 1959. Because we were staying in transient quarters at Bolling AFB, we thought it best to keep the boards on the house until we were ready to move in. Larry and Linda were a big help in getting the house ready. When our household goods arrived, we were ready to move in. Geneva with Jeanne and Tom came over and helped unpack boxes, wash dishes, etc. It was good to be home again!

Linda was sixteen and a half years old. She found that the high school in which our area was assigned was Oxon Hill High School. This had been the same as the one I graduated from in 1942 but was now in a new building. The worst part about her going to OHHS was the fact that the young people she came in contact with at church went to Surrattsville High School in Clinton, Maryland. She did make a few friends at OHHS as she finished her senior year after attending there for only one year. She took driver's education, and by the following summer she was working at Murphy's Dime Store in Oxon Hill, Maryland. Larry was fourteen; he went to the new junior high school, Lord Baltimore, not far away. The next year, he went to the new Friendly High School about half mile from home. Friendly didn't have a graduating class that first year, so Linda stayed at Oxon Hill High. She worked part time at Murphy's during hwe senior year.

Vikki Kay was four, and she attended play school at Oxon Hill High School the same year when Linda was a senior. My grandfather Dennison, Papa, was ill; he was first in the hospital and then in a nursing home. I would drop Vikki off at play school, drive to see him, and rush back to pick her up. Papa died the following spring (1971).

Ken was at the Data Systems Design Center in Suitland, but AFDSDC moved to the new Forrestal Building at 1000 Independence Avenue, Washington DC. They were going to move again to Maxwell AFB in Montgomery, Alabama, so Ken decided to retire rather than make another move as my parents really needed us now more than ever. He did so on September 1, 1970. The ceremony took place in the commander's office with a beautiful view of the Washington Monument. Ken had only been with the Air Force's headquarters for designing and testing all new computer applications a year. As the ranking NCO there, he apparently did some great things; maybe he will mention them in his bio later in this book because he walked away with all the top awards that outfit had to offer.

Ken applied for a job with the Department of Agriculture and thought he was going to get it as they really wanted him for a job in which he was highly skilled. The problem was he did not have enough formal education in computers to satisfy their criteria. Then a freeze on hiring in government service came about, preventing any of his other applications being considered.

Chief Master Sergeant Jack Hargons appeared on the scene to take Ken's job at the Air Force Data Systems Design Center in Washington, DC. Ken and Jack were assigned together the first six years from tech school through three assignments all the way to the Philippines. Now after all these years Jack came to replace Ken, and he stayed for the full thirty years, moving with the design center to Alabama.

Ken took Beth and Jack house hunting, and the real estate office manager suggested he take their sales course which was starting soon. He did, and he started to work for Larry Eul Realtor. From there, he went with F. L. Jenkins Realtor, then Ruth Robbins Realtor, and Coldwell Banker Realty when they bought that company. He will cover these areas in more detail in his bio, but he retired from Coldwell Banker on December 31, 1990, as the senior business consultant for the northeast region covering 13 states and 323 offices. Many offers came from government service as soon as the freeze on hiring was lifted, but Ken was too well ingrained in the civilian world to even consider any of them or to be interviewed. He feels that God had His hand in directing his final career.

My dad's arteriosclerosis was beginning to affect his memory. He would want to go home in the late afternoon, and there was no use telling him that he was at home. Mother would help him on with his jacket, if needed, and then call me. I would go over on the lane and meet him. If I drove him down to the church and back, he would be satisfied that he was home. Ken had to park the 1966 red Ford truck down by the house so he could see it, or he would think that someone had stolen it. It was a sad time for everyone. When he got too much for Mother, he went to Regency Nursing Home in Forestville. I had just had a complete hysterectomy, so Ken and Uncle Percy (Reggie's brother) took him to the Nursing Home. Uncle Percy said that was the hardest thing he ever had to do. My mother knew that would be the last time she would see him alive, so it was as if he died that day. Ken visited him often, as he was in that area doing real estate, and he would stop in and shave him and visit almost every day until he died.

Linda graduated from high school in 1971, and she enrolled in Frostburg State College (now University). She did well in college. She lived in the dorm for two years and then moved with her friend Barb to an apartment on Main Street in Frostburg, Maryland. She began to work part time at Stoop's Restaurant, about a block away. She purchased a 1970 green Chevrolet Nova to drive back and forth to college. In her senior year just after she had returned to college, my dad died on September 8, 1974. She drove home for the funeral. Larry took Work-Study in his senior year of high school and worked for Burgess Electrical Contractors. He liked it so well that we enrolled him in a correspondence school. He graduated from Friendly High School in 1973, and began to work for Burgess full time. He met Virginia Allen, nicknamed Ginger, in 1974. They decided to get married. Her parents, Bob and Esther Allen, came over to our house, and they were laughing as they came in the door. It seemed that they were friends of the people to whom I had rented the house when we went to Okinawa, and they had been to our home. Ginger and her sister, Christy, had played on the swing set that we had left in the backyard. Small world!

Larry and Ginger's wedding was on September 14, 1974, at the Catholic church in Beltsville. The reception was at Ginger's Uncle Ken and Aunt Bev's home in Fort Washington, Maryland. Linda came home from college for the wedding. Larry bought a 1970 fire- engine-red Pontiac GTO 400 as his first car. (In 2009, he found an exact replica, only green, and he bought it for old times' sake. He has restored it to like new condition.) They went to Deep Creek Lake in Western Maryland on their honeymoon. I must mention Larry's sudden interest in motorcycles.

It was 1970; Ken was in Malcolm Grow Hospital at Andrews Air Force Base for minor surgery (Ken says, "The only minor surgery is when it is on someone else.") Larry saw an ad in the paper for a used motorcycle. He called about it, found the owner was being transferred to Lebanon, and needed to sell immediately. So nothing would do but get his dad's permission before looking at it. We bought it with the understanding the fellow (a captain in the Air Force) would not only deliver the bike to our house but would also teach Larry to ride it. He rode that bike all over the front pasture, making a figure 8 path. He couldn't ride it on the road until he was 16 and had passed the motorcycle driver's test. It was a small Puch 125. In the meantime, he saw an ad for a Kawasaki 500 for sale. For some reason, I was elected to take him to see it. He liked it and bought it. He followed his dad home until he reached Friendly Hill, and then he passed him going up the hill before arriving home. He rode it up to Frostburg one weekend to see Linda when she was still in college.

He purchased an old mobile home on a lot in Wayson's Corner in southern Maryland. He and Ginger were living there when Bryan Kenneth was born. Larry and Ginger sold the trailer and bought a house in Clifton, Maryland, just below La Plata. It was there they were living when Wendy Michelle was born on February 19, 1978. (Wendy and Linda share the same date, only twenty-five years apart.) Since Ginger had to go to Sibley Hospital all the way across town to Northwest Washington, she wondered if she would make it if it snowed. No problem, and Linda was ecstatic to learn she had a niece born on her birth date. She was twenty-five, so Ken told her that it wouldn't make any difference. When she was a hundred, Wendy would be seventy-five; they both would be old fogies! Wendy won the heart of her grandpa as she had reddish hair.

Linda graduated on Mother's Day in May 1975 from Frostburg and returned home to look for a job in the sociology field. She passed the state test for social workers but learned she was way down the list even though she made a passing grade. Once again, jobs were hard to find. She worked as a waitress at Joe's El Rancho in Clinton while she worked on preparing for a try with the US government. She found that agencies were only hiring clerk- typists at the time. She took the clerk-typist test, and immediately the agencies started to call. She went on several interviews and accepted the job at Secret Service. She started at the GS-4 level but was soon promoted to the five levels. Then, she was offered an internship for advancement periodically. She became an intelligence research specialist. She had several interesting assignments while there, attending political convention at Madison Square Garden and traveling with President Reagan on his visit to Bonn, Germany, advancing to GS-11.

Vikki started schooling at Rose Valley Elementary School in Friendly at an open-classroom concept of teaching. It worked well for aggressive children, but Vikki was a little shy. She liked school and soon had several friends, mostly Caltor subdivision neighbors, Carrie Cole and Joanna Edwards. While in elementary school, she joined Allentownettes, a majorette group sponsored by Allentown Fire Department. She enjoyed it very much. She and I attended many functions where she participated every spring and summer, first as a group and then individually. It was fun, but after about three years, she stopped. She took horseback lessons for about six months and liked that. But she decided she didn't want a horse of her own, as had been her desire when she started taking lessons. She had some trouble with math early on, so we had a tutor come in for a few weeks. Once she got over that hurdle, she seemed to do OK. Her best year was seventh grade at Lord Baltimore Junior High. In eighth grade, she tore the cartilage of her knee playing soccer in gym class. What a time she had getting it to heal properly. She went through crutches, a couple of casts, and finally a knee brace. The doctor didn't want to operate because he felt it would heal on someone as young. She went on to Friendly High School where she had mononucleosis in tenth grade. I had taken her for a blood test, but it didn't show up. Finally, one morning she said that she was so tired she couldn't get out of bed. I took her for another test, and this time it showed up. She had to deal with that for a long time. She was assigned a home teacher because she missed so much. She made up algebra, so in the eleventh and twelfth grades, she took a two- year algebra class. Her home teacher was Rosalie Timmermeyer, so we hired her to help her through algebra. Her senior year, she took a nursing aide class offered at Crossland High School in Camp Springs. Since she had to find her own way to and from school, we bought her a 1978 Volkswagen Rabbit. She took the nursing class at Crossland in the morning and returned to Friendly to take English and algebra. She graduated from Friendly High School in 1984.

Larry and Ginger sold the house in Clifton and moved to Strawberry Hills in Bryans Road, Maryland. One Thanksgiving eve, he came home to inform Ginger that he had quit his job and was going in business for himself. Ronnie Wright Electric for whom he was working had gotten so large that Larry felt he had lost control of the jobs he had bid on. He leased a van and did surprisingly well. His first job was to install lights in the parking lot of a subdivision on Temple Hill Road. Dad suggested that he take the 1952 Ford tractor that had a lift on the back to assist in setting the light poles and other needs as he did the job. Larry learned to drive the tractor when his feet barely touched the pedals. Interestingly enough, Bryan also drove it as well as Jacob as the first motor-driven vehicle. It is still in the metal shed, ready to go on a moment's notice in 2010, although Larry has switched it over to a 12-volt system and upgraded the whole electrical system to eliminate the need for ignition points, etc.

Linda always wanted to live where there where mountains. Growing up in Colorado probably had something to do with that. In 1983 she found an opening at Kirtland Air Force Base in Albuquerque, New Mexico. She transferred from the Secret Service to the Department of the Air Force with a grade increase to GS- 12. This later became a job from which she progressed to GS-13 prior to retirement with something like thirty-three years of total government service when she reached the age of fifty-five. Like her dad, she walked away with every award possible from both the Air Force, Department of Defense, and the community and the state of New Mexico. The family all slipped in to surprise her as she was hosting a luncheon for all her staff members.

Vikki decided to go to Prince George's Community College to become a nurse. She soon decided that she wanted a degree in nursing. The counselor worked with her to assure she had all the right courses to transfer to a four-year college. It took her three years to get all the credits, and she was accepted at the University of Maryland School of Nursing in Baltimore, Maryland (UMAB). We moved her into an apartment in student housing. We also bought her a Ford Escort to drive home because we didn't feel the VW Rabbit could take too many trips from Baltimore. It had begun to wear out, leaving her stranded.

Vikki met Rob Powell, a serviceman stationed at Andrews Air Force Base, shortly after she started to college. He worked with Yolande's husband, Bob. Vikki came home most weekends while she was in Baltimore, not to see us but to see Rob. He spent Christmas with us in 1987. He even fixed waffles for breakfast. In February, he called and wanted to talk to both of us. He said that he wanted to ask Vikki to marry him, and he showed us the ring. We were pleased. He rented a limo, went to her apartment in Baltimore to pick her up, and had the limo park while he popped the question. She was so excited that she shouted out the window to the first couple passing by that she just became engaged. Interesting thing was they were still there when the couple returned and brought them a little memento. They originally planned to get married after she finished nursing school. The Air Force was encouraging personnel who were in a surplus career field to take an early release. Rob was an outdoor electrical lineman, and there were too many in the service at that time, so he took an early out. He had worked occasionally for Larry while in the service, so he went to work for him. He had to get an apartment. It was then that he and Vikki asked if they could get married that summer. We agreed if she would finish her nursing school and get a degree.

So on August 20, 1988, the wedding was held at Providence United Methodist Church in Friendly, Maryland. Linda was her maid of honor. As bad as Linda hated humidity, she wondered why Vikki had picked a day in August! Rob's parents, his grandma Dot, his uncle and aunt, his sister, and his cousin flew in from California about a week before the wedding. They had a ball riding the subway and seeing Washington DC for the first time. Ken loaned them his Fleetwood Cadillac to drive while they were in the area. Vikki and Rob went to the Poconos in Pennsylvania for their honeymoon. Ken was a Business Management Consultant for Coldwell Banker, and that was one of the areas he served, so he knew about the resort area there where many honeymoons take place each year. And some couples come back year after year. A week later, Vikki started her senior year in the school of nursing.

Vikki graduated the following May of 1999. There was a pinning ceremony for nurses, and then another day was the graduation for all at the professional campus. I had the honor of presenting Vikki with a Gideon Medical Nurse New Testament, Psalms and Proverbs. Rob and Vikki had bought a mobile home in Laurel, Maryland, so that was closer for her to drive to Baltimore for the classes she had there. Her main clinical was at the National Institute of Health in Bethesda, Maryland. That is where she went to work after she graduated. When she had worked a year and passed the Maryland board, she and Rob sold the trailer and moved to Palmdale, California. She went to work in Lancaster Hospital, about fifteen miles away, and Rob went to work for a local electrical contracting company. They bought a house in Palmdale at 38645 Angele Trumpet Court on the same street as his cousin Tom.

Backing up to make note of some trips we took while Vikki was still at home. We flew to Dallas in December 1971 to see Ken's relatives. This was the first time they had seen Vikki. We had been there at Christmas in 1965 before she was born. We also flew to Daytona Beach, Florida, in August 1972 to go to Palm Coast to check on a lot we had purchased. We were glad to find that it was not underwater! We rented a car and drove to Disney World. We also drove to St. Cloud to see Harlan and Louisa Miller. In 1975, we drove to Dallas to see the relatives so Ken could attend the Lions Clubs International Convention. (Ken joined the Oxon Hill Lions Club in 1974. Both he and I are now Lifetime members of Lions Clubs International.) On the way to Dallas, we stopped in Tennessee to see Phil and Vera Phillips. We took a walk through their farm, but Vikki was the only one covered with ticks when we returned. Had to put her in a tub and wash them off! When Vikki was seventeen, we flew to Dallas to see relatives there, then we went to Lubbock to see Edna and Dennis, and to Denver to see all the friends there. When we left Denver in 1966, I was six months pregnant, so we thought the folks there may like to see the finished product. These are just a few of the trips we wanted to make note of that we took with Vikki.

Linda and Gene Stillman were married on October 21, 1989, at the base chapel in Kirtland Air Force Base, New Mexico. Gene was a major in the Air Force, and they were able to make their own arrangements. His parents, Fremont and Florence, flew in from San Antonio; his sister and family came. So did his aunt from Minnesota and family and friends, and Evie Smith and family from Grand Junction, Colorado. All our family flew in from Maryland. Vikki was Linda's matron of honor, and Linda wore Vikki's wedding dress. It was a great family gathering. They went on a cruise to the Caribbean for their honeymoon.

Mother slipped in the bedroom and broke her hip when she was eighty years old. The inside of her thigh hurt, so she thought she had pulled a muscle. After walking around for over two weeks, she decided she better see a doctor. The X-ray showed that the ball was about out of socket. Surgery required two or three nails or screws to be placed. She recovered quickly and only required one session of physical therapy. I had put Beverly in Clinton Nursing Home. Ken, John Skinner, Larry, and Ginger worked hard to paint the inside of Mother's house while she was in the hospital. We really had to rush when she was going to be released so soon. Beverly stayed in the nursing home. I took Mother to see her two or three times a week until Beverly died suddenly in March 1983 of a ruptured intestine. Mother stayed in her own home and took care of herself and her affairs until May 1992. She had a slight heart attack due to a leaking heart valve, and she died of congestive heart failure. She was only in the hospital for four days and visited with her brother Maurice and Shirley a few hours before she died.

In addition to Daddy, who passed away in 1974, Beverly in 1983, and Mother in 1992, other family members who died are as follows: On the Dennison side: Papa in 1971 at 92; Aunt Elizabeth (second cousin on Taylor side) in 1975 of malignant brain tumor; Uncle Millard of lung congestion; Uncle Irmon of leukemia; Aunt Hilda (second cousin on Thorne side) of Parkinson's; and Aunt Estelle of a stroke.

On the Taylor side: Aunt Clara of breast cancer; Aunt Bernice of stomach cancer; Aunt Edith of myasthenia gravis; Uncle Calvin of injuries possibly resulting from being pistol-whipped during a robbery at his Friendly store; Uncle Raleigh of congestive heart failure; Aunt Beulah of ruptured bowel at age 92; Uncle Percy probably of arteriosclerosis at age 95; and Aunt May of Alzheimer's. Ken's sister Corda died in 1950 and his mother in 1953, both from liver cancer.

The next death in his family was his sister Edna's, who died in 1989 of congestive heart failure. Then it was his sister Ruth, who died in 1994 of colon cancer. His brother, Jack, died of prostate cancer; his sister Bea, died of a long illness of back problems. The longest to live in the Deal family was his sister Tony who died on June 17, 2010, at the ripe old age of 101. She just stopped taking food for a few days prior to her death. Ken and I are the only ones left of our immediate family. That is why we are making a special effort to record some data that may otherwise be lost forever. We hope it proves to be worth the effort to those who follow.

We were so fortunate to have so many friends and relatives who came to spend a night or two with us in Maryland. We may miss a few, but we want to make note of the following who made special effort to make the trip. Ken's sisters Bea and Edna flew in together for several days, as did his brother Jack. Ken took them down to Trinity Lutheran Cemetery near Weyer's Cave, Virginia, to see the huge memorial erected to Michael Keinardt (Koiner), a distant relative. (Rebecca Koiner married Captain George Deal.) Ann (Ken's niece) and Bill Winterhalter with Will, Ken, and Holly came a couple times from Ohio. Then, in 1988, Ann came with her sister Helen Etter, and Helen's daughter, Janice, and her two children, Shannon and Jason. (Ann and Helen are Ken's only two nieces.) Bill, Silver Poteete, and Darrell came one time in the winter hoping to see snow.

Bill and Silver came again later. Harlan and Louisa Miller converted an old Greyhound bus into a neat motor home. They would arrive without warning and blow that air horn! One time, they were pulling a trailer with two motorcycles and went downtown DC to sightsee. Janet had her husband with them that time. When we heard the air horn, we always knew it was the Millers. One time they came, and we all went to the drive-in church on Sunday morning. The crew jumped out and went for more donuts thinking they had a busload of people. Jim and Margaret Valk came by on their way to England. We took them to see some of the places they wanted to see in DC, like the White House, etc.

Verne and Dot Archey flew in when Verne worked for Frontier Airlines. Their daughter, Nancy, visited once when she was a teenager attending a conference in DC, and then again about four years later when she received a commission as a second lieutenant in the Air Force Nurse Corps and was stationed at Malcolm Grow Hospital at Andrews Air Force Base. She came out to the farm with a group of three or four nurses to visit and have dinner with us. Dick and Carol Smith visited when in from Bellingham, Washington, when they were making several stops on the East Coast. Chester and Edna Kipisz visited when they drove from Seattle to his home in Michigan and down to Arlington National Cemetery where her parents were buried. Lew and Mary Ellen Bradley visited along with son, Duane, when Duane got out of the Navy, and they were heading back to Colorado. Harold and Betty Brauer drove in from Westminster, Colorado, when they were seeing some of the sights on the East Coast. Eva Van Arsdale visited a couple times when she was attending a mental health conference, and Jim also came one time. Kathleen Wilkowske visited several times when she was stationed in the area, and one or two times, she had her mother, Norma, with her. Paul Krisik came once when he was working at Aberdeen, Maryland, and the family was in Newport News, Virginia. Anne and Gerhard Wust with their son, Martin, came twice from Germany when they were visiting Civil War sites. Martin is a Civil War buff even though he was born in Germany. Jean and Buddy Smart and Betty and

Ed Dye came by from time to time as they were visiting family since they both live in Virginia. (We have visited all these folks at one time or another in their respective homes.)

We received an invitation to attend the wedding of Debbie Denney in Richmond, Virginia. We decided to go and stayed with Betty and Ed Dye in Midlothian. It was the first time we saw Bill and Nell Denney since we left Germany. It was great seeing the whole family again and attending the Debbie's wedding as we remember when she was born back at McChord Air Force Base in Tacoma, Washington.

Ken's second career for twenty years was in real estate. He worked for local brokers and then had his own company—Friendly Properties—at 10,000 Old Fort Road. The sales manager was Charlie Weaver, and the theme on his paperwork was "Specializing in Friendly Service." He also managed offices for Routh Robbins across Andrews Air Force Base, and when Coldwell Banker bought the Company, he managed the Oxon Hill office. He will cover the details in his bio, but I recall that during those years, he became a two-million-dollar agent when the price of home ranged from $19,000 to $39,000. He was also the Realtor of the Year for Prince George's County, the Community Service Person of the Year for the county, as well as a four-time winner of the Lion of the Year award. The last five years of his second career was at the Coldwell Banker Affiliate headquarters for the northeast region, where he was the senior management consultant for thirteen states and over three hundred offices.

Ken joined the Oxon Hill Lions Club in 1974. He was the King Lion of his Club in 1980 to 1981. I was Queen Lioness of my club and was a charter member. Ken was appointed by Lions Clubs International as the Guiding Lion for a year to start our club on the right foot. My club later elected to become a Lions Club when women were authorized to be Lions. It became known as the Oxon Hill Friendly Lions Club, and the old Oxon Hill

Lions Club chartered in 1948 merged with our club. We both became Melvin Jones Fellows, the highest award given by Lions Clubs International. Unfortunately, many of the Lions died, moved away as we did, and just grew older, so the club turned in its charter in 2009. We were able to celebrate fifty years of community service in 1998.

Ken joined Gideons International on May of 1978, and I joined Gideons International Auxiliary a couple of years later. We continue to enjoy the work of the Gideons and have held numerous positions at both camp and state levels. The fellowship of dedicated Gideons working together to share God's Word has been a blessing. Ken's involvement with prison ministry in Maryland and Colorado will also be covered in his bio. Ken began attending Christian Business Men's Committee (CBMC) breakfast meetings when he first entered real estate. He is also a lifetime member of CBMC, holding various positions locally and regionally. Ken served on the planning committee for the conference for three years. The one in 1995 was held at Messiah College near Carlisle, Pennsylvania. Prior to that, he organized summer meetings for families at Sandy Cove near North East, Maryland, where Christian Business Men Committee members and their families had a week long family time-outs from five different states.

We each have held many positions at Providence United Methodist Church. I was president of the United Methodist Women for four years. The new sanctuary was built during the bicentennial celebration of the country in that time. I also held the position of health and welfare representative for a number of years and worked with the Sunday school and Vacation Bible School. Ken was the church treasurer for several years. When Rev. Gordon Clews was our pastor, his wife, Eleanora, once asked Ken to fill in as a substitute adult Sunday school teacher while she worked with the youth. She never came back, and he substituted for nineteen years.

Ken retired from his second career in real estate along with Mack McCready, one of his consultants, and Bob Hagestrom, his boss, on December 31, 1990. We had been told that the best way to begin retirement was to leave town for a while. So we planned the first trip to the Rio Grande Valley in South Texas in mid-January of 1991. Ken thought it would be nice to take some video as a reminder of our first trip, so he numbered the first tape as Trip No. 1. We are now up to Trip No. 35. He began to make copies of the tapes for our children. We are slow learners; we did that for a long time before we realized that they were too nice to tell us it did not interest them nearly as much as it did us.

We stopped in the Dallas area to see relatives, and then we took off South. We stopped at Georgetown to see my cousin Winnie's daughter, Sharon. She was not home; we found out later we missed her by a few minutes. We stopped to see Hunter and Jeanine Estep in Austin. It was the first time we'd seen them since he retired from the State Department and they moved to Austin, Texas. We went on to San Antonio where we stayed with Jack and Beth Hargons. We had not seen them since they left DC. It was Jack who replaced Ken when he retired from the Air Force, and Jack was now retired from the Air Force but was working at Randolph Air Force Base. Jack drove us to Fort Sam Houston so I could look for the buildings where I worked back in 1944. Ken also spent nine days at Fort Sam when he was drafted into the army. That is where he received his first Gideon Testament. He had no idea who the Gideons were at that time.

We went down the river walk, but it was so cold and windy that we soon gave up on the walking along the river. Besides, the river was drained for cleaning. We went to see Linda's in-laws, Fremont and Florence Stillman. They drove us over to the San Antonio shoe factory where we bought our first SAS shoes. Then we spent the night with Bill and Nell Denney who lived near Lackland Air Force Base. The next morning, we drove to

Lackland to see Ken's great- nephew, Jim Etter, who worked at the service station on base. Ken found what appeared to be his old barracks where he took basic training; it used to be called San Antonio Aviation Cadet Center (SAAC) before it was named Lackland. We traveled to the house of Jim's mother in Weslaco, Texas. That is Helen Etter, Ken's niece. We stayed a few days with Helen and went on to spend a week in a Time Share in Brownsville, Texas. Our Canadian friends, Stuart and Gwen Simpson, have a mobile home in Weslaco where they spent the winters. We invited them over to Brownsville to spend the night and watch the Super Bowl. It was a great evening! The next day, we went to the zoo before they went back to Weslaco. While at Brownsville, we drove over to South Padre Island and went through the Confederate Air Force Museum at Harlingen Air Force Base. We went through the Stillman house downtown. That was particularly interesting since Linda was now a Stillman. This Stillman was from upper-state New York and had been instrumental in establishing Brownsville, Texas.

We went back to Helen's for a couple more days before starting back East. When we left Weslaco, we stopped at Helen's daughter Janice's home northeast of Houston near Dayton, Texas. We tried to find Ken's friend Hal Renneberg with whom he worked in both Denver and Europe and who lived north of Houston. Apparently, we were on the right road, but we turned around too soon. It rained too hard for us to make the trip to the space center; since the part of it that we wanted to see was closed.

Next, we headed for Joaquin, Texas, to see Mack and Janice McCreary, Ken's old church and high school fishing buddy. What a time Ken had there. Mack met us at the Sears catalog store in a small Louisiana town; I think it was Logansport because he knew we would never find his home back in the woods on the bank of Lake Toledo Bend. They baited the lines with minnows and something called fish sticks which are no longer legal. The next morning, Mack ran the boat and a heavy video camera that Larry loaned us while Ken took the fish off the line. He still cherishes that video as they caught forty-nine crappies and a host of catfish. He enjoyed watching Mack fillet the fish in his up-to-date fish house.

It is hard to say how many trips we made to Mack and Jan's over the years, but each has been a wonderful experience. They still have many tales to tell of growing up in the Lucas and Parker area of Texas. Ken will no doubt add to this story in his bio. Mack iced down fish for us to take to our nest stop. He always sent us away with items from his garden or from the lake, packing with all our car could hold.

Our next stop was at my cousin Jeanne Cotton's home in Monroe, Louisiana. Jeanne had fixed dinner when we arrived, and we had a nice visit with her and her husband, R. L. Then we drove along the Gulf of Mexico to Niceville, Florida. There was no oil on the beach in those days. We spent the night with Bob and Joan Hagstrom. Bob, Ken's old boss, had retired from Coldwell Banker the same time Ken did. They lived in a nice area, right on a golf course and not far from the water. When we left Niceville, we went north through Florala (Doris Cousino's hometown) to Montgomery, Alabama, to Kathleen Wilkowske's. Kathleen had retired as a colonel and was going to college to be a nutrition specialist (dietician). She took us to dinner at Maxwell Air Force Base after church on Sunday. While she studied, we visited Dave and Joyce Clark. We had not seen them since the Data Systems Design Center moved to Alabama. They had been our sponsors when we came back from Germany. Dave was a master sergeant who worked for Ken, and it was great to see them again. We went to Tuscaloosa to see Buddy and Sarah Gray. Buddy was a blind fellow whom Ken had helped in Maryland. Buddy always gave Ken credit for leading him to know the Lord. He and Sarah own a music store and have quite a business. They took us to lunch before we started on East. Ken will have coverage in his bio about Buddy whom he taught to be a real estate agent. This was a thirty-two-day trip, but it was packed with visits and sightseeing.

In my draft, copies of which have been furnished to our children, I cover many more trips. Ken also videotaped all these trips. We have decided to exclude the detail of those trips from this book since the draft copies and/or videos can be reviewed by children and grandchildren. We will pick up in Section Three a brief coverage of our move from Maryland to Colorado in 1997 and the years up to 2013.

SECTION THREE

CHAPTER THREE

1997–2013
Grand Junction, Colorado

The Taylors and Dennisons pretty much stayed in the eastern part of the United States. Although we are not absolutely sure, we believe the Taylors came from England. We believe the Dennisons came from Ireland. Both settled in Prince George's County, Maryland.

We have tracked the Deals and Rubles back to Germany, with the Deals first settling in Lancaster County, Pennsylvania, and the Rubles settling in Augusta County, Virginia.

We have not been able to find written records of why the Deals moved from Pennsylvania to Virginia to Missouri and finally to Texas.

The move from Pennsylvania to Virginia took place when Ken's great-great-grandparents were into their seventies; the great- grandparents moved to Missouri during midlife years, and the grandparents moved to Texas when they were about nineteen or maybe twenty years of age.

So we thought it may be wise to explain why we moved to Grand Junction, Colorado, from Friendly, Maryland, when we were in our seventies. We hope this book will be read by our great-great- grandchildren and perhaps their children on down the line, and like us, they may want to know why their ancestors made a cross- country move when they too were in their seventies.

We were fortunate to have the pleasure of having our grandchildren Bryan Kenneth and Wendy Michelle close by when they were growing up in Maryland. Bernt Rennie Powell, son of our youngest daughter, Vikki Kay, was born in Palmdale, California; our oldest daughter, Linda Lee, was in Albuquerque, New Mexico.

Following Ken's retirement, we took a nine-thousand-mile trip through twenty-two states in 1992, keeping in mind that we may want to retire in a city smaller than the metropolitan area of Washington DC. We spent five years in the metropolitan area of Denver in the 1960s while in the Air Force and remembered that we enjoyed Colorado.

Grand Junction's population in 1997 was about forty-five thousand, and the metro area probably totaled seventy-five thousand. There was a bus and a train station, an airport, two nice hospitals plus the Veterans Affairs Hospital and several retirement facilities accommodating seniors of various health levels. It appeared we could get home from any location in town within fifteen minutes. We were also between our two daughters' homes in New Mexico and California.

That is why we made the move. We did not know of a single friend in Grand Junction, Colorado, prior to our arrival on June 5, 1997. We soon learned that Evie Smith, who attended Linda and Gene Stillman's wedding, lived in Grand Junction. We also learned that a former pastor couple that we had in Westminster, Colorado, Pat and Walt Boigegrain, were living in the Redlands area following retirement as the district superintendent of the United Methodist Churches.

Although Ken never mentioned this before, he felt a strong calling that the Lord had a mission for him in Grand Junction. He hopes that he has been obedient to that calling.

We reserved a week in a timeshare exchange at Powderhorn Resort on top of the Grand Mesa in April 1997 and contacted Paul Nelson of the Coldwell Banker Home Owners real estate office. We gave Paul our specifications, and to be sure of our satisfaction, he selected homes in all the metropolitan areas where there were homes for sale that met our requirements. On the second day, we selected our first and second choice and made an offer on the first choice, which was then accepted by the owners of a new home they had lived in for only six months. Their two sets of children both moved to Boulder, Colorado, so they wanted to move also. They wanted to leave in May, so we settled the paperwork by mail and began the process of packing in our home where we lived for twenty-nine years.

Larry and Bryan loaded our household goods into a large U-Haul truck and drove across the country. They arrived a day or so earlier than we did. They had the truck unloaded, and many of the things they placed are still in the same location.

When we were in Grand Junction earlier in the year, we noticed that the Lions Club was sponsoring a health fair, and they were using the fellowship hall of the United Methodist Church at 30 and F Roads. We participated in that with all the tests, etc., that were offered so we may be able to find local doctors. We noticed that the church also sponsored and housed a senior day care center, so we thought this as one possibility.

However, we decided to visit six other local churches, and Crossroads UMC was our first visit. Denomination was not our first priority. We wanted a home church that was both mission and community minded with stable adult education and one that was friendly. To be sure of our choice, we visited all the local churches one Sunday one at a time. Crossroads best fit our needs even though we had to pass several churches on the way from our home. Interestingly, the pastor wanted nothing to do with the Gideons. Ken learned the reason and eventually won him over. We are now on our second pastor following Rev.

Doug McKee. There was Dr. Wes Kendall, now retired, and Rev. Karen D. Hurst, who has been with Crossroads UMC the last five years. Both have been supportive of the Gideons International, a ministry we are both active in now for over thirty-two years. However, as previously noted in this book, we still have strong ties to Providence-Fort Washington UMC in Friendly, Maryland. They later sponsored our sixtieth anniversary with the help of our children in 2009.

We have taken a lot of trips since arriving in Colorado, details of which are included in some thirty-five videos and a journal kept by Shirley. We highlight a few cruises for the record.

The first one was with the McChord AFB in Tacoma, Washington, a military group we named the McChordites. We went to the Mexican Riviera with stops in Cabo San Lucas, Mazatlan, and Puerto Vallarta.

In 2000, we flew to Fairbanks, Alaska, took the land tour for seven days, and then took the train to Anchorage. We boarded one of the Ocean Princess liners to cruise the Inner Passageway to Vancouver, British Columbia. This was in celebration of our fiftieth anniversary.

Next, we flew fourteen hours from Los Angeles, California to Sydney, Australia. We boarded another one of the Princess ships and enjoyed stops in Melbourne, Tasmania, where we saw the Tasmania devil and many other wildlife native to the island of Hobart, where we also petted the koala and fed the kangaroos. Then, it was on to New Zealand where we had several stops at both the South and North Islands, ending our cruise at Auckland. The flight back to Los Angeles was only eleven hours.

We drove to Fort Lauderdale, Florida, with many stops along the way to visit friends and relatives and boarded another Princess ship to the Panama Canal. We had stops at Jamaica, Costa Rica, Grand Cayman, and Cozumel. Ken had always wanted to see the Panama Canal (we should never have given it away), and I always wanted to see the Mayan ruins, so the trip satisfied us both.

One more! Vikki planned a trip to the Mexican Riviera so her son, Bernt, could go with her before he got too old to go with his mother. We also went, as did Linda and Jon. We all did our own thing during the day and had dinner together. We were really impressed with Bernt. He learned the ship from stem to stern. He also knew how to place the best orders for all the various courses at dinner. You might say he was our mentor. Bernt had been on a previous cruise to Alaska with his Powell grandparents, and he knew the ropes.

It was a joy to attend Linda's retirement from the Air Force after some thirty-two or thirty-three years of civil service. The whole family slipped in on her during a farewell lunch she was hosting for several staff members with whom she worked. We stayed over for the formal retirement ceremony in April of 2008.

Next, the whole family flew and drove to California to participate in Vikki Kay and Michael Murphy's wedding on August 8, 2008.

On a sad note, there were trips to Texas for funerals for three of Ken's siblings: Beatrice Moore in 1998, John Arlee (Jack) 2001, and Leona (Tony) Poteete in 2010.

We have enjoyed using Linda's mountain house on many occasions. In fact, that is where we are writing this book. High up in the New Mexico mountains west of Las Vegas, out of range of cell phone, television, e-mail, neighbors, etc. Except for a little wildlife, there is not much to distract us.

These are just a few of the highlights of our years in Grand Junction, Colorado.

SECTION FOUR

CHAPTER FOUR

Ken's Bio 1926–2015

Virgle Kenneth Deal's Earliest Memories

I was born on December 5, 1926, to Annie Elizabeth and John Newton Deal, Jr., the last of ten children. My mother said that if I had been first, there would not have been another nine. I hope that prepares you for this biographical sketch! My earliest memory is being called Kenneth by my mother, Annie Elizabeth Deal. Her maiden name was Ruble. She was born near Staunton, Virginia, on May 29, 1879; she died at my sister Leona (Tony) Poteete's home in Dallas, Texas, in November 1953. Next, and I am not sure which came first, are two events that have forever stuck in my mind.

One was seeing my grandmother Margaret "Maggie" Eagleman Deal in her coffin after she passed away on August 1930. I do not recall seeing her alive, but it was a lasting memory I have of seeing her, probably because she was the first person I had ever seen after she died.

The other was when my sister Ruth was carrying me down the stairs of our farmhouse when lightning struck our house. A ball of fire about the size of a softball bounced down the steps we were on, crossed over the floor, and knocked the battery-operated telephone loose from the wall. There must have been a noise associated with that strike, but I do not remember. For some reason, I was less scared than any of the family members;

I suppose that is one of those cases where ignorance is bliss. Fortunately, it was my sister Ruth who was holding me in her arms because it seems to me that of all my sisters, she was the calmest under stress. She outlived three husbands, raised many stepchildren and four fine boys of her own, and went to be with the Lord in a calm and reverent manner. The burn marks on those steps alongside us are also burned into my memory. If the fireball had been just a few inches right of where they were it is not likely I would be here some eighty-nine years later to tell about it. I have never seen a ball of fire like that the rest of my life.

My father, John Newton Deal, Jr., referred to by his friends as JN, had his right leg amputated just three weeks before I was born. My next recollection was standing by his bed during a later illness from which he was not expected to recover. I must have been about four at the time. He did recover, and he lived until I was sixteen. He was born on July 3, 1877, and died in February 1943. The home where he was born on Farm Road 2153 between Allen and Lucas, Texas, in Collin County still stands at the time of this writing in 2010. The farmhouse on the Deal property about two miles away is no longer there. In its place is a huge home, along with other huge homes spread out over the sixty-acre farm. The farmhouse was where Dad died, and it was purchased and moved to the east side of Lucas and is still in use at this writing.

I was the last of a family of ten. My mother was forty-seven, and my father was forty-nine. There were 9½ years between me and the next to last, my brother John Arlee (Jack). Hardly anyone was looking for another baby except my grandma Deal. My sisters vowed they would have nothing to do with raising another kid. Grandma Deal straightened them out by telling them the Lord had given her a vision that he had a purpose for that child. So when I came along, I must have been a favorite. All my baby teeth rotted out due to the candy they fed to me, and my mother hardly knew she had a baby. My sisters all report that after I arrived, they spoiled me rotten. That rotten part will show up in the "Early Childhood" chapter. Three of my sisters had married and had children of their own before I was born. I had a nephew and two nieces, so I was an uncle when I was born. There were two stillborn; one was an infant boy born on December 1903, and one was an infant girl born somewhere between sisters Ruth and Leona as best I can figure out. My oldest sister, Viola Lake Deal, was born in 1899, and she died in 1917 of a ruptured appendix. She was married to Joe Gilland and had one child, Wanda, who enjoyed spending a week with us every summer. We tried to time that week to be the same time my other niece Helen visited from Crystal City. Both nieces, being a little older than me, would often spend time trying to teach me about girls, how to treat them, etc. Wanda married a man named Stebbins. I never got to know her, and she died sometime in her forties. She had several miscarriages but had no children. Viola was the other redhead in the family, so the first and last had red hair. She died almost ten years before I was born. My niece Helen was born to Corda Hardaway, and my nephew Eugene was born to Edna Chandler before I was born.

CHAPTER FIVE

Kenneth's Early Childhood

As early as I can recall, conversing with my father, he called me Kenos. Only when writing did he refer to me as Kenneth, and most often he spelled it Kennith. If he had a weakness in spelling, it is one of his traits I picked up, and I continue to live with it even today. My mother and sisters always referred to me as Kenneth. Brother Jack must have had at least a dozen different names for me, and he used them all. I was nine years old before I knew that my first name was Virgil. I do not ever recall any family member ever referring to me as Virgil.

It was my aunt Surreldie Deal, wife of Uncle Ed Deal, who was present at my birth, who suggested I be named Virgil. She had a son named Virgil. So my sister Tony, who was seventeen, said, "Let's call him Kenneth." I was nine years old before I knew I had a first name; I always thought it was Kenneth. There is a chapter that comes later in my military service that explains why I spelled it Virgle instead of Virgil.

Since Tony gave me my name, it is time to explain that I gave her the name Tony, which stuck with her for a hundred and one years with family and friends. I could not pronounce Leona. My attempts to do so resulted in Oney or Tony. So the name Tony stuck with her all these years, and like me, most people never knew her name was Leona. Sister Ruth, with whom she grew up closest in age, was the only sister who continued to refer to her as Leona. My sister Beatrice (Bea) always referred to me as Kent and did so until she died.

I don't know how my brother John Arlee Deal acquired the nickname Jack. Once again, I was a teenager before I learned that Jack was not his real name. Jack was the first boy to live through a string of girls. He tormented them every chance he got. So when I came along, he took one look at me and said, "Well, I guess they will know how to raise boys by the time he grows up." My dad would often say in jest that he "had ten children, all boys except two."

Grandpa George Ruble lived with us. I think his wife was a Simmons; however, I was not real sure about that. There were four girls in his family—Aunts Lillian, Izer, and Eller and my mother, Annie Elizabeth. I have spent a lot of time with little success tracking the Ruble name. Not from records but from what I learned as a child, the family moved from near Staunton, Virginia by a covered wagon when my mother was about three. So that would be sometime around 1881. My grandma Ruble was a schoolteacher. She died at a young age. I don't know if my mother was the oldest child or not. She married my dad at a very young age, and some—if not all—of her sisters and my grandpa Ruble came to live with them until the girls married off. This is all subject to verification and correction should records ever be revealed. As best I can determine, Grandpa Ruble was there for the birth of all ten of us because he gave each child a nickname. I have forgotten the names he gave to the other children, but my nickname was Buck. He died at age 84, I believe I must have been about four. It was prior to our old farmhouse burning down in February 1932.

The one thing Grandpa Ruble taught me that I still use today is how to stay awake and not fall out of the chair. He spent a lot of time sitting in a rocking chair on the porch of our Texas-style home, which had a porch around its two sides. With his right hand, he would clasp the two middle fingers of his left hand. I called him Bompa. I recall his answer when I asked him why he did that. "Well, Buck," he said, "If my hand slips off the fingers, it wakes me up, and I don't fall out of the chair." I use it in church; try it, it works!

I remember that Bompa disappeared. I thought it strange that no one seemed to be concerned, so I asked, "What happened to Bompa?" He had a custom of going to Dallas every summer. He had a regular route there, going from door to door and sharpening knives and scissors, apparently for the same customers year after year. He made enough money to supply his tobacco and other needs all winter. Bompa was tall and straight, much like my sister Bea. If what I include in the genealogy section and here can ever be verified and/or corrected, it is my desire that some future generation who has an interest will do so. My sisters tell me that one of Bompa's daily laughs was watching me bounce across the floor on my rear end. I never crawled. Sitting upright, using my hands as a lever, I bounced across the floor. People would stop in front of our house to watch me go bouncing across the porch. We had an early Texas-style house with a wraparound porch, and apparently, I could negotiate the corner and make a round-trip much to the amusement of onlookers. Years later, in the 1950s, I had to have a cyst and part of the bone removed from the end of my spine. Sister Tony married Berle Poteete on March 29, 1929. I was very young, and Tony remembered that I followed her around all day saying, "Tony, I don't want you to go." On each of their visits, she brought candy, and I'm told that when I saw their car coming, I would call out, "There comes Tony, Berle, and Tandy." My baby teeth all rotted out from the treatment of spoiling sisters.

Sister Ruth took me over as a bed partner as soon as I was weaned from my mother. I don't know how long that lasted, but she recalled feeding me buttermilk at night, and I would go right to sleep. I do recall that just before she married, she would show me pictures at night until I fell asleep. It may be why I like pictures and photography today. She married Douglas C. Ross, whom we all called Pike. I don't know where that name came from, but we were not the only ones to use it. His first wife died and left him with a houseful of children. Some of the children were older, some were about the same age as Ruth, and some were younger. Dorothy and Gladys (Chubby was all I knew her by for years) became my playmates. They lived on the next farm down the road. I do recall how mad I was at Pike. He was a big tease, and he took my bed partner away. I became very fond of him when my mother was finally able to get me to ignore his teasing, then he quit teasing, of course.

My mother's wisdom never ceased to amaze me, considering her education was limited to the third grade. It is somewhat of a mystery to me how she arrived at her Biblical knowledge. I do not recall seeing her spend as much time reading the Bible as my dad did. She was even a source for ministers who knew of something in the Bible but were at a loss as to where to find it. This could very well be one of the best gifts she passed on to me.

Sister Beatrice is the only one of my sisters whom I can recall being courted. Horace W. Moore (Jake to me and most everyone else) was Bea's boyfriend. They visited in the room that we called a parlor. I always showed up and sat on the floor until he gave me a piece of chewing gum. He often referred to me as Punkin; no one else ever called me that. I wouldn't leave until I had my gum, so he always brought some. I became furiously mad at him when he married Bea, and they took off to Oklahoma on their honeymoon. I had lost Tony and Ruth, and now Bea was the last to go. I eventually got over my being mad and became very close to Jake. He was good to me, and he treated me like a brother.

Dad needed a lot of help on our two farms, and his big drawing card was having a house full of pretty girls. Pike Ross rented a farm that joined our lower farm, but all other brothers-in-law worked for my dad. This included Joe Gilland, Dennis Chandler, J. D. "Jake" Hardaway, Berle Poteete, and Jake Moore. I recall my sister Tony explain how strict my dad was with all the girls. He provided all the goodies like popcorn, a record player and records, ingredients for candy-making, entertainment, etc. The catch was they had to do it at home in the parlor and kitchen. As a result, they each married at very young ages; I suppose it was to be able to get out of the house. I think each of them were married in the house by Rev. Ben Snider. Dad thought he had a reputation of never having a couple that he married divorce.

When Tony and Berle married on March 29, 1929, Berle gave Reverend Snider a five-dollar bill, and he said, "Thank you." In those days, the going rate for weddings and funerals was two dollars, and Berle expected three dollars in change. This put a crimp in their honeymoon planned in McKinney, Texas, ten miles away, where rooms must have been one dollar. My aunt Lillian lived in McKinney, and she let them stay with her. She had a son, Leon "Bud" Beard, and daughter, Venita, who were cousins and good friends of all the Deal children. I believe that Bud's recent death may very well be the last of all the cousins from the Ruble side. I recall that when I graduated from high school, Bud Beard was home on leave from the navy. I was so surprised when he gave me a kit that contained all the bathroom needs one could use. I used it throughout my military service during the time when I lived in the barracks. I always enjoyed his stories. The last one he told me shortly before he died was a time when he and Jack were playing with guns that had live ammunition. My mother caught them pointing the guns at each other and whipped the tar out of both of them. I can attest to the fact that she could do that. Sisters Tony and Ruth told me how they showed my red bottom to Dad, and he consented to let them rotate staying out of the field and taking care of me so I would not be beat up from my temper tantrums, for which my mother takes credit beating out of me.

My brother Jack, who was just older enough than me to be a big brother, had a real streak of mischief in him, and he used it on me and his sisters. Jack and I were always very different from each other. He had a musical talent that never rubbed off on me. His talent was noticed by his older sister Ruth. He would beat out a tune on an old pie plate or use tin cans and sticks to make music. Ruth saved up her money and purchased a guitar for $4 from the Sears Roebuck catalog. I don't know how old Jack may have been then, but he was never without one until he died. His crippled fingers finally prevented him from playing during the last years of his life. Jack was just a half year short of being ten years older than me; he would tease me until I got mad then hold me where I could not do anything about it. Of course, much to his amusement, I would get even madder. I was just the water boy when Jack was working in the field.

He would tell me that I was eating my "white bread." That must have been a term used to tell youngsters that they had it easy now but their day was coming. I was always asking Mom, "What does eating my white bread mean?" I don't recall anyone else ever using that term; it may have originated with Jack, as many of his jokes were his alone. He could make them up faster than I could remember them, and in his last years, he could tell the same one over and over whether he could remember anything else or not.

I recall that occasionally, maybe once a year, we would be visited by Corda, Helen, and J. D. Hardaway who lived in Crystal City, Texas, the spinach capital of the world. Popeye's statue still sits there in the town. This was prior to Anne's birth as she came along some thirteen years after Helen. And my sister Edna, Eugene, and Dennis Chandler would visit from Hale Center, Texas. This was prior to Carl D.'s birth, as he too came along several years after Eugene. Except for his mother, we all called Eugene Gene. He was born about three weeks before I was born. He was a good-looking boy, and if one could be meaner than me, it was Gene. We got into lots of trouble. I don't know if I taught Gene to smoke or if it was he who taught me, but by the time I was five, I was smoking corn silks, cotton leaves, coffee grounds, grape vine roots, etc. Between us, we set the barn on fire smoking. I recall that it started in the cottonseed bin, and our furious kicking to put out the fire moved it over into the corn crib, and it quickly spread to the hay loft. The bucket brigade began; nearby farmers all pitched in to help. They were able to move the shocks of Highgear and bales of hay out of the barn before the flames spread by knocking one end out of it. Believe it or not, this did not stop me from smoking. I set the garage on fire, but my sister Bea managed to save it from burning down. She had just come home from some event with her good shoes on, and Dad was encouraging her to run up in that garage and pour water on the fire. Bea had a mind of her own and was not about to run up in the fire with her good shoes on, but somehow she managed to get the fire out. I headed for the peach orchard to hide and wait until things cooled off.

I recall playing jail with Helen. We had an old smoke house. I locked her up in the smoke house and went in the house to get some bread and water to feed her. She kind of panicked in that smoke house and screamed until I let her out. All the time, I was trying to feed her bread and water of which she wanted no part. Helen saw a lot of movies, but mine were limited to a few Westerns I had seen at the state and Texas theaters in McKinney. She liked to play a game of identifying movie stars. Well, the stars she saw bore no resemblance to the ones I saw, so the games did not go well.

She was one of the most beautiful girls I ever saw. I recall Gene Chandler saying, "Why did she have to be my cousin?" I carried her photo with me when I went into the service, and when guys would pull out pictures of their girlfriends, I would pull out Helen's picture and would lie about my girlfriend. It was fun confessing all that to her years later.

Our farmhouse on what we called the lower farm was about two miles from the upper farm; it caught fire from either the chimney or from Delco wires from which the rats chewed the insulation off in February 1932. No, I was not smoking this time; I was under the house gathering eggs. We had a door-to-door peddler named Key Long who came once a week. I always got candy when Mom sold the eggs to him in exchange for various groceries, and there was always leftover change which I could use up for any candy I choose. As a youngster of five, I knew the day of the week the peddler came and managed to find more eggs that day than any other day of the week.

While under the house, I could hear family members calling for me. I thought the peddler must have come early, so I made my way out from under the house. As I ran across the front yard, the roof of the porch caved in just behind me. I never broke an egg and nursed those eggs all the way through the burning of the house. Those were the only things I saved along with a strainer pan used to hold the eggs. The family did not know where I was. Mom, Dad, Bea, and Jack have all said many times that if they had not seen me in twenty years, they would not have been happier than when they saw me run across the yard.

The next morning, I recall that all that was standing was Mama's kitchen stove in a pile of smoking rubble. Not much was saved from that fire as the victor roller, as we called it, a machine with a crank handle that played records when it was wound up, became lodged in the door; they could not get it out or in. This resulted in some of those beautiful old oval-shaped pictures of my grandparents being consumed in the fire. As a result, no photos of my dad's parents have ever shown up. I am told that he looked much like my Dad as well as Uncles Ed, Will, and Roy, who were all short with a lot of dark hair. Each had a mustache except Roy, who was the youngest.

In those days, I could purchase a bag of Bull Durham or Golden Grain tobacco for a nickel, complete with cigarette paper to roll my own. I liked Golden Grain best, but I had a hard time buying it at the store because it was a very mild tobacco and the store keeper knew that I was buying it for myself instead of my dad. Prince Albert was ten cents a can, and it worked best for me. I could hide it under the bridge just before school, and it would stay dry, so I could pick it up and smoke on the way home then hide it again before I got home.

Dad chewed tobacco. He liked a brand called Brown Mule. I tried it but didn't like it. He did not smoke except for the occasional cigar. Jack smoked, and I watched to see where he threw his cigarette butts so I could collect them and reroll into my own. This went on for a couple of years. I recall smoking coffee grounds rolled in a piece of a brown paper bag. They were hard to keep lit. One had to draw hard to keep the fire going. I drew them down my throat and became strangled. I recall busting the lock off the outhouse because I did not want to die in that outdoor privy. Another close call was when I smoked a grape vine which was still kind of green. They needed to be dead or completely dry to be smoked. My throat closed up so tight I could hardly breathe.

The crowning blow came when my dad gave me a cigar. I went with him to take a bale of cotton to the gin. We were in the wagon pulled by a team of mules. About the only time he smoked was on a trip out in the open air such as this. He pitched a cigar back to me. They cost a nickel a piece in those days. I held it for about a mile before he told me, "Go ahead and light it up. I know you smoke everything you can get your hand on." So I did. I could feel myself getting sick, but I could not give up because it tasted different from anything I had smoked. The more I smoked, the sicker I became. I was too sick to get out of the wagon when we arrived home. I can hear him now as he entered the house. "Annie, go get your son. He is in the wagon, too sick to get out." He was on crutches, so there was no way he could carry me to the house. That was the cure for me at seven. Never have seen the need to start again. My smoking experience was between ages five and seven; setting a couple of good fires, almost being strangled, and becoming extremely sick saved many dollars and left me with pretty good lungs now in my eighties.

After that experience, I did experiment with a little more Brown Mule and Day's Work chewing tobacco, swallowing just enough to know there was not much future in that. I experimented with snuff, but I never could get the hang of that, so it was a short experiment. Many times I have wondered what may have happened to me if the variety of drugs and money on today's market were available back in the thirties.

Folks my age grew up during what is commonly known today as the Great Depression. The beauty of that was that we did not know there was a depression. The word did not seem to be in our vocabulary until later in life. We knew beyond doubt that things were not easy, but we thought they had always been that way, and we were no different. My dad was a good farmer, and according to stories told by my older sisters, he made lots of money in his early life. I'll include some of those in the next chapter when I recall events of his life. Both Shirley and I were in similar situations even though we were miles apart. She may have had a more difficult struggle than I had growing up. It seems to stay with her while I do my best to leave it all behind. It has been her austere methods that have helped us avoid extreme hardships. Obviously, that period of time has had a major effect on our lifestyle, and we both consider that it was sort of a blessing because we would not have the comfort we have today without experiencing similar periods where money was very tight in our married life.

We both knew how and had the discipline to handle economic conditions. So when we speak of those depression years, we are not complaining or bragging; we are just stating the facts and how economic conditions of those days differ. For some who read this in future years, the same or worse conditions may very well prevail, and we feel it should be a part of our history. I don't like to make the prediction, but I can vision here in 2010 that several generations who have not felt the effects of the Great Depression may be in for one of the rudest awakenings of their young lives. Those of us who experienced the Great Depression may very well consider that era a picnic compared to what is ahead.

Our kids have heard and can repeat and complete the sentence when it is started—how I could go to town with fifteen cents, see a movie at the state or Texas theater for five cents, buy a hamburger for five cents, and drink all the root beer I could hold for five cents. If I was lucky enough to have a quarter, there was ten cents to purchase three shotgun shells.

There is another story that fits in here. I remember when my dad purchased a single-barrel, twelve-gauge shotgun for $7.95. That gun is still in my inventory. I was a little small to shoot it when he first brought it home. I don't know how old I was when he let me shoot it for the first time. It kicked me back a few steps, and he admonished me not to let Mama know I tried it. The next year, he let me shoot it again; I dug in, knowing that if I didn't handle it right, there would be no more shooting until next year. I recall my left foot coming off the ground, but I managed to get it back down without backing off. So I had arrived and could shoot the shotgun. The three shells I could purchase for a dime were very important. I could bring home a rabbit, take one to Stokley Armstrong, the local veterinarian who would give me dime, and I could miss one rabbit. The dime would purchase three more shells. Since I allowed myself to miss only one rabbit out of three, I became a very good shot at a very early age. One of the ribbons in my military case is for my expertise as a sharpshooter, with a level of accuracy attributed to only one in a hundred. Not bad for a one-eye gunslinger!

CHAPTER SIX

My Dad, John Newton Deal, Jr.

As a child, I knew that my dad must have been one of a kind by listening to all the neighbors and various friends and family members, especially my sisters and brother. That did not seem important to me at the time as it does today; otherwise, I would certainly have asked more questions about my dad. He didn't talk a lot, but it was wise to listen. This will be the hardest chapter of our book for me because my eyes will be clouded with tears. Speaking of tears, the only time I ever saw my dad cry was when he was reading the Bible. When I asked him why the Bible made him cry, he responded, "Kenos, that is one thing I cannot explain. It is my hope that someday you will also understand." Didn't make much sense to me, so I tried reading both the Old and New Testament with no emotional effect.

I have now lived some twenty-five years longer than he lived, taught adult Sunday school for three years in Denver and for over twenty years in Friendly, Maryland. I know why tears came to his eyes. It took years, but yes, I finally understand. It's not the words but the effect of the Holy Spirit after having read the words. I am sure he would agree. He may have known what Paul wrote in 1 Corinthians 2:14, "But the natural man received not the things of the Spirit of God; for they are foolishness unto him: neither can he know them, because they are spiritually discerned" (KJV). He probably also knew what John meant in

John 6:44, "No man can come to me, except the Father which hath sent me draws him; and I will raise him up at the last day" (KJV).

I was fortunate to have him for about sixteen years. He died in our home on the farm on February 1943. However, my sisters and brother had him for a much longer time, and my mother lived another ten years after his death. So much of what I learned about him came from those sources.

Dad was very much closemouthed in that he never wasted words. When he spoke, he had something to say; there was very little small talk with him, but did he have a voice!

As was mentioned earlier, his right leg was amputated just three weeks before I was born. Once his leg was removed, he never ever weighed again. He was not a tall man, nor was he heavily built, and he would not weigh as much as a hundred pounds after he lost his leg.

We had two farms, sixty acres each, located about two miles apart from house to house. The farms were different from each other; they were identical only in shape and size. They had no names as one often sees on ranches in Texas. They were always referred to as the upper and lower place. I was born, like the other nine, on the lower place. After the house burned, we lived for a short time in a house on the nearby Hogue farm. Then, we moved to the old house on the upper place. This would be the house I lived in when I started to school. Unfortunately, there are no photos of that house, and photos of the house that burned are only partial ones.

It was one of my jobs to shuttle back and forth between the two farms for whatever was needed at Dad's beck and call. In fact I was his chief gofer. Dad never once in his life asked me to walk or go on an errand. It was always without fail, "Run." Dad had the strongest voice of any person I have ever known. When the occasion rose, he could easily be heard from one farm to the other. That is one of his traits that was never passed on to me. There were others that I can see both in me and in our children and grandchildren, especially in our great-grandchild Jacob Kenneth.

I did not know what perfection was in those days, but it is now clear that he was a near total perfectionist. He had a habit of worrying excessively, and he perspired excessively too. He was early for all events, very strong in his arms, honest to the point of almost disgusting, totally dependable, and hard of hearing, at least during my life time.

As a kid, I did not know what legend meant, much less how it applied to him as others spoke about him. His brothers told me that he was the best baseball pitcher in the county, if not the state. I kind of learned that on my own later when I played ball. They also told me that he was the most powerful and accurate slingshot thrower of all time. He was accurate with either a shotgun or a rifle. He taught me to shoot at the top of a rabbit's ears as he ran away from me, and I would almost always hit him. When I was able to do that with a .22 I knew that he was telling me correctly. I watched him kill a buzzard flying in circles in a single shot with a rifle. He could shoot the rubber top off an insulin bottle without breaking the bottle. So I know that the things I was told by others must have been true.

Cotton was picked by hand in those days and he had the reputation of being the best in the county. He would scoot along between two rows pulling a cotton sack while I picked one row. His old black hat with a hole in the very front where he always grasp it is all you could see in the cotton patch. I would weigh and empty his sack which always had twice as much as I had in mine. He gave credit in his arms as having come from the leg that he lost. I don't know if that is possible or not, but I have seen him take two twenty- four-pound sacks of flour (that is the way flour came in those days), hold them straight up over his head, and lower them to shoulder level and hold them there.

More than once, I have seen him take a quart fruit jar that Mama could not open and twist the top off, breaking the glass jar top into pieces.

Dad did not know he was a diabetic until he slipped on a butterbean hull, cracked his leg, which the doctor did not recognize until it had set up gangrene. His leg had to be amputated, and it was then determined that he was diabetic. Less was known about diabetes in those days; insulin had just come into being, and it was administered by a syringe and needle. When I was big enough to pinch his arm or one remaining leg, it was my job three times a day to assist with his shot. I have a vivid memory of those small little bottles because it was my job to run to Allen, which was four miles away, and pick one up each week. Those little bottles were no more than two or three inches tall with a rubber stopper where the needle was inserted. They cost $1.25 each, and I got a nickel ice cream cone from the druggist Mr. Cundiff each trip I made to Allen. Those are the bottles that I mentioned which he could shoot the rubber stopper off without breaking. I broke many bottles, but I never achieved his skill.

Dad had a great sense of humor. He did some things which were funny in the eyes of others. My brother Jack recalled some of them every time we visited him. All of my sisters used to break out in that southern Texas twang, laughing when they related experiences that happened long before I was born. Jack and Dad wore the same size of clothes and what was commonly called overalls, which was a blue denim material that had a bib-like front with glacis that came over the shoulder that buttoned or otherwise latched to the top part of the bib on both sides. Dad always had to fold up the right leg and tuck it in his back pocket. On occasions when he miscalculated his swing over the fence, the leg of the trousers on the missing leg would become caught in the barb-wire fence, and as he went over the fence, it would pull him back like a rubber band. Instead of stopping to unhook the pants leg from the wire, he would just jerk it until it came loose, sometimes tearing or ripping the pants leg clear to the end of the trousers.

You may gather by this time that he was extremely impatient. Mother, on the other hand, was cool as a cucumber. Even Dad could not jar her out of her pace. "Get a move on you, Annie," is a phrase all of us kids remember well. Dad could jump a fence higher than most people could by placing his crutches at just the right spot and swing his body over the fence, then he would hobble out on one leg until he could balance himself with his crutches. By then he would be far ahead of anyone who was either opening a gate or crawling through the fence.

Dad was the fish fryer in our house. I have seen him place that stub of a leg on the stove to balance himself and fry fish. He knew exactly how to do it and when the fish were ready. Catfish in deep fat will come to the top when it is exactly right, and he would have them out of the pan the second it rose to the top. He was the only fisherman I ever knew who built a fire before he put his hook in the water. He would have a fish in the pan by the time the fish stopped wiggling. I never had that much faith I would catch one. Dad knew that catfish can be good or it can have a muddy taste if he is fishing in the wrong waters. No use spending a lot of time catching fish that nobody likes. He could motivate me when I was hoeing Johnson grass or chopping down sunflowers by saying, "When we finish this field, we are going fishing." Somehow, the field always got finished sooner.

There were times I would be working toward dark and would hear his voice from a mile away, "Kenos, come to supper." There were a few things Dad could not stand. An opera star singing on the radio with a high-pitched screaming voice was one. Instead of just turning the radio off, it went right out the window, and of course, I have to go outside and turn it off before bringing it back inside the house. It was battery operated. We had no electricity on the upper farm and of course none on the lower farm after the house burned. We had some electricity there with the Delco system located in the garage. As a kid, I had no idea how dangerous it was for me to be smoking in the garage with all those batteries, etc. I'll bring Dad into this record many times as different subjects are covered. Early in their marriage, when the house and garage were new, Dad was teaching my mom to drive. It is reported they were making good progress just driving around on the farm. When she drove into the garage, instead of stepping on the brake pedal, she just yelled out, "Whoa." The car went through the back of the garage, knocking out the whole end of the garage. She never tried to drive again.

CHAPTER SEVEN

Kenneth's Later Years in School

Lucas School was about two miles from our house on the upper place. Our farmhouse sat on one of the highest hills in Collin County. At night, we could see the lights of McKinney, ten miles north; of Plano, nine miles southwest; and of Rockwall, eighteen miles southeast. Other towns or communities like Parker, Murphy, Lucas, and Allen were not big enough to even have lights in those days. I walked to school except for the first day when Mama convinced the Jones boy on the next farm to let me ride with him on his horse. I had to climb up on the mailbox in order to get on the horse behind him. That was a scary ride. I walked home and never rode with him again. If I cut diagonally through our sixty-acre farm, I could cut off about half a mile. It all depended on whether it was muddy or if crops had just been planted or if corn or cotton was so high that walking was a problem.

When I started schooling in 1933, all roads for four or more miles in all directions were dirt (mud) when it rained. The grown- ups had a saying when I was a kid: "Collin County has the blackest land and the whitest people in all Texas."

My first grade teacher, Mrs. Horton, was a saint. She never gave up on me, although the principal, Mr. Clarence Horton, found that a paddle, switch, and on one occasion a baseball bat spoke for him. I don't remember how many kids were in the first grade, but the entire school population of eleven grades was only sixty. When I started to school, one could graduate from high school at Lucas, and several did every year until the school was reduced to an elementary school by the time I was in the fifth grade.

Parker, where all the other Deal kids went to school, was similar. Somewhere along the line, I think about the ninth grade, those kids would then go to Wylie to finish high school. The nearest any of my sisters and brother came to graduating from high school was my sister Tony who went to Wylie; she was a star basketball player, and she completed the tenth grade. There were other schools in the general area that were similar to Lucas and Parker, Branch, Lovejoy, Nevada, and Dump. We played ball against all those. Allen was a little bigger than these, serving the same purpose as Wylie in that some kids went there to finish high school. McKinney and Plano each had a high school for whites and a high school for blacks. The principal of the white school also served as the principal of the black school.

I had the distinction of being the only redhead in a school of sixty. At recess, the bigger kids picked on me. I didn't mind being called Red. But when they found they could make me mad by calling me a redheaded woodpecker or by accusing me of getting a suntan through a screen wire, they had a fight on their hands. I was as close to a solid freckle as one could be. Having fair skin and being out in that Texas sun would cause me to burn unless I was full of freckles. After recess, the only thing that kept me from crying at my desk was a color poster with pictures of birds. I would look at it until I could regain my composure. Jack had to quit school when he was nine to kind of run the farm since Dad had lost his right leg at that time. At nine years old, he harnessed up old Blue and Beck and bedded up a sixty-acre farm with that team of mules. I can hardly imagine that even today. He asked me about school after the first week, and I told him I was finished with school; a week was enough, and since he quit in the third grade, I was quitting too.

Jack was about sixteen years old when I started to school, and he already knew what he missed. He was determined that I was going to school. All of my sisters had the same determination since none had finished high school. They made it a part of their business to see that I finished high school. My thoughts were, "How am I going to do eleven years of this? One week is enough." The first day of the second week, I came home crying and kind of beaten up. So Jack taught me how to fight and insisted that I warp their arp, as he called it. Following his instruction, I entered the next week of school with far more determination than was necessary. Jack's instructions were to warn them once then to beat the tar out of them one at a time until they get the message. So before the school bell rang, I beat up the first boy who called me a redheaded woodpecker. I don't even remember warning him once like Jack said; I just beat the tar out of him.

When lunchtime came, I beat up another one before I had my lunch. This went on for two or three days while Mrs. Horton tried to reason with me that "they didn't mean anything" and that they were just teasing me. Then the bigger boys who could beat me up found they could start a fight real easy, and no matter how big they were, I would attack only to be beaten up myself. It was time for new tactics, and Jack was my instructor. He fashioned the handle of an old washtub into shape to fit my right and left hands, which in fact gave me a homemade set of knuckles as they were known in those days. Mine would fit in my front pockets. He practiced with me to learn how to conceal this weapon, still have access to it, use it quick, and place it back in my pocket without being detected. I did have the discipline to use it only on boys who were bigger than me.

This became a mystery not only to the teachers but to others in the school as well, and then the main problem ceased. A new problem arose in that when a new kid came to our school, the older boys would coax him to call me a redheaded woodpecker.

This would usually happen on the first day he was in our school, and he would go home with a knot on his head which required explanations from the parents and the teacher and ultimately me. By midyear, I had achieved a notorious reputation. However, no one challenged me, and my homemade tools lost their usefulness.

I recall that Jack attended one of those old-time revivals because he was asked to be part of the music, one of his real talents. However, the Holy Spirit captured him during those meetings. He told me, "Son, I have to unlearn some of the things I taught you. I'm a Christian now. Most everything I have taught to you is wrong." Well, that didn't make a very good impression on me; I had learned to enjoy being mischievous. It was a few years later at a Baptist revival that the Holy Spirit caught up with me. That will be covered in a later chapter.

My mother was a snuff dipper, and she purchased glass jars of snuff. I think it was Eli Garret that she liked, and she could spare thirty-five cents from her egg money. When money was real scarce, she would buy small cans for either five or ten cents, depending on the size. When she finished with one of those small cans, I would fill one with a mixture of cocoa and sugar which tasted pretty good. Then I would use another small can about the same size and sneak the real thing from the glass jar. With both cans in my pockets, I would pretend I was using snuff. I would pass it around to a couple of boys and wait for some unsuspecting little girl to ask if she could try it. I'd quickly explain that this was real he-man stuff, not for girls. When she begged for a snort, I'd pull out the real stuff. This would do her in for the day; the next day, her mother would be at school, and I would wind up in the cloak room. That is where the teacher took boys to get spanked. I recall coming out of the cloak room holding up my snuff box and asking if "anyone else want a snort," only to be marched back in the cloak room for another lashing. That made me think twice about whether this was a good idea or not.

Later in the day, still a little miffed at the teacher for not understanding my theories, while I was standing at the blackboard, I found it tempting to reach back with the toe of my shoe and gently slide the chair back far enough for the teacher to miss it. Both legs went up in the air. Then I did my best to help her up. I would have gotten away with that if a second teacher in the next room had not been watching. We had one big room with dividers that made the room into four rooms with adjoining doors. As I recall, one teacher would teach first, third, fifth, and seventh grades. Another would teach second, fourth, sixth, and eighth grades, and a third would teach eighth, ninth, tenth, and eleventh grades. Students would remain put, and the teachers would move around so one room of students would hear the lessons of several different grades being taught while we were supposed to be studying. It was an arrangement not likely to be found in the US today, but this method may very likely still be in use in some foreign countries.

I recall that one day a week, everything was opened into one large room, and we had a rally-type songfest. This was usually when we had a baseball, softball, or basketball game scheduled. We always sang a few religious songs, and there was almost always a prayer and the Pledge of Allegiance. We liked it when the leader split up the verses with different grades singing different verses. Some grades may have as few as three or four students because the total school population was only sixty when I first started to school. This may seem a little weird to the reader today, but that is how it was.

We only had three, sometimes four, teachers. By the time I completed eighth grade, there were major changes. Lucas was no longer a high school, and eighth grade was as far as one could go at Lucas. The teacher, Miss Adams, who caught me in the act mentioned above, married during the summer and became pregnant before school started. She threatened to quit teaching at Lucas if I came into class, so I was promoted to third grade where Mrs. Horton had to deal with me all over again. Bless her; I hope she is in heaven when I get there so I can apologize to her. It will be a surprise to her if she sees me there too. Apologize was not in my vocabulary in those days.

If there is a good point to this story, it was when I was a junior at Plano, a high school of over four hundred students from grades one to eleven. I was awarded the Citizenship Award, competing with all eleven grades in what was called deportment in grade school and citizenship in high school. My grade from all the teachers averaged 99.2 percent, and the funny part of it was I did not even apply to be considered as other students did. The principal, learning of my deportment in the first grade, tracked down the teacher some sixty miles away and had her come to make the presentation of that award to me. I think I still may have that little emblem given to me during the war years, about 1942. Just like my mother said time and time again about my temper tantrums, "I beat it out of him and he turned out to be a pretty good boy after all". Mrs. Horton never said it, but she must have at least thought about it several times. She told me that the thing I did she liked best was when I cracked a hardboiled egg from my lunch sack on my forehead and then convinced some boy that he could not do that. When he bragged that he could, I would reach in my lunch sack and give him a fresh egg. It was hard to do that without getting egg on your face.

CHAPTER EIGHT

Kenneth's First Years in School

I continue to go to school at Lucas through the seventh grade. At that time, seventh grade was the completion of grade school. The rules changed later, and there were eight grades in grade school and four in high school.

While I was in high school, there was a time when everyone in school jumped a year, and those just starting first grade had to go twelve years. I don't remember, but it may have been about my junior year when that took place. Having skipped the second grade and moved up a year with the rule changes, I graduated from the twelfth grade and only went to school for ten years. All of my life, that has been a hindrance to me by missing one whole year of school, and it showed up in my high school years more than anywhere else. I think that is one of many reasons why Shirley is so much smarter than me. I never thoroughly learned the rules of grammar, the English language, or how to spell, so she has taught me more in those areas than I learned in school.

Mr. and Mrs. Clarence Horton moved to another school, and Mr. and Mrs. Clement Alexander moved into the house across from the school and became our new teachers along with Miss Holbrook. I recall the first day of school in the fourth grade. The teachers were doing things a little different. Mrs. Alexander, a beautiful lady, taught some subjects, Miss Holbrook taught some, and Mr. Alexander taught math to everyone. That may not be exactly right, but I recall that there was a different pattern from past years where one teacher taught a class that included all subjects related to a specific grade.

Mr. Alexander asked me to stay after school for a visit. As I waited for the big bell on a long pole outside to ring, thoughts began to run through my mind. Well, I thought, he has been given the lowdown on me and I'm in for a lecture. I stayed put in my seat and began to wonder if he was even coming in. I never knew if he had been briefed on me or not, but all indications led me to that conclusion.

He came in, picked up a piece of chalk, looked me straight in the eye, and said, "There are going to be some changes here at Lucas beginning this year, and you are going to play a major role in those changes." His long pause, as we walked slowly around the room, only heightened my interest and put my mind in overdrive. "Yup," I thought, "here it comes, rules, regulations, conditions, threats, and who knows what else."

He turned to the blackboard and wrote number 1 on the board and paused briefly, again only to cause my mind to shift gears trying to second-guess what rule number one was going to be. "Lucas," he wrote, "is going to have a track team, and the team is going to place number one in the county." I didn't have the slightest idea what a track team was, and I wondered where I fit into that conversation. Then with a slight pause, he wrote number 2, laid the chalk down, and began that slow pace around the room again.

When he arrived back at the board, he both announced and wrote, "Lucas will win the regional softball championship." I didn't know there was a region or a championship. We had just lost our baseball team as we were no longer a high school, and all the big boys had left Lucas to go to high school. Then he wrote number 3 and began slowly pacing around the room again. By now, I was sure he had asked the wrong boy to stay after school. On his way back to the blackboard, he casually said, "Lucas is going to have a basketball team that scares the socks off the other schools in the area." Then without further comment, number 4 appeared, which merely read, "We have a lot of work to do."

I spoke for the first time, "Sir, I don't know about the first three, but you sure are right about number 4."

"Well," he said, "number 5 is the answer."

I waited for him to put it up there on the board, but he didn't write. We both waited and stared each other down. I had relaxed considerably by this time.

Looking me straight in the eye and putting the chalk down, he said, "You, my friend, is the answer."

"Me?" I exclaimed in surprise.

Before I could continue, he said, "Yes, you, and we are starting today."

"I want you to leave now and run home. Tomorrow morning, I want you to run to school. You can start by trotting, but by the end of the week, I want you to be running all the way, both ways." When I was dismissed, I left the school yard running. Down the road, I slowed to a trot. As I turned up the lane for the last quarter mile up the hill to home, I glanced back; a car was just turning around where the lane intersected the road.

"Yap." It was him, and he gave me friendly Texas wave, where the index finger extended up from the steering wheel. On a visit to Texas in 2010, while driving on a country road, I noticed that the Texas wave has not been replaced. Farmers who meet on the road still use it as they did back in the 1930s. I was glad that I had made good time, had not slowed down to walk, and still had enough steam to climb that last leg of the journey uphill at a good clip. My dad's early instructions to run from one farm to the other and to run to Allen and back permitted me to make the two-mile journey to and from school without practice or working up to the task. I had been running several miles every week before Mr. Alexander ever knew me.

The first thing I did when I got home was ask Jack, "What is a track team?"

He responded, "That is when you run in everybody else's tracks." He didn't know any more than I what a track team was, but I could always count on Jack for answer. May not be correct, but he had an answer.

Lucas's track team won for Collin County, and little Kenneth led the county. I'm not sure they even kept time in minutes and seconds in those days. If they did, I was not aware of any times. All I knew was that the guy who crossed the finish line first was the winner. Just prior to the bang that started the race, Mr. Alexander whispered in my ear, "I want you to run just as fast as you can for the first half of the race, then just gradually increase your speed to the finish line." I was way out in front at the finish. The race was over before I realized what he had said. I was very little and lightweight as my growing did not really commence until I was about fourteen. I do recall that when it came time to go to high school, three high schools talked to my dad about enrolling me.

Dad's sense of humor showed up again. "Well, if one of those schools has an elevator, I guess we will use it because I think Kenos will have to have an elevator to ever get in high school."

This is probably a good place to reflect on the coaching I received in my ball-playing days. It was a combination between my dad and Mr. Alexander that made me one of the most sought-after students by the three high schools in our area.

Ball practice at home began after a full day's work in the field. The mules had to be unharnessed, fed, and watered. We had an old broken down wagon sitting in the feed lot near the barn. Each mule and the old horse mule had a certain place at the table which was the bed of the wagon. One of my jobs was to shuck the corn and dump it in the wagon bed which was just the right height for the mules to eat from in a standing position. We had a watering tank near the well that held 120 gallons. It was my and Jack's job to rotate drawing up buckets of water from the well and dumping it in the tank. We had some of the best water in the county at the upper farm which came from a white rock jug, as it was called then, which was a reservoir at the bottom of the well to hold the water. Although my first teeth rotted out at the lower farm, my new teeth were strong from all the fluoride in this well. My teeth will get some coverage in the military section of this book. Four mules who have been working since noon in the hot Texas sun can drink many buckets of cool fresh water. Then there would be firewood to split and bring in for the next day's cooking along with a bucket of corn cobs used to start the fire, eggs to gather, and one, sometimes two, cows to milk, supper to eat—all before it was ball coaching time.

Dad had been to some of the practice games that we played with what was called the outsiders. Those were the farmers who gathered at Dave Morrow's store to play dominos. (On a trip to Lucas in 2010, I noticed that Dave's store has been restored and is one of the historical sites in Lucas.) Dad noticed that when I was playing third base, I sometimes bounced the ball to first base, resulting in the runner being safe at first. He also noticed that I did not charge the ball coming from the hitter at the plate, and he also noticed that I could not hit the ball hard enough to get it over the outfielder. Along with this, he could see that I was a fast runner.

Dad began to coach me, taking all these observations into consideration. We found a hard rubber ball the size of a baseball. He could sit on the front porch and throw the ball against the side of the barn and have me charge it as it came off the barn. It was kind of funny because he had a fly swatter and while I was chasing the ball, he would kill flies. When I first began to charge the ball, I came off balance, and I was close to crashing into the barn. He taught me how to charge and be in a throwing position which took the danger of crashing into the barn away and cut the time necessary to get rid of the ball. When he let go of the ball, he would count up to six. That is when he expected the ball to back in his hands as though he was the first baseman. If I could beat the number consistently, I would be throwing the runner out.

He kept account of the number of throws, and the goal was that I have one hundred error-free catches. If I missed one time, the count started over, and we went for another hundred. I was not very fond of this rule. His objective was for me to gain confidence that I could charge every ball with the assurance that I was going to catch it. Well, it worked. As added assurance that I could throw a runner out, I was moved to shortstop. Between the shorter distance to throw to first and the ability to charge the ball and my almost error-free fielding, I became just what Mr. Alexander had in mind.

Then the hard part came. I wanted to swing the bat as hard as I could. Most of the time, I hit a fly ball right into the hands of various outfielders. Dad began to coach me to swing just hard enough to get the ball over the infielders and short of the outfielders. While I learned this method, I did not like it. He instructed me to try to count the threads on the ball as it was coming from the pitcher. I thought this was a bit crazy. What he was really telling me to do was to keep my eye on the ball all the way until it made contact with the bat. When Dad was not at the practice sessions we had with the domino players, I went back to swinging hard, hoping to get the ball past the outfielders. Jack was often one of the domino players, and he would tell on me.

When I finally mastered this method of hitting, my times of getting on base improved. We didn't keep averages; I didn't even know they existed. Then the next phase was "smart running." Dad coached me on how to run smart and steal bases when the time was right. The rules at that time for softball were that the runner must keep one foot on the base until the ball crossed the plate before you could attempt to run. This is different for softball than it is for baseball, where the runner can take whatever lead he can get away with. Dad would watch the catchers and determine what the chances were of stealing from first to second base. He knew that I was the fastest runner on both teams, so he would signal with one of his crutches when I was to steal. It worked, and Mr. Alexander always scheduled me as the lead-off batter, hoping that I would get on base, steal second, and be in scoring position with no outs.

When we played another team away from home, Mr. Alexander would drive by our house and pick Dad up to help with the coaching. I liked that because I would get a ride home after the game. It did not always work because Dad would often be out in the field plowing. When he was not there, I would fall back into swinging the bat for a homerun, only to hit a fly ball directly in the hands of the outfielders. I hit only one homerun in my lifetime of playing ball. It may have even been a foul ball, but it counted. Swinging probably as hard as I could, I hit a ball that went straight up in the air. I took off running, and the catcher and pitcher scrambled after the ball, and it hit the ground. I don't know if it was the catcher or the pitcher that picked it up and threw to second base because I was between bases when the ball came down. He overthrew the ball to second, and I never slowed down. I came all the way home on what should have been an out and may very well have been a foul ball. Beauty of it all was that it was a game-winning run for Lucas. We had only one umpire in those days, usually chosen from one of the domino players. He was usually harder on us than on the other team for some reason, and he always stood behind the pitcher instead of behind the catcher as they do today. He called all the outs as well as the balls and strikes.

Just as Mr. Alexander's rules explained earlier, Lucas

became the regional champions. And as he predicted, I was an important member of the team. Junior "Mack" McCreary, a member of my Sunday school class, was the pitcher on the Parker softball team that we played several times during the season. He is still my fishing buddy; he lives on the Toledo Bend Lake in Joaquin, Texas. We both attended and graduated from Plano High in 1944. I recall that when I came up to the plate and had that determined look in my eyes, he could not help from laughing. I was dead serious, and there he was laughing at me. He was good enough to fan me out a few times at the plate. It was the dual coaching of my dad and Mr. Alexander that made me one of the best shortstops in Collin County. I guess that is why I enjoyed watching Cal Ripken of the Baltimore Orioles play during the years we lived in Maryland. The Colorado Rockies has a budding star in that position, and I enjoy watching Towliwiske at short. Baseball consumes many hours of both Shirley and I, and I often wonder how Dad would have enjoyed baseball on television.

I was not an asset to the Lucas basketball team. We did do well some years, but we never won any championships. I recall one year, the only game we won was with Frisco, and it was the only game I did not play in at all. In recent years, Frisco was the fastest growing city in Texas, but population was way short of a thousand back in the 1930s. We did not have a football team at Lucas, but we played among ourselves, and Mr. Alexander coached us as if we playing in an AAA team. It was a blessing to have this experience to learn the game.

My grades were barely average through these years. I am sure that I should have had worse grades than were reported. Mr. Alexander had a rule that if you did not miss a day's school during the reporting period—which was four weeks at that time—you did not get a D. I know that I got many Cs that should have been Ds because I did not miss a day. Skipping a grade was only part of the reason for this; I was what may be described today as a slow learner. I recall that it only snowed to a point of not having school one time. He called our house on the old battery phone because he knew I would be on my way. Our ring was a short and two longs. When this happened, I would be out all day hunting rabbits, and my mother would have much preferred I be in school. I would skin rabbits and nail them up by their hind legs on the smoke house wall and let the wild taste get out of them by the night's freeze. She could cook rabbit for breakfast or any other meal. They were especially good after a night's freeze. Along about the fourth grade, my best childhood friend came on the scene.

CHAPTER NINE

Best Friends

Perhaps you are wondering who, if anyone, would like to be my friend! I was not a bad kid, just trained like an attack dog. I was always looking for a leader, never opting to be the leader myself and unless pushed into it. During the later years of my life, that changed.

I really had no friends my age except for a few nephews, and they lived what was considered far away in those days. I remember Willie Jones who lived on Uncle Roy's farm as our closest neighbor. Willie was about five years older than me. He had a horse, and I rode with him on the farm. He was the one with whom I rode on my first day of school, when I had to climb up on the mailbox to mount the horse. We had a mule I could ride on the farm. That mule would not leave the farm. He knew the property lines, and there was no way I could get that mule to cross the line. Sometimes I would just ride the mule in the five-acre pasture fenced in around the barn. Our cow—or cows when we had two—always Jerseys, grazed in the pasture along with the mules.

There was a little black boy about my age who lived two miles away with his farm labor parents who would visit me. I knew he was black, which did not bother me at all. I had a little problem understanding why Mom and Dad discouraged becoming close friends with him. I noticed they would not let him drink from the same water dipper. On one occasion, I invited him in for lunch; Mama set a nice plate of food for him on a different table from us. I did not understand that, and it was later explained to me that colored people did not eat with white people. You will have to remember that this was about 1935 in Texas. That was eighty years before this writing. Many things have changed for the better since then. Some of my best friends in later years have been black.

My nephew Billy Joe Poteete, Tony and Berle's only son, was about three years younger than me. Although he lived in Dallas, thirty miles away, we had many good times together. I did the funeral service for his mother, Tony, who died at age 101 on June 17, 2010. Bill was eighty-five on his last birthday, and he still lives in Dallas with his wife, Silver. During the summer months, we would spend a week with each other out on the farm and then a week together in Dallas. I remember that the first time I ever saw a toothbrush was when Bill came to spend a week with us. He bought a toothbrush and a can of Pepsodent tooth powder. That was news to me, so I got an old willow limb, made a brush out of it, and used some of his powder. It started my using a toothbrush for the first time in my life.

One of Berle's milk route customers gave Bill a dog which he brought with him to the farm for a week. It was a real fancy dog called a China-eyed screw-tailed bulldog. I can see that dog now; he had bright blue eyes and a screwed-up tail. Bill really loved that dog. He may have been worth more than the farm, but I had no idea of his value. We took that dog swimming, and Bill thought he was drowning when he was just swimming along in an old farm tank full of turtles and crawdads. We had a lot of fun with that dog.

In the last chapter, I mentioned my best friend. Well, he came on the scene about this time. His name was George "Junior" Deskin. He went by Junior which I thought was his real name. I don't know where the Deskin family came from, but they moved into a farmhouse owned by Gene and Margaret

Biggs. Margaret was the daughter of Aunt Annie Stratton, who was Dad's sister. There were several family members in addition to Junior. His dad was George. I cannot remember his mother's name but seems like Vivian should be about right. They had several daughters. There were Violet, Velma, and Verna Mae, and it seems like there was one more. Junior also had a younger brother, Floyd, who was a few years younger than me. Verna Mae was around my age, and I was kind of sweet on her. Jack married Velma, a beautiful young lady, somewhere around 1936–37, and John Arlee Deal was born. We all called him Arlee as he grew up. I was with John Arlee at Tony's funeral on June 21, 2010. Jack was so proud of Arlee and would have enjoyed seeing what a big nice-looking man he became. John Arlee married Loretta, and he has a nice Deal family who will help to carry on the Deal name. Mrs. Deskin was an Indian from Oklahoma. I believe she was a full-blooded Indian. She had the warmest smile. She was especially good to me. George, her husband, a non-Indian, was a very nice man. He died, I believe of a heart attack, and several of his children developed heart problems in later years and died of a heart attack. George Jr., Velma, Floyd, and Verna Mae all had heart problems.

Junior Deskin was a year or maybe two older than me and was several inches taller, and we were best friends. He spent many nights at my house, and we had many meals together. He and I were both coached by my dad to be ball players. Junior was a natural. He became the catcher on our softball team, the only person around who could catch a new pitcher, Ed Moore, who came to our school at Lucas. I remember that Mama reserved a few nickels out of her egg money to buy softball gloves for me and Junior. We bought pancake-type mitts for fifty cents each. Everyone made fun of them until they saw how effective they were. We could not afford regular ball gloves with fingers in them like most kids had. Mama sold her excess butter for twenty cents a pound, and the demand was great as she molded it up in a wooden mold, and the customers got about a pound and a quarter of fresh butter. Eggs were also twenty cents a dozen.

My job was to milk the cows, churn the clabber into buttermilk, and make the butter, gather the eggs, slop the pigs, and cut and bring in firewood. Junior was always a helper if he was around. There was no such thing as an allowance; it was expected of all farm boys and girls to do the chores. Mama would color stripe eggs with bluing, an item used with laundry, and set them under hens who would sit on them until they hatched baby chicks. I think it took three weeks for an egg to hatch into a baby chick. The blue-striped eggs were the ones we left in the nest. However, other chickens would use the nest to lay an egg when the old setting hen was out for food and water. My job was to lift the old setting hen up and gather the non-striped eggs that other chickens may have laid in her nest.

I recall there was one old setting hen who never liked to be disturbed by my feeling around her nest for the fresh eggs. She took about fifty cents worth of hide off the top of my hand with her bill. I promptly went to the house and got Dad's twelve-gauge shotgun and blew her off the nest, eggs and all. This did not go over well with Mama, while Dad thought it was the funniest thing that happened in a long time.

Junior and I made many slingshots. This was a forked limb from a tree that fit comfortably in one hand. Using old rubber inner tubes, we sliced two strips of rubber about three quarters of an inch wide and about twelve to fifteen inches long. One end of the rubber strip was fastened over one side of the fork and another over the other side, tied with a good strong chord. At the end of the rubber strips, a tongue cut from an old shoe was attached by another good strong chord. In those days, they were commonly known as nigger shooters. I never saw anyone shoot another person with one, so I don't know how that name came about. It never would be used today; I think these can be purchased in a store now made from metal or wood instead of an old tree limb. Junior and I became good hunters. He could slip up on a rabbit and see them better than any person I knew. It may have been his Indian nature. He was a good shot, and we brought home much game for Mama to cook. I recall that when Junior came to our school, he was in the third grade and was much taller than other third graders. After about a week in school, the teachers decided that he should be moved up to the fourth grade. One day, the teacher brought him over and explained that he was too advanced to be in the third grade. He was being promoted to the fourth grade during the middle of the year. I began the ovation by clapping my hands, and the whole room of kids in all grades joined in the celebration. Junior was scared that he could not keep up with a class well into the year, but I assured him that I would help him. Fortunately, he did not know how poor a student I was. Junior did well, and I barely passed that year. It may have been one of the hardest years for me in all my school years.

Junior and I were buddies, playmates, teammates all through the seventh grade. I believe that he was also the best basketball player in the county. He was tall and lean and was a sure shot from just about anywhere, and it was he who made our team one to be feared. He was equally a good softball player, a power hitter, a super catcher with a strong arm. Nobody jumped on me when Junior was around. When we graduated from grade school, I tried my best to get Junior to go to high school with me. He had his mind set on joining the CCC (Civilian Conservation Corps), and nothing seemed to stop him. The CCC was one of the best government services in President Franklin D. Roosevelt's New Deal program to help pull the country out of the Great Depression. I believe the pay was $36 a month with a mandatory allotment to be sent home in the amount of $18 to help parents. The army supervised the program, so when World War II was declared, the program phased out, but the boys were already trained and could go right into the army. Many things we enjoy today were built by the CCC boys. An example is the twenty-three-mile road that goes through the Colorado monument. I don't know how he got in at his age, but he did. He spent three years in the CCC, coming out just in time to go into military service. I don't know if he joined or if he was drafted, but he was in the Third Army with General Patton. Junior was in the first wave going into Normandy Beach and was wounded on June 6, 1944. I was working at Ray Woods Tire Company in Dallas, having just graduated from high school on May 29. I was the first person to get the news that he had been wounded in battle, first by telephone then by telegram. I never have figured out why I was the one notified. He must have put me down as the person to be notified as his parents lived on a rural route with no telephone.

Junior was discharged as a buck sergeant about the time I was drafted near the end of World War II. When I was at my first duty station, Andrews Air Force Base Maryland, I visited Junior in Red Lion, Pennsylvania, several times. He married a girl named Anne, and they had one daughter. I was a PFC (private first class), and Junior asked me to put his uniform on with all those ribbons and sergeant stripes. He insisted that we go out to some function with it on. I did not want to do it, but he insisted. I was afraid someone would ask me about the Purple Heart and battle ribbons, but no one did. I recall how comfortable I was when I got out of his uniform and put my little old one-stripe uniform back on. Several visits were made while he was still alive, and the last visit was just after a baby girl had been born. Years later, Shirley and I stopped to look him up and found that he had died of a heart attack but that he had a grandson. When I met his grandson, I did a double take. He was the exact image of Junior when I first met him. I believe his name was George. He had the same quiet mannerism, and he stood the same way. He informed me that Junior died of a heart attack a few years back. Then, after I retired from the air force, one of the real estate brokers I serviced was in Red Lion, Pennsylvania. I looked up Anne Deskin and took her to dinner and met the grown-up daughter I had last seen as a new baby. Yes, Junior was my best friend. In honor of his military service, I sponsored a plaque for him at the World War II Museum in New Orleans, Louisiana. I had a lot of friends that should be mentioned, but Junior was the best of the best. He was sweet on my niece Helen, who visited us during cotton-picking time. They corresponded for a while after he went into the service.

CHAPTER TEN

Early Church Days

My sisters told me stories about early church days, long before I was born, when the family all lived on the lower place near Parker. Lewis Road now runs alongside the old farm, and it is much like the unpaved road that I remember.

Before automobiles made their appearance in that part of the country, Dad would hitch up the wagon to a team of mules, and the whole family would go to the Christian church at Lucas a little over two miles away. They also went to the Corinth Presbyterian Church when there was a revival or a preacher whom Dad knew would be preaching there. The Presbyterian church built in 1923 still stands and appears in excellent shape in 2015. It is on the site of the oldest and first Presbyterian church in Collin County, Texas, in continuous use since 1846. I strongly suspect this may be the oldest church in continuous use in the state of Texas. With the exception of me, the entire family belonged to the Christian church. I became a Baptist at about age fourteen then became a transplanted Methodist after marrying Shirley.

Sister Tony recalls that she told Mama to listen to Jack when they were singing "Standing on the Promises of God My Savior." Tony said that "he is not singing that right." Jack was singing it his way, "Standing on the Promises of My Goddamn Savior." Not that he was being disrespectful, but that was what it sounded like to him since he was too young to read the words.

When I came along, Dad had purchased a new 1926 Willys-Knight car so they were beyond going by wagon and team. Let's deviate here and talk about that car before getting back to church. Tony was standing in the doorway when the salesman brought the car out to the farm. He set the steering wheel in a lock position, started the car, and let it run around in the yard in a circle all by itself while he talked to Dad. That sold Dad on the car. Tony went back to the kitchen to tell Mama that Dad was writing a check. Mama responded, "If John has decided to buy that car, all the king's horses won't stop him." Years ago, I saw a 1926 Willis in a car museum in Bozeman, Montana.

I have heard my sisters talk about the time when Dad would round the corner up at Mr. and Mrs. John Harvell's, the edge of our farm, and he would turn on the cut off, which sent the exhaust straight through the pipe without going through the muffler. The roar of the car could be heard a mile away, and everybody knew that John was coming home. You could set the table and get ready for supper. This is the car that Ruth drove to Plano to pick up hired help to pick cotton as mentioned in an earlier chapter. Tony was with her to do the book work and pay the help.

When I was fourteen, I attended several revival meetings at the Lucas Baptist Church. I joined one evening. I recall telling Mama the next morning at breakfast that I joined the church and asked if that was OK. She responded with an assurance that it was fine. Dad never said a word, which surprised me. I think he was happy but disappointed that I had joined a Baptist church instead of the Christian church a hundred yards up the road where everyone else were members. I suppose the only reason I did not is that the revival was not at that church.

Mrs. Hallie Biggs was my teacher, and I tried not to miss a Sunday. My first car, a 1929 Chevy, which I will discuss in another chapter, was used to drop Dad off at the Christian church and pick him up when my Baptist church was over. Hallie Biggs was married to Shorty Biggs. I never knew his real or first name, but he had two pretty daughters. He owned and operated the store next to the Baptist church. Billy Jean was my age and was a redhead. Her sister Elizabeth was older. I was in the same grade as Billy Jean from the fourth through the seventh grade, and then she went to McKinney High School when I went to Plano. For some reason, she switched from McKinney to Plano her senior year, so we graduated together. It may have been because the bus no longer served her area. I'm not sure she was ever happy about that as she never attended any of the high school reunions.

Junior McCreary was in my Sunday school class, and we attended off and on until we both graduated from high school. His mother, Clara McCreary, obtained a promise from him that he would always be a member of that church, and he told me in 2010 that he was still a member although he attends the Baptist church on Joaquin, Texas. The church moved into a new building several years ago, and Shirley and I have attended in the new building. The old church building is now used to sell antiques and fish worms. Junior and I were both baptized in a muddy creek full of crawfish.

CHAPTER ELEVEN

Kenneth's First Year in High School

We lived in the middle of a triangle of three high schools. Allen was the closest, four miles west. Plano was the next closest, nine miles southwest, and McKinney was ten miles north. I learned at a later date that my teacher Mr. Alexander was contacted by the principals in all three schools. Two of the three came to see Dad. His preference was Plano because he liked Mr. E. A. Sigler the best. However, common sense dictated that I go to Allen, the closest of the three. The first day of school, I walked down the end of our property to catch the bus. The bus then continued down the road about a quarter of a mile to pick up the Ross children. That would be Sister Ruth and Pike's children; during the summer, they moved from a farm near Allen to another farm he rented near us. I went to Allen for two days and listened to all the teachers' rules.

Dad was approached by someone at the Allen school who told him that due to some routing agreement with other schools, I would have to catch the bus up at the corner of the roads where Parker and Allen intersected. That was about one and half miles farther than at the corner of our property. Then, I would ride over the same road I had walked on when the bus came to pick up the Ross children. There was some special dispensation granted for the bus to pick up the Ross children in front of their house because they had all been going to Allen for years. These were the Ross children by his first marriage that were in high school. Dad thought that was the craziest thing he had ever heard, so he jumped at the chance to send me to Plano. I cannot help but believe that God had His hand in me going to Plano instead of Allen. If you read the rest of our history, I think you will agree that Dad made a good decision. (In 2016, Allen HS has 783 in Rose Parade.)

So school started over again for me. When I stepped on the Plano school bus, a cheer went up, which really made me feel good. Mr. George Goode, the driver, had been picking me up and dropping me off at Lucas the last two years of my schooling there, saving me about a mile and a half walk or run to school. I don't know if he was supposed to do that or not, but I asked him if he could pick Jimmy Moore up also, and he did when Jimmy was in grade school at Lucas.

Plano had been in school two days, of course. Mr. Sigler took me under his arm personally, and we selected my courses. He found a place for me to sit in the study hall, got my books, and showed me where my classrooms were. I was off and running in high school as a freshman.

No one explained to me that the seniors had control of the freshmen. I learned soon enough that freshmen were gofers, among other things, for seniors. There was an occasional trip through the belt line and chores to do for them. I took it in stride and not at all like my first year in school at Lucas. The Lord has been looking out for me ever since Grandma Deal sent those prayers aloft for me before I was born. When it rained, the bus could not travel our dirt road, and I had to walk an extra three miles to catch the bus on the white rock road. The last year of high school, the road was white rocked, but by then, I was living in the school. I will explain that arrangement in later chapter.

In my first year of high school, I took math, English, general science, and vocational agriculture. My agriculture teacher was

Mr. E. A. Randles. He was one of the best teachers I ever had. It was through his encouragement and help, along with my brother and sisters, that I was able to finish high school. I was the only one of us ten kids who did.

There was a new strain of onions coming available. They were called sweet Barbosa. It cost $25 to buy the onion sets for one acre. The money was not available, and I didn't know if I could chisel a whole acre from my dad, but Mr. Randles arranged for both. He arranged a loan from the First National Bank of Plano at 4 percent interest. I did have an account there. Dad insisted on opening an account for $5, so if I ever needed something, I could write a check. Incidentally, since that day my account was opened, I have never been completely broke. It was several years after Shirley and I were married that I closed that account. Mr. Randles also convinced my dad that I should have an acre of land. When the onion sets arrived, they were so big that they did not have a full hundred count, and my onion patch measured only six tenths of an acre.

There was some kind of a problem in South Texas in 1940, which caused the onion crop to fail down there. So prices were up, and my onions were in demand. When harvested, I brought home a check for $75 after paying my bank loan off. Interestingly enough, the balance of the farm that year netted just short of $100 in cash crops. This made a believer out of Dad. Plano High School, or Mr. Randles, could do no wrong in his eyes.

Mr. Randles said to me, "Let's order one hundred of the best egg-laying chickens on the market today." So they were ordered from Springfield, Missouri, and they cost twenty-six cents each. A sack of baby chick food would cost about $4, and Dad and I would have to build a special brooder place for them. This consisted of a sheet metal bottom, size four by eight, with board sides twelve inches high, and a top that had an opening right in the middle with hatch-type doors. I had to dig a trench, put in a flu, and put a kerosene lamp in the trench under the brooder so the chicks could keep warm. I also had to use some quart fruit jars to which I attached a special feeder head to let water flow through a circular area for the chicks to drink. I had to buy a bottle of tablets that turned the water a light blue color.

Mama and Dad, who always let the old hens raise the chicks, thought this all very strange. And to pay twenty-six cents for chicks a thousand miles away was very risky. When I explained to Dad that at least ninety-six would be pullets and no more than four roosters, he had the silliest grin. Mr. Randles had his confidence, and if it was his idea, it was all right with him. I wanted to take some of the $75 I made with the onions to pay for this investment, but Mr. Randles said no. "Let's go to the bank again and get a loan."

Dad thought this was really strange; suppose those chicks die on the way from Missouri or freeze to death. Mr. Randles explained that I was now a paying customer.

"Let's do this as a business. You will work a little harder at it that way to be sure you are profitable."

When those chicks arrived, Dad took a look at them and said, "They all look alike. How can you tell which ones are the roosters?"

I showed him the procedure I had been taught. I could tell that he was skeptical. As the chicks grew, it became clear which ones were roosters. As I remember, we had six instead of the four that were promised. I only lost ten baby chicks through the cold winter. Mama always raised Rhode Island Reds which were a large meaty chickens; they made great fryers for fried chicken.

My little single-comb white Leghorns were small beside the red ones Mama raised. These new chickens began to lay eggs at about five months. The eggs were so small in the beginning that we were ashamed to sell them at first. They were white as opposed to Mama's chickens which had large brown eggs. In a few weeks, they began to lay larger eggs, and they were coming so much faster than Mama's chickens. I remember Dad asking if they were supposed to lay two eggs a day because they were right at 100 percent at producing an egg a day. This was another big surprise to my parents.

Mr. Key Long, the door-to-door peddler, asked if he could have first choice at buying the eggs, but we began to get more than he could handle. He increased his route in Dallas to handle more. Mr. Long peddled the eggs he got from us, and he brought his grocery items to housewives in Dallas who liked farm-fresh eggs. They began to ask for those white eggs at a demand he could not supply, so he increased the price by a nickel a dozen for white eggs, and he passed the increase back to us by giving us twenty-five cents a dozen for white eggs and twenty cents for brown eggs. We now had an income from those new chickens over and above the cost of our groceries. Mama and Dad were really impressed as this was the first time in dealing with Mr. Long that they ever came out ahead.

Next, Mr. Randles suggested that I buy a registered heifer that I could have bred by a registered bull. Of course, the costs was nothing like what Dad paid for heifers at McKinney when they had what was called first Monday. On the first Monday of the month, farmers brought their wares to a special lot in McKinney where they traded, bought, and sold everything from turnips to steers. Then, they played dominos until it was time to go home. That is usually when I spent my fifteen cents for a movie, hamburger, and root beer. Dad had the reputation of being the best domino player in the city. And by legend, friends claimed he was the best in Texas. He could tell by the way other people played and remembered who played which domino and what they had in their hand near the end of each hand. Junior Deskin would team up with me and play Dad. He could beat both of us together. Didn't seem to matter what kind of a hand he drew, we didn't have a chance.

Dad's top price for a new little heifer calf was between ten and fifteen dollars. When I bought one for thirty-five dollars, he thought I was out of my mind. I explained that I had to pay more because it was a registered animal, kind of like the chickens I bought earlier. Dad had been a farmer all his life, and although he was a good farmer, he farmed by the seat of his pants. I was bringing into being a new type of that he never experienced.

Shortly after I brought that thirty-five-dollar heifer home, she got out and joined Mr. Albert Chumley's pasture; he had lots of green pasture and plenty of water. Mr. Chumley convinced me to let her stay and grow up with his herd, and I would not have to feed and water her. He did not charge me, so that saved some money and work.

Dad's health had been failing for several years. It now reached the point where he could no longer handle the farm as Jack had married and I was in school. He rented our farm to Mr. Jones, the next farmer over from us who had just bought a new tractor. It was a John Deere; Popping Johnnie, we called it. So with the reduced farm income, the income from my chickens, the calves from my registered heifer, and Mama's butter sales were all we had to survive on. Mr. Randles arranged for me to have a registered Duroc gilt pig with no cost to me except for half the first litter of pigs. The pig only had two baby pigs, which was very unusual. All the farmer got back was one pig. Out of all Mr. Randles's suggestions, this was the only transaction that did not prove profitable. You probably realize now why Mr. Randles was one of the reasons I was able to graduate from high school and why Plano High School was the best choice for me. In later years Allen High School grew to be one of the largest High Schools in Texas. In 2016 they had he largest band in the parade of roses.

CHAPTER TWELVE

Kenneth's First Car

I bought my first car from my brother Jack for $15. It was more like a gift than a purchase. Jack had been working for the Work Progress Administration (WPA); it was another of FDR's projects to build roads, parks, and bridges that was launched during the Great Depression. I believe that he made $30 a month, and although it was as a lot of work, Jack had a new name for most everything. He coined the phrase for WPA as "We Piddle Around." It was formed in 1935 and was dissolved in 1943. I believe it was around 1940 when Jack began working for the WPA. My brother- in-law Jake Moore also worked for the WPA, building bridges. He was a good mechanic. He put in a new set of rings and gaskets and tuned the motor. Jake told me this was the first year that Chevy made a six-cylinder, and it had a quick clutch and a loose axle which made it easy to break an axle if you released the clutch too fast. This was good advice because for the most part, I had to learn to drive it all by myself; Mama never drove, and Dad had only one leg, prohibiting him from driving.

Having the $9 necessary to put Texas license plates on and still have money for gas was the biggest problem. I could buy east Texas white gas for nine and nine-tenths cents a gallon. So for a dollar bill, I could get ten gallons of gas and a penny's worth of candy. Later on, when the war started, gas was rationed; we could get four gallons a week with A gas stamps. Some farmers who had a truck were issued B stamps that I think gave them authorization to get five gallons. Defense workers and some others were entitled to C stamps that gave them extra gas to get to and from the factories and larger trucks used T stamps. Someone told me that if I mixed one gallon of Naphtali with four gallons of kerosene, I could use it instead of gas. I used it once and created a toxic smell and plenty of smoke going down the road. Everybody knew it was me. I decided that was not the best idea. I never had enough money for both gas and girls, so except when they were hitchhiking, I never carried girls. I had been driving about a year when my dad insisted I get a driver's license. I knew that my car would never pass the test, and I was not old enough. One had to be sixteen in Texas at that time and pass the driver's test with a car that also passed.

Dad talked to the justice of the peace, explaining that I was the only one at home who could drive; with his one leg in evidence, he obtained permission for me to have a license at around fourteen or fifteen.

When Fred Petway went to get his driver's license renewed, I went with him. He had a 1940 Chevy. I passed the test using Fred's car. The part I remember was when the policeman riding in the front told me to stop. Fred was in the backseat. He came right over the top into the front with us. The policeman said, "That was enough. Anyone who stop that fast should have a license. Take me back to the station." I never finished the driver's test but was issued a license a couple years ahead of schedule.

Fred Petway was the son of Aunt Bird Petway. Shirley and I remember visiting her on our first trip to Texas after we married. She was ill and was lying in bed, and she looked like a little angel. She was my dad's sister. She and her sister Annie were the only ones in my dad's family who had a college education. I never knew which school back east they attended and from which they graduated.

The last words of the policeman were, "Son, I never found out how well you could drive, but God knows you sure can stop."

I have had a driver's license in several different states and a few foreign countries, and yes, I still know how to stop.

I recall that I rewired the wires from the dimmer switch to the horn. When I stepped on the dimmer switch located on the left side of the clutch on the floorboard, the horn would blow. I always enjoyed when I had passengers who could not figure out how I could blow the horn without using the horn button. When I used the horn button, the lights dimmed. I kept the car a couple of years, and I could not muster up the $9 required for a license plate. Let it sit for about a year, and there was a need for scrap metal to fight the war. I sold it for scrap metal for the same $15 that I paid for it. So my high school years were without a car. Eating was more essential than having a car.

CHAPTER THIRTEEN

Kenneth's Second Year in High School

Dad insisted that I take another year of vocational agriculture, and that was fine with me because we received one and a half credits, and this would give me three credits for two years.

Second year students got to go on field trips to run the survey for terrace lines, dehorn cattle, castrate pigs, vaccinate cattle, and all sorts of things on other people's farms. Sometimes we went to the county fair to judge cattle, sheep, etc. I also took biology, and we did laboratory experiments. I also took algebra. I don't know why because I never did understand it. Don't remember how I passed it. English was my fourth subject. Didn't understand that very well either. Skipping a year in grade school showed up in areas like math and English.

There were a lot of activities in which our class members were able to participate that I could not attend. Picnics, dances, field trips, etc. that cost money. Plano was the richest town in Collin County at that time, and many of my classmates were from wealthy families. I could not even afford a raincoat. I recall the teachers letting me stand by the radiators used to heat the room to dry my clothes. I volunteered to empty the wastebaskets because some kids threw good paper away, and I could salvage what I needed in stubby pencils and paper to do what I had to do in class.

Dad's diabetic spells required Dr. Perry to come give him

a shot, and that cost $4. We were living off my chicken's eggs and Mama's butter. We always had meat from one or two hogs and a calf we slaughtered along with all the garden items that Mama canned. I remember when we asked Cappy Wilson to remove our phone that cost $1.75 a month. She refused to take it out, but we never got a bill after that. Postcards were a penny, and first-class letters cost three cents. Our communication was mostly on penny postcards. My sister Tony could put a letter on a postcard. If fact, she continued to do so after postcards went up in price.

CHAPTER FOURTEEN

Kenneth's Sports Career

P lano High was a powerhouse in sports, probably the most feared by other schools in the county. Winning the state championships were almost common in football and basketball, and the girls had a powerful basketball team as well.

It was difficult to call my association with sports any kind of a career after I left Lucas grade school. The only award I ever won was associated with the track team while at Lucas, although I was considered by many to be the best softball shortstop in the county while in grade school.

The football coach at Plano was my biology teacher, Mr. Crabtree. Football practice started early in the fall even before the first day of school. I had to work on the farm, and I had to miss the first few weeks of school one year in order to get our cotton out of the field. Practice was after school, and I had to catch the bus within about five minutes after the bell rang because our home was nine miles from school. I often gathered a wagonload of corn or picked a sack or two of cotton before dark after getting home from school. Mr. Crabtree approached me about being on the football team since Mr. Sigler told him about me being on the track team and playing ball at Lucas.

I explained that I would not be able to practice and that I only weighed 126 pounds anyway; I would not be an asset to the team as every player was bigger and heavier than I was. He surprised me by telling me that he knew I could catch a pass and that I was faster than greased lighting. He said I would like us to talk about some special arrangements that may work for both of us.

I couldn't imagine what that might be because I was a horrible basketball player and had never played tennis, volleyball, or any sports except softball. I had the most unusual experience in sports in that I was not actually on the team. It worked to some extent because he would slip me in quickly without much notice, hoping I could get the ball and get a few steps ahead. When that happened, no one could catch me, and it was a sure score. If I failed to get the ball and get ahead and was hit by a linebacker, it would knock the breath out of me, and I'd be no good for the rest of the game. I only did this a few times. I was not able to participate in my junior and senior years because I lived in the school, and I was the custodian, which occupied all my time. Mr. Crabtree had left Plano, and Mr. Williams was now the coach; none of those special arrangements would have worked.

I love to watch football today, and over the years, I have explained the rules and various tactics to Shirley; she also enjoys watching the game and rooting for the home teams. It was the Redskins in Washington for years, then it was the Denver Broncos from 1997–2013. Now it is the Redskins again. She also likes baseball, and she spends hours watching and rooting for the Colorado Rockies. Now it is the Washington Nationals. Like football, I have explained the rules and tactics used by the managers to her, which has improved her desire to watch the games. Plano had an excellent baseball team, but I never was on the team for the same reasons I could not be a regular player on the football team.

CHAPTER FIFTEEN

Kenneth's Third and Fourth Years in High School

Mr. Sigler told me about a new program that the state was initiating. He would like to have me in the program. It was administered by the state of Texas in Austin, and it paid $6 a month for a student helper. Our janitor, Shorty Cox, was having some illness; he needed help, so he gave me the job of sweeping down the stairs on each end of the school building then sweeping the basement floor. I could do it during the last period of school which happened to be a study period for me. I jumped at the chance to do this and earn $6 a month. I found that I could do much more than that in the forty-five minutes, so I asked Shorty what else I could do to help him. I learned how to fire the steam boiler, oil the floors, gather up all the waste paper and put it in the furnace, etc. Shorty thought that was great. It took a couple months for the $6 to kick in as the check came from Austin.

The $6 was in addition to Dad's first Social Security check. It was called Old Age Security pension. Dad turned sixty-five on July 3, 1942, so he was eligible. This also took a few months to kick in after his application, and his first check of $22 started near the end of the year. Dad died on February 1943, so he only received four checks—less than a hundred dollars—before he died.

It was now my responsibility as a sixteen-year-old to be

the old man of the house and farm. Mother was also sick and was barely able to attend the funeral. I had to make all the arrangements and notify all the kinfolks, and it was wartime, so things were not easy to get done. The night Dad died, Fred Petway took me to McKinney to notify my sister Bea and Jake. They did not have a phone. Fred also took me to Virgil, my namesake, and Pauline Deal. They let me use their phone to send telegrams to my sister Edna and Dennis in Hale Center, Texas, and sister Corda and J. D. Hardaway in Crystal City, Texas.

I recall brother-in-law Dennis saying that the wording in my telegram was just what he needed to get a gas station to open up and sell gas to him. In those days, gas stations were regulated by the Office of Price Administration (OPA), even regarding the hours of operation. My parents had paid $1.25 a month for years to the Massey-Harris Funeral Home for what was called burial insurance. This was a blessing because I did not have to pay for either of their funerals. There may have been some extra cost involved, I don't know, but there never was a bill for either of their funerals.

I recall Mama saying, "If I can only live until Kenneth is old enough to take care of himself." Well, she did live another ten years, and as a teenager, I supported her. Shirley and I supported her from the time we were married in 1949 until she died on November 1953. School was not easy the year Dad died. Shorty Cox, the custodian, became seriously ill, and he was admitted to the hospital. Doctors said he would be out for weeks following surgery and then would be on limited work schedule, if he was able to return at all. There was no health insurance in those days. Shorty told Mr. Sigler not to hire a janitor but to give the job to me until he was able to return. His monthly salary was $125, and there was no such thing as sick leave or other types of compensation. Shorty also kept things up during the three summer months when school was out, and that is when his vacation was scheduled.

Mr. Sigler was aware of both Shorty and my financial needs, so he made the decision to share Shorty's salary by giving me $50 and $75 to Shorty and let me stay in Shorty's room in the basement of the school. I was also Mrs. Cox's helper. They lived a block from the school and a block from downtown, so I did her shopping and took care of her needs at home while Shorty was ill. Shorty had a cot and a hot plate in his work room in the basement of the school. I was given all the keys to the building and the gymnasium which included the homemaker economics room and also the vocational agriculture room.

This was a major lifestyle change for me. I could go home on the weekend but not before all the forty-two rooms were cleaned and all the doors secured. Then there was either a nine-mile walk or a ride on the interurban from Plano to Allen, with which I would walk only four miles. The fare was fifteen cents, and the roundtrip ticket for a quarter.

Once I was home, there was shopping to do for Mama at Dave Morrow's store at Lucas, two miles away. Then on Sunday afternoon, it was a nine-mile hike back to Plano or four to Allen, where I would ride the interurban back to Plano and get ready to fire up the boiler for Monday morning. Shorty told me about cleaning the flues of the boiler once a week, but he never taught me how to do it. It was a job he did on the weekend when the boiler was cooled down. The first time I did what I understood him to tell me, I cleaned the large black flue that took the smoke up the chimney. What a job that was, only to learn that was not the flues.

The flues were the forty long round cylinders that led from the firebox to the back of the boiler. Each of them carried the heat through the boiler to make the steam and in the course of the week there was a buildup of soot that had to be punched out with a long handle that had a metal brush on one end. The soot accumulated in the back of the boiler where it could be removed by opening a set of double doors. Coal cinders had to be removed from the firebox as they fell through grates in the firebox, and this was also a weekly job. Not an easy one because they had to be carried up steps to the basement then up to the first level and placed in a wheelbarrow and toted off to the cinder pile in back of the gym.

I had some long hours in that I was up at 5:00 a.m. to start the boiler and have the forty-two school rooms warm when the first set of kids arrived. Between classes, there were chores to do such as feeding the boiler to keep the steam pressure up. When school was out in the afternoon, there were all those rooms to clean, wastepaper to haul down to the boiler room to help start the fire the next morning, and my own meals to worry about. Very little time was left for homework or studying.

Shorty Cox came home from the hospital. He tried to come back to his old job. He asked that I continue to be paid $50 a month since he could not do very much. I continued to live in the school building. Shorty found that he could not take care of the boiler or carry anything heavy. Arrangements were made for Shorty to retire. He told me that I could have the job the rest of my life if I wanted it, but then he added, "Don't take it. You've got what it takes to have a great future."

Forty years later, in 1984, I took Shirley by the old school house. A tear came to my eye when I saw the carved plaque on the building. It was now called the Cox building, named after Shorty, and it was now the administration building for the Plano School District. The Plano school system evolved into eleven high schools due to population growth.

There was an old janitor using a buffing machine. Thoughts ran through my mind. That could be me if I had not taken Shorty's advice.

Teachers understood my role, and when I came to class late, they knew I been down firing the boiler to keep the steam pressure up. When I came in with soot on my nose, they would just smile. This was the year I was awarded the Citizenship of the Year award during graduation ceremonies. I was so sorry Mama was not well enough to attend. I hired a young girl who lived in the Deskins' old farmhouse on Gene Biggs's farm to stop in and check on Mom in the morning and again on the way home from school. Do not remember her name. She drew some water from the well for her. She was also to stop by on the way home from school, draw some more water, gather the eggs, and check on Mama. I paid her $10 a month from my $50 salary. Mr. Jones, who was now renting our farm, also checked on Mama from time to time; once a year, there was a little rent money from the cotton and corn that he raised on the farm, like one-third of the gross sales. This permitted us to pay the taxes and have a little leftover.

My senior year found me once again living in the school building. I had the job down pretty well by now. The hours were long, and there was no time for movies, fun, girls, sports, or any of the senior activities. Although I could have walked up to the movie that cost fifteen cents, I never went to a single one. Both time and money were too important. Fortunately, I had enough credits that I only took the essential subjects to graduate because there was no time to do a lot of homework. I missed some classes that would have been nice to have. I lost out on all the class activities, parties, picnics, proms, and sports events.

I developed a health problem that must have been associated with stress. A sudden loud noise caused me to jump up and faint. I was carried from the classroom and from the study hall a couple of times down to my room in the basement. Students and teachers became very concerned, and they were careful to see that a door did not slam shut or any loud noise take place. The flag on the stage in a large container blew over once, and I rose up and just keeled over. Interesting that after I finished school, the problem went away. The first reunion

I was able to attend was our forty-fifth. During the forty-fifth school reunion, several commented that they did not think I would live very long and were surprised I was there. Then when I co-conducted the fiftieth, fifty-second, and fifty-fifth reunions and ran the sixtieth reunion, they continued to comment on how shy I was during school days. It was not that I was so shy; I just had responsibilities they did not have. So now, at this point in my life, at eighty-nine, I have outlived twenty-nine of my forty-two classmates. Plano, Texas, had the only millionaires in Collin County when I went to school. Some classmates were children of business owners and bankers and were from well-to-do families. Some had brand-new cars they drove to school from where they lived half a mile away. I remember admiring a 1940 Ford coupe. The owner wanted a coupe, so he could only carry one girl at a time. Some of the students discarded good used pencils, pens, and paper in wastebaskets. Since my job included emptying the wastebaskets, I found all the school materials I needed which had been discarded by more affluent students.

I could have had the janitorial job at Plano following graduation, but I took Shorty's advice and turned it down. Graduation was on May 29, 1944, and Mama was well enough to come. I arranged for a neighbor to take us to Allen where we rode the interurban which was a single car like a streetcar but was operated on a track, and it went like a train from city to city. There is one that sits at the station now as a memory of the old system. Each time I see it, I wonder if it was one that I ever rode between Plano and Allen. There were not enough vacant seats, so I got one for Mama, and I stood up for the trip which was about five or six miles. I can still see the smile on Mama's face as she watched her only child going for graduation.

I had a new suit that cost $19.00 and a new hat that cost $1.70 and a set of eye glasses that cost $9.00. Tony and Berle along with cousin Bud and Roberta Beard met us at Plano for the graduation. I arranged for someone to take Mama home that evening, and I went to the big city of Dallas with Tony and Berle after graduation while other graduates were discussing the colleges they planned to attend. I felt that I was lucky to graduate from high school. Although after three years of vocational agriculture, my heart was set on becoming a veterinarian. That was out of the question for me. A couple of the boys planned to volunteer for military service as World War II was still very much alive in 1944.

CHAPTER SIXTEEN

Kenneth's First Brush in the Big City

Brother-in-law Berle Poteete took me to look for a job the next day. In the only place we went—and I don't know why we went there as it was across town from where he lived—the manager hired me on the spot.

It was a night job at Ray Wood's Tire Company located at Ross and Haskell Avenues in Dallas. I remember that it was 4400 Ross Avenue, exactly twenty blocks from Ray Woods Auto Company at Ross Avenue and Pearl Street. The general manager, Fred H. Johnson, hired me to come to work that very evening of May 30, 1944. The hours were from 8:00 p.m. to 8:00 a.m. I was to be off every other Sunday, and the pay was $130 a month. Payday was every two weeks. I was glad to take the job.

Berle showed me where to catch the streetcar two blocks away on Live Oak Street. I would have to ask for a transfer because I would have to change cars at Lamar and Main and ride a second streetcar to the end of the line at Second Avenue and Hatcher Street. Then I would walk about a mile to his home at 3125 Vannerson Drive. Tony and Berle let me live with them and Bill until I could accumulate enough money to rent an apartment and bring Mama to Dallas. They were always so good to me, and they did not charge room and board. They let me have a fan during the day so I could sleep, and they washed my clothes and fed me for a few months. I can recall how funny Tony thought it was when I commented after a few paydays that money was piling up on me. I was only spending money for car fare. Berle told me I could buy six streetcar tokens for a quarter; otherwise, the fare was six cents cash.

I recall my very first night. I didn't know how long it would take to get to the station, so I left early. When I arrived, Fred Johnson introduced me to the night manager, Mr. Thacker. He was a farmer who worked there when his farm work was caught up for the season. When farm work started up again, he went back to the farm. I did not know anything about service station work or anything about the city of Dallas.

My first assignment was to take a can of gas and a lady to her car about a block away and get her car started for her. I was to charge seventy-five cents for the service call and twenty-cents for the gas. We sold regular gas for 16.9 cents and ethyl (high test) for 19.9 cents per gallon. So I took a can of gas and a lady in distress a block or so from the station. Lack of gas was not the problem. Her car would not start after putting the gas in the tank. I didn't know about priming the carburetor, and she didn't know about putting the car in gear and releasing the clutch if the car was pushed so that it may start. She asked me to push her home, so I pushed her car with the truck. The truck was a 1942 Ford with heavy-duty bumpers. She turned a few corners, and I continued to drive up behind her and push, thinking just any minute she would turn into her driveway. It was miles before she reached home. All I knew to charge her was for the service call and the gas. I didn't know there was a ten cents a mile charge for each mile over the first mile.

I had no idea where I was, but I drove and drove, trying to find the gas station. Nothing looked familiar, and it was at night. I lost sense of direction. I remember getting out of the truck and looking at the address on the side of the truck. The service trucks were black with a white cab. I was too embarrassed to ask anyone how to find my own station. Finally, I struck out in a straight line hoping to cross either Haskell or Ross Avenue.

When I found Ross Avenue, it was a sight for sore eyes. I turned and hoped that I was going in the right direction. I came up on Ray Woods Auto Company, and everything looked different. I did not know that he had a used car lot at Ross and Pearl Avenues. It was twenty blocks from the tire company. Everything was closed, and there was no one to ask, so I went on down the street looking for Haskell Avenue.

When I pulled into the station, the manager was so glad to see me that he didn't even fuss about the fee I collected. He thought I had absconded with the truck and he would never see me or the truck again. It seemed like hours had passed since he sent me on that call. I vowed to myself that I was going to learn Dallas like the back of my hand, and I did. In a matter of days, you could not lose me anywhere in Dallas. Many folks stopped in the station for directions, and I could tell them how to get where they were going. Other service station men would refer them to me to give directions. My next assignment was to fix a flat tire. Except for the flats on my old 1929 Chevy which had a split rim, I had never fixed a flat tire especially on rims I had never seen before. I learned fast how to fix flats because that is what we did from about midnight until dawn after the traffic slowed down. We fixed flats for fifty cents. Tires were rationed, and they wore thin, so there were many flats to fix. People who had a flat tire would put the spare tire on and drop off the flat tire to be fixed. They picked up the repaired tire the next day. We charged twenty-five cents to put it back on their car and replace their spare tire back in the spare tire rack of the car.

I got about as dirty as a person could get in twelve hours. Tony washed my clothes. I would wear one set to work, change at work to another set, then change back to the set I wore to work to go home. So the clothes I wore at work for several days became very dirty.

I did not know who Ray Woods (the owner) was. He stopped in to use the payphone after I had been working for several weeks. He never used our regular company lines, just put a nickel in the payphone which set on a table in the lobby and used the phone. I was selling a new battery to a young lady who had just had a battery charge. We charged batteries for thirty minutes for one dollar. We had charged her battery, and I tested it after the charge. It had a dead cell, and I explained to her that it would start the car fine now, but the dead cell would pull it down. It probably would not start in the morning. I explained that she really needed a new battery, and if she wanted to have the battery replaced, I would not charge her a dollar for the battery charge. We had two types of batteries, those with wooden cells and those with glass cells. She wanted to know the difference. I explained that the glass cells were better as they did not deteriorate in hot or cold weather like the wood cells. I had no idea if that was right or not, but there was a three-dollar difference, so I thought that was as good an answer as any for someone who didn't know as much as I knew.

Ray Woods was listening to all my sales pitch. I had no idea why he was hanging around with a smile on his face. I thought he must have had some good news on the phone. This young lady, probably in her early thirties, was cute and had a cute smile like she understood everything I was saying. I pointed out that the tread on her tires were worn and that she should let us recap her tires. She had no idea what a recapped tire was. I showed her a tire that we had recapped with new synthetic rubber, and she thought that would be an excellent idea. We charged $7 to recap the common size. At that time, it was 600 by 16. A full recap that extended down the side of the tire wall about two or three inches was $11. She wanted to know the difference, and again, I explained that a full recap was not likely to come unglued and peel off. It had the look of a new tire. She wanted to know how she could do that as she worked every day and needed her car. I explained that we were the only all-night service center in Dallas; we could do it for her at night, and it would be ready for her in the morning.

She said, "How would I be able to do that? I work at the defense factory building airplanes. There is no time off to do things like that." I explained that I would take her home in the service truck and pick her up in the morning, and she would have a new set of recaps which would give her many safe trips to the factory and back.

"Really?" she said. "Would you do that?"

"Yes, and we could even install new seat covers while your tires are being recapped."

"How much will all of this cost?"

"Let me total it up for you. While all that is being done, we could put a Simonize glaze on your car, change the oil, and lubricate it for you. You will not have to miss an hour's work."

By this time, Ray Woods was hysterical. He thought I was putting on a show for him, but I had no idea who he was.

Ray Woods called Fred Johnson the next morning and said, "I want Little Red to be the night manager when Bob Thacker goes back to the farm."

Fred told Ray that I had only been working a few weeks, and I was just seventeen years old.

Fred was interrupted by Ray telling him, "I don't care about any of that. Make that kid the manager and give him a raise."

Fred took a personal interest in me and began to train me. He knew there may be a problem as I was the newest and youngest person on the night crew. Help was scarce during the war, and he did not want to lose a single person. He was afraid some of the older help would leave. Mr. Thacker thought it would be a good idea, and he really needed to get back to the farm. He also took a personal interest, and as soon as he gave the word to Fred, the job was mine. Before I hardly knew it, I was the night service manager of the biggest service station in Dallas.

We had eight gas pumps and three driveways by the pumps. We were the only full service station with two service trucks who stayed open twenty-four hours a day, seven days a week in Dallas. I was just seventeen years old, and I had a crew who recapped tires, installed seat covers, made road service calls, and pumped gas. The mechanical shop was closed at night, but I had two service truck drivers who were on the road most of the night fixing flats, towing cars, and pumping gas when they were not on the road.

I began to learn a lot about people. I handled the money, and it was not long before I detected some of the employees were stealing money collected from the customers. I could hardly believe my eyes. I discussed this with Fred, the general manager.

He said, "Just watch them closely and confront them when you see it happening." Help was so scarce he was reluctant to fire any of them.

December came, and my eighteenth birthday was on the fifth. I had to register for the draft within a certain number of days. My "greetings" letter from President Truman followed with instructions to report for induction on January 29, 1945. I felt that my short civilian career from June until January was over. I had made enough money to rent an apartment and move Mama to 226 North Peak Street. It was a block off the streetcar line, and it stopped a block away from the station. I thought this would be a good place for Mama if I went in the army. I was just concerned how I may be able to pay for it on army pay. I think it was only $21 a month at that time.

I failed the physical at the induction station. They were not taking people who had no vision in one eye. They told me I had to be able to shoot and aim with both eyes. I was classified as a 4-F. They told me that I would not be called up again for military service. This was a major blow to me. Ray Woods was happy to have me back as the night manager at the tire company. Mama was happy to know she would not be left alone. Several on the night crew were disappointed that I was coming back. Mediocrity was not a word in my vocabulary, not that I knew what it meant anyway.

I had made friends with a few more 4-Fs at the induction station. It seemed to me they were all good farm boys, and whatever defects they had that eliminated those from military service were not all that bad. I wondered what kind of service station attendants they would make. I discussed with Fred the possibility of hiring some of these boys.

He said to me, "Why don't you try one or two and see how they work out?"

That was all I needed to begin to replace some of the old guys whom I had caught stealing from the company. I began to interview the 4-Fs at the induction station and hired the ones I wanted who jumped at the chance to get off the farm. Soon, I had the youngest and hardest-working crew of any station in Dallas. I was so glad to get rid of the guys who did not have an interest in the company.

I convinced Ray Woods to send down some cars from the used car lot and let us spruce them up. He began to send down one car at a time. When the traffic slowed down around midnight, we would begin to polish, recap the tires, install new seat covers, and generally tune them up. I kept the night crew busy. We ran up a good bill for the auto company to pay to the tire company.

Next, I began to sell the cars before they could be returned to the auto lot. The car salesmen at the lot did not like this, and they tried to convince me to send people to them to make the sale as I was not collecting a commission. I didn't know what a commission was. I was just doing my job. Ray began to send down two cars at a time; one would come back and little

Red—as Ray called me—had sold the other one. There was no bargaining with me. I had the posted price, and if they wanted it, I sold it at that price. If they wanted to bargain, I told them I wasn't interested. The car was going back on the lot in the morning, and if they wanted to bargain, they would have to go to the lot and deal with a salesman.

Ray Woods decided to bring me to the auto company to sell cars. That was a big mistake for both of us. People were not interested in buying from a kid, and the old salesmen were not interested in having me there. The only good thing about it was that it was a day job instead of twelve hours at night.

Fred Johnson talked Ray into letting me come back to the station. I told Fred that if he would get some high-powered soap, I would have the guys wash down the large driveway after the traffic died down at night. Instead of soap, he found a chemical that was so strong it would eat away grease, gum, and ground in dirt when mixed with water. After a couple of nights, the driveway which, was referred to as the front, was looking like new. It gave the entire station a new look, and some customers would get out of their cars and look.

We had a lot of defense workers at the factory over in Fort Worth who stopped by almost daily for gas. Some began as early as four or five in the morning, and others would stop on the way home in the evening. Some worked the night shift as well. We had a lot of regulars. In those days, we pumped the gas; there were no automatic switches on the gas nozzles. We cleaned the windshields and checked the oil and tires, all for 16.9 cents a gallon.

There was a building adjoined to our station open from 7:00 a.m. until 11:00 p.m. Yes, it was the very first 7-Eleven store. The 7-Eleven headquarters is in Dallas, Texas. The company offices covers an entire block in downtown Dallas today. It was not even called 7-Eleven in the beginning. The name of the store was Crystal Ice. I talked to the manager about letting us sell coffee and donuts to gas customers before they opened at 7:00 a.m. He would not let us sell them. He would set out a coffee pot and the day-old donuts for our crew, and we could plug it in and help ourselves after they closed at 11:00 p.m. The night crew seemed to be making money for the company. The day crew was losing money. Fred decided to make me the day manager to see if he could turn it around.

I was glad to be moved to days, and I enjoyed my job there until I caught the daytime bookkeeper in a scheme. She had been working for months, maybe years, before I started to work there. I liked the lady very much. Her name was Mrs. Long, and her husband stopped by for gas regularly. Ray and Fred were discussing why the station was not making money, and I could not figure how the station was not profitable. So I began to keep my own records. This was a good lesson for me, because in later years, I did the same thing while working for Coldwell Banker Real Estate.

When I revealed my sales records, they did not agree with what was being reported. This went on for a few weeks, and no one knew I was keeping records except Fred, so he began to watch what was happening. It didn't take long to see that Mrs. Long was draining off funds every day except the weekends when she was not working. As soon as he verified that $1,700 was missing, he called in the auditor, and Mrs. Long quietly vanished. I never knew where she went or what happened, but I got all the accolades since I had a duplicate record of all sales. Shortly thereafter, we had a robbery back in the recapping shop, and I was buzzed up front to call the police Like a fool, I took out after the robber, caught him a half block away, and tackled him right on the sidewalk. He was a fairly small black boy, and through sheer determination, I was dragging him back to the station when a couple of helpers arrived. We didn't have to call the police because they stopped by at our station regularly to use the phone. We let them use the business phone without charge, so they didn't have to use a nickel in the payphone. The same policeman helped me in another case a few days later.

A customer came in and bought the most expensive battery we had and gave me a check. We made daily deposits, and the check bounced right away. The customer brought the battery back for a cash refund. I kept him there filling out papers until we could get the police there. He was wanted on numerous charges, so I got the battery back. Both Ray and Fred were impressed, and I was pleased that we were the ones who put the bite on that fellow. I remember that fellow just looked at me and finally said, "How can a dumb- looking kid like you be so smart?" The policeman just winked as he put him in the patrol car. Our storefront was never robbed because policemen hung out there all hours of the night.

It was now early 1945, and I had been promoted as day manager of Ray Woods Tire Company just prior to the death of President Franklin D. Roosevelt in April. Once again, I was the youngest person on the team at eighteen. In addition to the general manager and two ladies in the office, we had one grease monkey (who did all the lubes and grease jobs), two mechanics, and one helper. We also had two working in the tire recap shop, one doing seat covers, and three working the front. Fixing flats was part of working the front and pumping gas. There were two service truck drivers and a car washer who helped in the recap shop or seat cover department when needed. My hours had been reduced to eight, and I now had a day off every week instead of every other week. I spent a lot of time coordinating everything with the night manager. It was a lot of responsibility for a kid who had only been out of school less than a year.

When I rented the apartment where we lived on Peak Street, the owner was reluctant to rent it to me because rent was payable weekly at $8 a week. While he was trying to figure some way to turn me down by collecting a month in advance,

I gave him a hundred dollars and said don't bother us until we are down to the last week. First time in my life that I ever had a hundred dollars, much less one to spare. I still remember the look on his face. Right away, he wanted to make me house manager and collect his rent. "Nothing doing," I said, "I have enough responsibility as the day manager of Dallas' largest service station."

CHAPTER SEVENTEEN

World War II Was Over

T he news broke that the US had dropped an enormous bomb on Japan. I didn't think much about it, but a few days later, the second atomic bomb was dropped. Both Hiroshima and Nagasaki had been virtually wiped out. I will insert a brief statement here that will be more fully covered in a later chapter. In less than six months, I was drafted in to the army. They took me this time whether I could see with both eyes or not. I still have the battle plan that was to be used for the invasion of Japan beginning on March 1946, so I would have been right in the middle of that invasion had the two bombs not been dropped.

Before the war, Ray Woods was the biggest dealer of General tires in Dallas. His logo was "Ray Woods and General Tires goes a long way to make friends." It was on all our service trucks, invoices, etc. I thought for sure that he would stay a general tire dealer when tires were no longer rationed.

I don't know if he went to the Cooper Tire Company in Ohio or if they contacted him. Through some negotiations, he became the distributor of Cooper Tires for all 254 counties in Texas. He also became the automobile dealer for Kaiser-Frazer, a new brand of cars that was planning to come out at the end of the war. I think the company had geared up to build vehicles for defense and had retooled to build cars.

Building began at the car lot for a new showroom and service department. At the station, we cleared out space for storing tires in the back lot which had been fenced in. It covered about a quarter of an acre where we washed cars, stored customers' cars that had been serviced, etc. By this time, I had hired both my brother Jack and brother-in-law Berle who had been working the night shift at Zane's Freight Company. Something happened there—either management change or layoffs, I'm not sure—but they were both glad to leave, and I was glad to have them both at the station. After I went in the service, Berle went to work for Lone Star Gas Company. Brother Jack opened his own service station in West Dallas. It was near where he lived at 3520 West Turtle Creek Boulevard. It was close enough to the Trinity River, so he could also fish.

It was August 14, 1945, when President Truman announced the war with Japan was over, exactly ten years prior to the birth of our son, Larry Kenneth Deal. People came into the service station, tearing up and destroying their gas ration stamps and saying "Filler up!" I was afraid the station was going to burn down. We had not been officially advised that gas rationing was over, but everybody seemed to take it for granted, especially our customers.

I took the position of letting the attendants fill up the cars and to see if a customer would give up his or her ration book with us giving them a receipt. I had to be sure I could continue to order fuel. Ours was a Mobil station with the sign of the flying red horse rotating. We had competitive prices, the best service in North Dallas—and twelve gas pumps—increased from eight when I started there, and five bays. From the office, all I could see were car tops across the front in gridlock positions. Denying the gasoline at this point could have created a mutiny. All sirens in Dallas must have been cranked up wide open. The only way we could tell the phone was ringing was by the flashing lights on the buttons.

I coordinated with the Gulf station directly across the side street on Haskell Avenue, and they were doing the same thing. We kept the same prices at both stations. They would send business to us for items they did not do such as mechanical repairs, seat covers, and tire recapping.

We never did get an official word that gas rationing was over, and when the Mobil tanker came to fill our tanks, I wondered what was going to happen. By this time in the war, it was necessary to have the license number written on gas stamps, and they had to be pasted into sheets for easy counting. I had a jumbled-up mess, and I let him top off all the tanks before I discussed it with the driver. We had only a few charge tickets in those days, and what we did was different from today. We only took Mobil credit charges, and they had to be written out on Mobil forms with name, address, and account number and had to be signed. They were a mess, and we did not encourage them at all. Only a few customers used them. Our profit was three cents a gallon on regular gas and five cents on ethyl. The Mobil gas truck driver said just give me what you have, and we'll call it even. Such relief!

During gas rationing, it was necessary to paste or glue stamps on specific sheets about the size of a hundred postage stamps, certify that no gas had been dispensed into any other vehicle other than the one whose license plate number appeared on the stamp, and maybe a few other things that I cannot remember. One thing I do remember was that you had to have either a check or the money for the total delivery. There was no running an account or pay later plan. Our rent payment to Mobil for the station was based on the volume of gas we sold. All of a sudden, we were selling enough gas that the rent was almost nothing.

The announcement that Japan had surrendered came on September 2, 1945, and all hell broke out in Dallas. Air raid warning signals and sirens went off all over the city. Every policeman turned on his red lights and sirens. Dallas had a master control of traffic lights when an emergency vehicle was in a certain part of the city. All traffic lights turned red, and there was an audible ring or buzzer in each one. Whoever controlled these turned them on for the entire city of Dallas. Ration books were going up in smoke for sugar, meat, and coffee—everything that had been rationed. Just when we thought everything was calming down, drivers began to do crazy things like running over street buttons. Hubcaps were flying all up and down the street.

No one told us we could sell tires without ration certificates, but we got the first carload of tires that came to Dallas. I never knew how many tires a boxcar held, and I wish I still had the first invoice. All I can remember is that I dispatched all our service trucks, and they ran all day hauling tires. That was a mistake because this shut down my road service, and by now, we were the only station in Dallas doing twenty-four-hour road service. There was an eighteen wheeler on the auto lot that should have been used instead of the service trucks. Stations all over town were calling to see if we would wholesale tires to them, but we only sold to the Gulf station across the street.

In those days, there were not many different size tires like in 2015. Most all cars had a sixteen-inch wheel, and the standard size was 600 by 16. A few heavy cars used 650 and 700 by 16. Most were four-ply. There were a few six-ply tires. All used tubes at this time, and most tires and tubes were made from synthetic rubber, not real rubber which is used to make tires today. Fortunately, Cooper Tire Company had given us the exact variety we needed. Our bays were so full of people getting tires, one could not get in to buy gas without waiting in line. Some may remember the 1970s when gas lines were evidence of the gas shortage.

Another mistake I made was allowing the service truck drivers to go to people's houses or places of business and put new tires on for them. The drivers made out like bandits on tips doing this, and it was hard to get them to go on a service call.

Ray Woods had all 254 counties in Texas to set up distributors. He was so pleased at our success that he gave me thirty-six counties in Texas to set up Cooper Tire distributers. I had no idea what franchising was, and I often thought that if I had the knowledge then that I gained in later years with Coldwell Banker Residential Affiliates, what a difference it would have made. However, on second thought, it would have slowed me down considerably. This resulted in giving up my service manager job and beginning a new way of life.

Ray Woods gave me a brand new company car. A new Kaiser from the very first caravan of new 1946s that came late in 1945. I was given an almost unlimited expense account. I turned in receipts for purchases of $25 or more. What a contrast to the expense arrangements I had fifty years later with Coldwell Banker. I could do nothing wrong in his eyes, even when I backed one Cadillac into another Cadillac in his showroom. He had four very pretty daughters and no sons. He would invite me out to his house when I hauled SMU's (Southern Methodist University) mascot, a Mustang that he furnished, to the football games. I was too busy for girls or just about anything else. For the first time in my life, I had use of a new car and had money in my pocket, but I had no extra time for doing all the things I missed while growing up.

CHAPTER EIGHTEEN

Kenneth's Greetings Letter

A few weeks after my nineteenth birthday, a letter came in the mail from President Harry S. Truman. And just like the letter that came a year earlier, it said, "Greetings."

I had ten days' notice to report to the pre-induction station located at Fair Park just off Second Avenue in Dallas. My physical was in preparation to entering the army. Having been turned down exactly one year earlier to the day, on January 29, 1945, due to having vision in only one eye, I paid little attention to this notice. The war was over now, although it had not been declared over, so I believed this was just a routine check. Earlier, just prior to my eighteenth birthday in 1944, I tried to join the navy. The navy required a birth certificate. There was no way I could get a birth certificate before my eighteenth birthday. The process took several months. I had to find a non-relative who could certify to personal knowledge of my birth and a certified copy of a Texas census record that included me. This was tougher than being born to parents who were forty-seven and forty-nine years old.

When the reporting day arrived on January 29, 1946, I casually stopped by the induction station, cancelling only one of the three appointments for the day. What a shock! There was a room full of boys my age. They had handbags, suitcases, etc. I seemed to be the only one who did not think he was going somewhere. Oh well, I thought, as soon as they check me out, they will just renew my 4-F status. Or better yet, they would change my status to "Not needed," so I would not have to give up a couple hours every year going through all this.

As the process began, they marched us to lunch at a restaurant a block or so away. They had us picking up cigarette butts just for the experience of it as the corporal who was in charge said. I began to become more and more concerned that these guys meant business. The fact that I could only see the big E with my left eye did not even faze the young soldier doing the eye test. A few stations later, I was standing in front of a panel of officers, three or four young captains all doing the same thing. They were looking over a set of papers for each person. A young captain had a stamp with a big red border, and he stamped it on about half a dozen sheets of paper in a folder. He closed folder and handed it to me. With a big smile, he said, "You are in the army now."

What a shock! He instructed me to take a seat in the next room. It was a large room about half full of guys sitting there with folders. Most of them were excited and were carrying on with enthusiasm. I took a seat and opened the folder. Every page was stamped with a big red letters. "Limited Service." I had never heard of that branch of service. The guys all around me did not have that stamp on their records. I approached a weary looking sergeant who seemed to be in charge of the room and asked him if that meant I could go.

He gave me a weary smile and said, "Yes, that means you can go. There will be a bus here about 5:00 p.m. to take you to Fort Sam Houston where you will be processed into the army." I responded, "My papers say 'Limited Service,' and no one else seems to have that stamp on their folder."

He interrupted me, "That just means there will be some limits on what kind of assignments you will have in the army."

I began to walk out of the room and found a phone only to be called by the sergeant, "Where do you think you are going, soldier?" I told him I had to find a phone and cancel some appointments.

He took me to a room where a young lady was typing records as fast as she could type. I asked if I could use the phone. She told me to go ahead and talk as long as I could because she did not have time to answer the phone, and that would keep it from ringing.

As I began to make calls, she could tell my disappointment, but she did not know the half of it. I had three boxcars of tires on the way from Ohio and all sorts of unfinished business. I did not have a toothbrush with me, much less an overnight bag. Mama would have dinner ready, and I would not be coming home. My brother-in-law Berle Poteete was my best source to take on some personal chores for me. I asked Berle to call both Mama and my company. He told them that I would not be coming home and that soon I would be on my way to Fort Sam Houston in San Antonio, Texas.

Later that evening, we boarded one of those three buses. It was the only bus I had ever seen that had board seats and no back cushions. Never saw another one like it anywhere. They did not feed us before we left, but the busses made a few pit stops along the way, and we would purchase candy bars, sodas, etc. We arrived at Fort Sam just after daylight, and they unloaded us at a dining hall. They apparently did not know we were coming because there was very little food available.

My first meal was on a tin tray with partitions, but only two of them had food. Corned beef hash and a boiled potato were all there were on the tray. I took a seat at a long table that had a bench on each side for a seat. Two black soldiers came up, and one sat on one side and one on the other. That did not bother me, but it sure was different. They both had stripes on their sleeves and were waiting to be discharged. I did not start any conversation.

One of them said, "Glad you are here, soldier. That means I will be getting out sooner." I didn't know what that meant but casually mentioned that I probably won't be here long either.

This drew a smile from one of them as he said, "May be longer than you think."

He was right. If either of them would have told me that twenty- five years later I would be getting out, it would have been a hilarious conversation.

Following what the army called breakfast, we were lined up outside the mess hall in a column of fours. A smart and cocky soldier about five feet tall came up to take charge of us. He had two stripes and a T above the stripes. I didn't know what that meant. I learned later that he was a corporal with a designation of T, which meant he had some kind of a technical rating. We were all in civilian clothes, and he acted like we should know how to march, make corners, and all sort of stuff. I think he just wanted to show off. Our first stop was in a building where we were to undergo a physical. He told us that some would be going home from here if we did not pass the physical. The rest would fall in and be marched to the quartermaster building where we would be issued clothes.

My ears perked up because I knew that I should not have passed the physical back in Dallas. If I was lucky, I would not even have to change clothes before heading back to Dallas. I arrived at the station for eye exams where a staff sergeant was in charge. I explained that I could not see out of my left eye. He told me to sit over in a corner. He said, "When you decide you can see, I will check you again." One after another passed through the eye exam station, and when he come to a slack period, he said, "Can you see yet, soldier?"

I responded, "No better than before."

Some more would pass through, and he would ask me again. My hair was beginning to get red, and I had a lot more of it then than I have now. I don't remember the words I used, but I probably wouldn't print them anyway. He just stamped my papers and sent me to the next station. I thought he had stamped failed, but he stamped passed.

The next station handed out a duffle bag and also what is known as a barracks bag. The latter was somewhere to put my civilian clothes in with an address tag to be completed so my civilian clothes could be sent home. The next person I saw, and I can almost visually see him now, was a man probably in is sixties or seventies dressed in a suit and hat. I remember the smile on his face when he handed me a little book and said, "God bless you." I thought it must be a rule book. This was strange; he was not in uniform, and he was wading around in mud up to his ankles. I thought he must be a preacher; no one else would be out there smiling and handing out books in the rain. He was a Gideon. I didn't know who Gideons were, and I had never seen or heard of one. If someone would have asked me who Gideons were, I would not have had the slightest idea. Little did I know that thirty-two years later, I would become one of them. The book he gave me was the New Testament, Psalms, and Proverbs. It went in the bottom of my duffle bag. Today, it is in my military award case. It is the only remaining item of those issued that day.

At the next station, I was asked, "How much do you weigh?"

I answered 130.

"What size is your waist?" I answered twenty-nine. "Your height?"

I answered five feet ten inches.

Wow! When I look back at those answers now, almost seventy years later in 2015, the waist is thirty-nine, the weight was 180, and I have shrunk almost three inches. A lot has changed since that first day in the army, but I still cannot see out of my left eye.

Next, we were assigned a serial number with instructions to memorize it because if we were still in the army a hundred years from now, that number would not change. I still remember the number 38777565. However, the instructions were not correct. It started out as just a number. Then a prefix RA was assigned for regular army. Later the prefix was AF for Army Air Force. And still later the number was changed to my Social Security number. Months later, when I came at Lowry Air Force Base in Denver, Colorado, rather late one night, the guard on duty asked me to recite my serial number backward. It was just as easy backward as it was forward. I spit it out so fast, 56577783, he thought I had practiced it and momentarily held me up at the gate until he checked some additional identification.

The first night in the army was a nightmare for me. I had nothing at all in the way of bathroom items. Guys in the barracks told me that the PX (Post Exchange) stayed open in the evenings and that it was just a few buildings away. I struck out for the PX to pick up shaving and toothpaste items, writing material, etc. The lights in the barracks, except for the latrine, were out when I returned. I did not note the number on the outside of my barracks and began to guess at which one I had been assigned. I went from building to building. They all looked alike. Bunks were stacked two high in a row on each side of the building.

CHAPTER NINETEEN

Kenneth's First Days in the Army

I t's now late in 2015, and a paper I wrote about my first days in the army showed up when we moved from Colorado to Maryland. I will insert it here exactly as it was written. I will correct some of the things I have already written from memory, and there will be some duplication of what has already been written. It is old and battered, but I had placed it in a sheet of plastic which somewhat preserved it now for almost seventy years. There will be a few explanations in italics for the purpose of clarification. This was typed on an old Royal typewriter around the middle of June 1946.

ARMY TRIPS ACROSS THE ROAD

It goes back to 29 Jan 46 where the Army and I first shared my life together. On that date I got an early start to the Induction Station, carrying my greeting papers I had received ten days prior. Walking out of the house was not half as hard as I had suspected it to be. After I was a few yards down the street a funny feeling was approaching that I may not be able to return home that night as I had planned. So feeling both glad and sorry, I continued to the car stop which was only a short distance from where I lived.

Having in my possession at that time $28.00 and two car tokens. I used to board the Cross-town Streetcar which took me within four blocks of my destination. After leaving the street car I began a slow pace and was picked up by a gentleman who took me directly in front of the Induction Station. (Funny, I don't remember that part at all.) Being the first to arrive, I began to walk around outside. Slowly, men about my age, some younger, began to arrive.

By this time it was daylight and the doors were opened from the inside. As we entered, some with small hand bags, shaving kits and some like myself, just me, myself, and I. We were directed where to go and wait. We all waited for about an hour, during this time many thoughts ran through my mind. Would they take me? Would they have me in the Navy or in the Army? Would I be disappointed if they didn't take me? How long would they keep me? Could I stand what the other men could? And several other thoughts that were too numerous to mention. (I do not remember that I had all of those thoughts!)

By this time, I noticed that some of the other boys were thinking on the same terms, while others did not have a care in the world. Soon the process of physical examination was underway. This consisted of written and oral questions as well as the physical consisting of ex-rays, blood test and all the so called routine questions. The only question in my mind was what they would say about my eyes, having clear vision in only one would no doubt cause me to be rejected as it was just exactly one year earlier. (My first draft notice was for January 29, 1945, exactly a year earlier.)

The final process brought me before two officers, one Army and one Navy. (Funny, I always thought it was four Army Captains) The Navy Officer received my records first, gave them a quick check over and looked up something in a little manual, then he passed it on to the Army Officer who gave them a quick check over and looked up something in a little manual. After satisfying himself, he stamped several pages. I could not see what he stamped so I was left in distress. It was getting close to chow time so they marched us away in groups to a restaurant several blocks away.

I waited for what seemed like hours where we were assembled in the largest room and remained standing. The first thing I knew we were being sworn in and it was 5pm. After picking up all the coke bottles, stacking all the chairs back against the wall, we were told we would be leaving at 9 pm. I had not expected to leave that night but I had no choice. I decided to go home and pack up a few things to take with me. As I started to leave, I was asked by a guard at the door; "Where do you think you're going soldier?" I told him I was going home but he convinced me that I was in the Army now, this was my home. So I just made a few phone calls and sat around until we took off. (These were to cancel appointments and give instructions to brother-in-law Berle Poteete as to what was happening.)

At 9 pm sharp, we loaded into GI busses for the all night ride to Fort Sam Houston, Texas. It was plenty cold and everyone was singing, that helped me to forget that I was leaving the city which was the best city in the world. (Wow, I forgot that I felt that way, but then I had not been in many cities. We left at 9 pm not 5 as I thought I remembered earlier.)

We arrived at Fort Sam the next morning about 7am, just before dawn. They unloaded us and marched to several places before they decided to take us to chow. My first Army chow was ground up meat and potatoes, an orange and a bottle of milk.

After chow, we were marched outside and were given a few instructions that were kind of harsh by a short cockeye little soldier, like not whistling at the girls, etc. Still in civilian clothes, we went to a large building where we the only thing we accomplished was our dog tags. It took only a short time to remember my serial number, it was quiet simple, and luckily I got an easy one. I put the remaining street car token I had on the chain of the dog tags and it is still on there to this day. (Believe it or not, it is still on there until this day.) During the last hour of daylight, we were issued two blankets, a pillow and pillowcase and two sheets, but no raincoat and it was still raining but that is better than what I sometimes get now. (Must have been at Lowry because sometimes we only issued one sheet that we folded over to make the bottom and top.) We were also given a towel and a shaving kit. (I don't remember that at all.) Being kind of excited and knowing the lights were going out at 9 pm I made arrangements to shave and found I needed shaving cream and tooth paste. I bounced out to the PX to get the needed items. I was disappointed about not being able to find any stationary. I started my journey back to the barracks. The Post was sure large, and it was raining then, the mud was slick as ice so I fell down and must have lost my sense of direction. I could not find my barracks. The buildings all looked alike and I had forgotten if I was upstairs or downstairs so becoming more panic all the time and knowing the lights were going out soon made it worse. I finally remembered that my barracks was the last on the end of the rows but there were rows as far as I could see and I did not even know if I was on the right end of the rows or not.

When I found a barracks where the faces looked familiar, I felt better. Someone called me "Red," then I thought that I must be in the right place but happened to think, everybody calls me Red. While I was gone, someone moved my Duffle Bag from upstairs to downstairs. Who and why, I have never known to this day, but I did find it. My clothes were muddy and so was I. The lights were due out in a few minutes, so I made my bed first, knowing that the lights in the latrine remained on all night. After that dreary day had passed, I slept well that night and was awakened at 5:30 am the next morning to find it was still raining. Before we marched to chow, I went outside and got the number of that barracks in case I became lost again and I still have that number in my address book.

Chow that morning was a little better but I got soaking wet standing in line in the rain. They took us out to drill after chow, in the rain. We did not learn much about drilling but after chow at noon we drilled some more. It was still raining. Later that afternoon they marched us to a supply building and issued raincoats. I made another attempt to find stationary but none was available. I borrowed some from one of the boys who had brought it from home and wrote home for a supply of stationary. (Sure don't remember that. Sister Tony must have though it very odd too but later three boxes caught up with me.) My return address was: Company C. WD PDC, Fort Sam Houston, Texas. (Shirley had come to work at Fort Sam in 1942 and had left in 1944 before I arrived.)

The first Sunday in the Army was my first tour of KP (Kitchen Police) duty which was from 4:00 am until 8 pm. It was my fifth day in the Army. The next Sunday, my sister came to see me and that was the happiest day I spent in the Army up to that time. (This was a visit from sister Corda, J. D. and Helen Hardaway from Crystal City, Texas.) The following week brought two more tours of KP duty and several days of drill. We had three formations daily and mail call which I never missed after I began to receive a few letters. The only clothes that fit were my shoes, I was disappointed in myself. I had expected to look kind of sharp but my baggy uniform looked kind of sick.

During the next week we had another tour of KP duty and not less than six shots and a vaccination before we were put on orders. I was assigned to the Army Air Corps and was being sent to Sheppard Field for Basic Training. Upon arrival we found training was stacked up and there was not enough room for us to begin basic. While we were waiting for ten days, three of which were spent on KP, we scrubbed floors, picked up cigarette butts and practiced "Falling in and out of the Barracks with a second lieutenant holding a stop watch." He was having fun teaching us how to come to attention when an Officer came in the barracks. He would slip in at all hours of the day and night just to see us come to attention. My mail was catching up with me. I received three boxes of stationary, but then I was able to buy stationary at Sheppard. Writing letters was my biggest pastime at nights except when we were drilling. One night we drilled all night because the barracks were not clean enough to suit that lieutenant. We were so crowded that we had to crawl into the end of our bunk. They were so close together it was a problem making the bed as we had to wait as each bunk was slid down far enough so we could get around it, and then move it so the next guy could make his bed. The Army was trying to process all of us young guys in so the old ones could be discharged. Many were discharged who had been through the war. Our shot records were all lost, left at Fort Sam Houston, or missing from our records. We received all of the shots again recorded on a new set of shot records. We were given orders to turn in all our bedding and pack up to be transferred back to San Antonio, Texas, that was all we knew. We had just come from there ten days ago. We all marched over to the depot which was a half mile and waited until noon for the troop train, only to find that the train won't be through until the next day. We packed up barracks bags and marched a half mile back to the barracks. While at Sheppard we had four "shake downs" checking for thieving. I lost a fatigue jacket with a Parker 36 pen that my brother Jack had given me two days before I entered the Army. The next day, we packed up and made the same trip again with our Duffle Bags and this time the troop train showed up. It was just like the one we rode up about ten days earlier. Gambling continued to be the main thing all the way back through Texas.

We arrived at Kelly Field about noon the next day. This was the most beautiful base I had seen so far. The Officers were kind and even helped unload our bags. I was assigned to Squadron "Q" Platoon 63. It was nice to see a place with pretty green grass and not so crowded. The chow was really good most of the time and the Mess Halls were nice and clean. (Actually, we were on the side of the base that is now called Lackland Air Force Base). It was known as San Antonio Aviation Cadet Center. (SACC) at that time. The base was being converted from Cadet training to Basic Training. Pilot training had either dropped off or terminated because the war ended. I was assigned to Squadron QQ, Flight 150 and remained there all the way through Basic Training. (I notice that I never mentioned here—probably did not know it at the time—that Sheppard was being converted to a basic training center for black soldiers. In 2006, I took the McChordites military reunion group for a tour of Lackland since some of them also went through basic there. The flight numbers were up to 3,150.)

We were there a few days before Basic started. They did not have enough NCO's so they took two men from each Flight and trained them to march. Most of the boys in my Flight were from Texas. KP was still another duty all through Basic. We were informed time after time, that as soon as Basic was completed that we would be given a furlough; and then go overseas, so we all had the same information showing up in our letters home. Our shot records from Sheppard never showed up so we had all those shots and boosters again. I was beginning to feel like a pin cushion.

As the hot Texas sun beamed down, we attended classes of all sorts. Some took interest in a few things, and a few dreamed the whole way through. During this time there were test given called Army General Classification Test, know as our AGCT score. Most of the grades were average, so I felt as good as most at 110. A few were very poor hoping it would help them get out of the Army. A few were superior due to higher education and some of those received assignments above their abilities. (Years later, I had an assignment back at Lackland to write the proficiency test for the accounting and finance career field in 1962, and we established that the score had to be 100 or better to qualify for this field.)

We were called up for classification with an "Army Choice" of about two to five jobs. This was an important decision to make. I had three choices: Weather Bureau, Clerk Typist, or Airplane Mechanic. (Gee, I had forgotten these choices since my career was none of them!) I chose Clerk Typist after hearing the job description and the training time for each one because I expected to be out within six months. I choose the one with the shortest training course which was at Lowry Air Force Base, Denver, Colorado for ten weeks. (As draftees, we had an obligation for the duration of the war plus six months. Although the war was over, it had not been declared over, so the six months was not to start until it had been declared over.)

Upon completion of Bivouac, which was four and half days out in the hills of Texas among rattle snakes and the hot sun, we had our marksman practice and several gas attacks that required our gas masks training along with a few classes on survival. I made Sharpshooter on the rifle and Marksman on the pistol while most boys just qualified. We were all glad to get back for a nice hot shower and some good chow. Our day of return was the last day of basic training. During basic we were restricted to the base for the first forty-five days due to a spread of Polio on the base. We learned that there was an awful race problem at Sheppard just after we shipped out to Lackland. (The disease polio may be a foreign term to my grandchildren and their children. Let's hope it never comes back because it was a crippling type disease that seems to be eradicated.)

My first trip to San Antonio, we called it (Sanan Twine), did not impress me very much. Breckenridge Park was a nice place, but I was not fond of San Antonio. I did take a ride in a canoe on the riverfront. (It is all considerably different now from what it was in the mid-1940s.) My first pay day in the Army was in the middle of March. They paid me $11.53 and I never to this day have figured how they came to such an odd sum for a month's pay. (I spent twenty-five years in finance after that, and I still don't know how they arrived at my first pay.) At the end of March I was paid again, this time it was a little better, $21.40 that represented $50.00 as a Private. Pay had increased from $21.00 to $50.00 a month between my first draft notice and the second draft notice. I had deductions of $22.00 for a Class "F" allotment to which the Army added $12.50 giving Mama $37.50 a month check. There were deductions for a Class "N" Insurance of $6.50 and a deduction of $0.10 for the Old Soldiers' Home. There was a laundry charge of $2.00. This became my standard pay for the first six months. Back commissions from Ray Woods Tire Company came to $880.00 during that same period.

After Basic we were sent to "AA" Squadron, Shipping and Receiving. Some were going and others were coming. We were going. We were there for ten days before shipping orders came. During this time, we were swimming and playing ball waiting for that promised furlough before going overseas. Neither the furlough nor overseas assignment came. When orders came through, we were paid at 0200 in the morning of the first day of April. (Gosh, I had forgotten, that must have been an April's Fool joke.) It was raining when we turned in our bedding and was being paid.

The Troop Train left at 0600, which is 6:00 am. An old worn out Sergeant put me in charge of the car I was in with about twenty others. I was told that I was the only one that could leave the car and that was for the purpose of getting candy, ice cream, cigarettes, etc. for the boys who wanted it. We were going through Fort Worth so I thought this would be a good chance to make a telephone call. When we arrived at Fort Worth, I had about $5.00 worth of supplies to get for boys in my car. After getting all of the supplies I began to search for an open phone booth but none could be found. Several dollars was lost and won by those gambling on the troop train as it moved up through Texas, Oklahoma, New Mexico and Colorado. (This was my first time out of Texas.) We were served food from a rolling diner car. Several of us worked in the kitchen car from time to time and the food was pretty good.

Sometime during the night, the train stopped and some of the cars were left behind to catch another engine that took them to Chanute Air Force Base, Illinois to the Sheet Metal School. The interesting thing about that was that some of the gamblers from our car were in one of those cars gambling. I would not let the lights stay on in our car past 10:00 pm so some left to gamble where the lights were still on. Since I was in charge of our car, I thought I may be in big trouble, as these boys duffle bags were in our car. The old sergeant brushed it all off, he said; "they will make Sheet Metal guys out of those guys and issue them some more clothes, don't worry about it." This changed their careers from whatever they were supposed to do. I was off the hook anyway as the ole sergeant didn't seem to care one way or the other. He must have been on his way out of the service, or he was a career guy who had been through the war and going for retirement.

(Well, this has been quite an exercise. There were so many things I had forgotten until I found this old yellow piece of paper written almost seventy years ago. Suppose that is a good sign for those reading this. You are never too young to start with your memories because memory does fade with the years.)

Continuing on, before I found the old paper

There was a combination of things we were called upon to do such as learning drill movements. It was not easy in the mud to learn how to do left or right face, about face, etc. We learned what KP (kitchen police) was all about. Modern-day practice is much different. I took our McChord group through one of the dining halls at Lackland AFB in 2006 and learned that there is no more KP. It is all done by contractors, and the food line is a long cafeteria with variety of food like you wouldn't believe. It must be different in today's combat areas, but I'm not sure of that. They could also be contractors. On September 1, 2015, I had been retired from the United States Air Force for forty-five years, so I am no longer qualified to report on today's activities. Wow! That is nineteen years longer than I was in the service.

My name was called out at one of the formations on Sunday morning. I was not expecting that because these formations were primarily for old soldiers with loads of stripes who were being mustered out of the army as fast as they could be processed. Kind of a surprised, I just knew they had decided to muster me out, so I headed for the platform where the sergeant told me that I visitors. He instructed me to go to the orderly room and get a pass for the day to be with my visitors.

I did not know where the orderly room was or what one even looked like. I saw my brother-in-law J. D. Hardaway standing off to the side. He, my sister Corda, and my niece Helen had driven up from Crystal City, Texas, to see me, and I did not know they knew I was there. I have forgotten how they knew, but I got in the car, and we drove off base. That was my first and only AWOL (absence without leave) time in my twenty-five years. I never got the pass that I was instructed to get because I did not know where to go or how to go about getting a pass.

We went to visit some friends my sister knew at their house where several other people were also visiting. There was an old master sergeant there who had hash marks (three years of service per mark) all the way up his sleeve with just enough room for his overseas bar (each bar represented six months overseas). He had a chest full of ribbons. I was wearing olive drabs with a field jacket, so I was out of uniform for being off post. I had no pass, and I was scared to death. He just smiled at me and said nothing. I suppose he was either waiting for retirement or perhaps had just retired. I smiled back and stayed clear of him, hoping he would just leave me alone, which he did. It was great to see my sister Corda that day; she had driven about two hundred miles and had to take me back to the post and drive back to Crystal City.

About the ninth day I was in the army, we had the opportunity to listen to an Army Air Force first lieutenant give a recruiting talk about the Army Air Force (AAF). Boy, was he good, all dressed up with the then Pinks. (I believe it was the best uniform the army has ever had.) He had wings and ribbons, and he was an excellent speaker. He told us about life in the Army Air Force, which was still part of the army at that time, just a different branch. His final pitch was that as draftees, we were in for the duration plus six months, and no one seem to know when the war would be declared over. We may be in a year, or it could be indefinitely. We had the option to reenlist in the air force for three years, and then we knew when our time was up. We also had a choice of overseas theatres to choose from, and we would be paid $100, mustering out pay when we left the army. He sold me and a host of others. My nine days in the army were up, and if I had been smart, I could have had my name straightened out to be Virgil instead of using Virgle all these years. Most forms that one completes in the military are formatted to ask for the last name, first name, and middle initial. I was called into the office of a captain who asked me how I spelled my first name. I looked at my dog tags which said "V-i-r-g-l-e." Since I never used that name and I don't remember ever printing or writing it until I came in the army, I had listed it on various papers several different ways, and it was becoming an administrative nightmare. He asked me to select a spelling and keep that for the next hundred years if I stayed in the Army Air Force that long. I think I had some idea of the impact of that decision, but he scared me, so I made a bad decision that stayed with me throughout my military career.

My new set of records had "Limited Service" stamped all over them. I kept my same serial number, but it now had RA in front of the number, which meant regular army. I was no longer considered an inductee but was now in the air force branch of the regular army. When the air force became a separate branch of its own in 1947, the prefix became AF.

CHAPTER TWENTY

Kenneth's Basic Training

The old paper "Army Trips across the Road" spilled over into basic, so kind of like "Limited Service," this chapter will cover only limited items that were not included in the earlier chapter.

This was the first time I realized there was such a difference between the north and the south. Our barracks quickly divided into Yankees on the north side and rebels on the south side of the barracks. We fought the Civil War over again, somewhat good natured, for six weeks of basic.

We tried to trip each other up on the general orders. The only way one could get a pass was to be able to recite whichever general order we were asked by the officer who issued the pass. If we missed the question, we did not qualify for the pass. Just like when the Lord comes again, we did not know which of the general orders would be asked, so the proper thing to do was learn them all. Believe it or not, the south enjoyed teaching the north and vice versa because both sides would try to teach the other side incorrectly so they would not get a pass. I remember that the question I was asked was General Order No. 5, "To quit my post only when properly relieved." The Yankee who was teaching me tried to get me to say, "To stay on my post until properly relieved." That was all it took to deny a pass.

I purchased my first camera on the first trip off base. It was a Kodak 110. I began to take my first pictures. I have been taking pictures ever since, but my cameras have been updated. Mama was so pleased to get some photos. She could not address envelopes well enough for them to reach me. I always addressed one, put a three- cent stamp on it, and included it in every letter I sent her. Shirley did this after we were married, but the price of the stamps was not the same. We did it as long as she could still write to us.

The troop train experience from Texas to Colorado was covered in a previous chapter, but I recall spending a lot of time looking out the window. This was my very first trip out of the state of Texas. I remember getting up in the middle of the night to see what New Mexico looked like. When our train came into Lowry Air Force Base near Denver, Colorado, I could see the front range of the Colorado Rockies from the door of the troop train.

I recall the lump in my throat when I thought about those boys who were supposed to be with us but were diverted to Chanute AFB, Illinois, during the middle of the night. If I had not demanded that the lights be turned out, resulting in them going to another car to continue their gambling, they would be with us in Colorado.

When I asked the old sergeant what to do with their duffle bags, he told me to turn them in to the supply sergeant. "Sarge," I said, "that will change their whole military specialty."

"Yap," he muttered, "Son, that is just your first command decision. You will make many in your military career, and we don't sweat the small stuff."

The old sergeant didn't know just how right he was, and I got the idea that he really didn't care. He was ancient in my eyes, must have been about forty years old, and he took everything in stride.

CHAPTER TWENTY-ONE

Kenneth's First Military Technical Training

There were many airmen trained at Lowry Air Force Base in various specialties. Each specialist had a series of numbers that were called military occupation specialist (MOS).

The numbers changed from time to time. Later in the air force, mine changed to Air Force Specialty Code (AFSC). The number on my records represented a clerk-typist. It was MOS 405, I believe; I am not sure because I didn't have it very long. I was told that there was a shortage of finance clerk-typist, and my specialty was being changed to fill this need, and the next class was starting soon. The clerk-typist class was full, and if I waited for the next class, it would delay my furlough and overseas assignment. That was enough for me to say, "Put me in the finance clerk-typist class." The clerk told me that the only difference was that I would be typing finance vouchers. Little did he know the difference. I firmly believe the Lord has His hand in this change.

Graduating from this finance class entitled me to have a MOS 623 instead of a 405. This is where I met Richard C. Hargons. We called him Jack until he died a few years ago. Jack was also in basic at the same time as me but was in a different flight. He and another fellow by the name of Kretsinger were in the same finance clerk- typist class. This was the beginning of a six-year period when Jack and I would be stationed together. Then, upon my retirement twenty- five years later, Jack came to replace me. He stayed for thirty years, and we were in contact with him right up until his death.

Jack looked like a sergeant should look even in those days, so he was put in charge of our flight to march us back and forth to class, to the mess hall, etc. It was kind of funny to us when they asked the sergeants to fall out and report on roll call, Jack fell out with the sergeants. Six months caught up with us during training, and we were all promoted to private first class (PFC). This meant we could wear one stripe on each sleeve.

I don't remember a lot of the details about the finance school. It was a full-day course five days a week. It included typing and learning about pay forms, how to compute pay and travel, write checks, etc. This is long before finance merged with accounting into one specialty called accounting and finance. This was a great opportunity to check out a new town—Denver, Colorado. Wow! What a place. It has changed from the way we knew it seventy years ago. I never suspected that I would be at the Accounting and Finance Center headquarters located downtown at 3800 York Street in Denver in the 1960s.

Graduation was a pleasant experience. All we had to do was wait for our overseas orders that would have our very first furlough built in on the way to the overseas depot. We did a lot of KP (kitchen police) which we had been excused from while in class. We watched the troop trains pull in with a new group of green horns, and we heckled them. I wondered how many of them should have gone to Chanute AFB instead of Lowry.

I had written letters home saying that I would be arriving in Dallas as soon as our orders were cut. I was anxious because we didn't get to come home after basic training as promised, and I had not been home since I left on January 29, 1946. We were hoping for orders at each formation because we were getting tired of policing the area, pulling KP, checking out bedding to incoming personnel, and doing anything else they could find for us to do.

Then the news came, orders were in, and names began to be read from our formation. "The following names are being ordered to such and such base." When they read my name along with Jack and Kretsinger, all grouped together, we could hardly wait for the destination. It was Greensboro, North Carolina, followed by a pause—that is the overseas depot for Europe. "This is not your final destination which will come after you are processed at Greensboro for a base in Europe."

We all celebrated and speculated where we may be going. We wrote home that we had ten whole days of leave plus travel time and that we would be home soon. The next morning, we asked the first sergeant if it was necessary for us to stand the formation since we had our orders. He informed us that our orders had been cancelled. It seems that the advance finance course (MOS 622) was about to start, and it was short of students for a full class. The top ten students in the just graduated 623 class were being diverted to fill the class. All three of us qualified to attend the advanced class. What a disappointment! This is one more diversion that may have had the Lord's blessing, but we sure didn't think so at the time.

The advanced finance course was for those who were already assigned to the finance office at various bases and were being sent from those offices for higher level of instruction. These were an assortment of different grades who were on temporary duty (TDY) to Lowry AFB and would be returning to their duty stations upon completion of the class. The advanced course was two weeks longer than the basic course. What a blow! Our leave home had to wait another three months. Another boy from a different basic class by the name of Cook was also put in the advance course.

The three of us decided to go to the base canteen and drown our sorrows with a few beers. Well into our stay at the canteen, I felt a blow to the back of my head. It knocked my glasses off, spilled my beer, and left a knot on the back of my head. The waitress had given me a better stiff arm than I ever got playing football. One of the fellows in the booth behind us had pinched the waitress. He ducked, and she hit me instead of him. She knew immediately that she hit the wrong person. I accepted her apology, but it seemed I never could do enough to ease her embarrassment. She grew to like me more than I was interested in her. She was at least ten years older than me but offered to be friends and do things together. I declined all the offers with the words "I'm shipping out." The incident gave us something to talk about besides what we perceived to be our troubles.

The advance course was excellent. We had the opportunity to talk real finance with those who were corporals and buck sergeants who had already been in the field, some for a year or more. We did not have to take typing this time or to march to class or the mess hall, and there was no KP as we could trail along with the big boys. We spent a lot of time in Denver. Somehow, we never did get to the mountains.

Almost immediately following graduation, orders came, and five of us were assigned to Andrews Army Air Field in Camp Springs, Maryland. No one from our class had been to Andrews. We had no idea where it was, and it seemed that no one else did either. The transportation people would issue a transportation request (TR) if we were going directly, but we all wanted to take our leave as it had been ten months since we left home. We were all smart now, and we knew about travel pay and constructive rail time and knew how to compute travel so that all five of us would report in at Andrews on the same day.

I remember that when I purchased my train ticket in Dallas to Andrews at Camp Springs, Maryland, none of the ticket agents knew where Camp Springs was located. They checked a few books and discussed between themselves whether to send me to Baltimore or to Washington DC. The decision was made to send me to Washington and let me figure out how to get there after I arrived. I was tired of writing home that I would soon be there. I just slipped in on everyone with no notice.

CHAPTER TWENTY-TWO

Kenneth's First Military Leave

I recall arriving in Dallas and catching a street car to the end of the line just like I did when I was living at Tony's. I walked about a mile up the sandy road and slipped in on my sister Tony. That evening, we went over to see my mother who lived with Jack in his little house at 3520 West Turtle Creek Boulevard in West Dallas. I stayed out on the porch while Tony, Berle, and Bill went inside only to hear Mama ask as soon as they came in, "Have you heard anything from Kenneth?"

I couldn't wait any longer; before they could answer, I came busting through the door in my full PFC uniform. I remember the tears of joy and how she referred to me as "my baby, my baby." I was the baby of the family. What a joyous time we had visiting. I plan to hear those words again someday, and it will be even more joyous I'm sure.

My first visit was to Ray Woods at his auto company. He gave me a new Frazer to drive while I was home on leave. He sold the service station to C. A. Christianson who had been released from the army as a lieutenant colonel about the time I went in the service. Ray decided that with both the new car dealership with Kaiser- Frazer and the tire distributorship with Cooper Tires, he no longer needed the service station. Ray told me he no longer had managers around like me, and it wasn't fun anymore. Besides, he had a service department with the car distributorship. He made some great offers to me if I was getting out of the service. My first thoughts were if I had not made that three-year commitment with the air force, I probably would be getting out about now, and he was ready to take me. I have to pause here and say that I have no regrets. I believe the Lord once again had His hand on my future, and it was not to be in the tire business. Ray later lost both distributorships. I have no idea what happened or why, but he gave me a car to drive each time I came home on leave. He knew I would have it washed, lubed, and oil changed each time before returning it to the company. Somewhere along the line, the Kaiser-Frazer auto company went out of business. I do not recall seeing one in old car museums. They just kind of vanished. Cooper Tires is still a major tire manufacturer after all these years. However, for the family members reading this, keep in mind that Shirley would not have been in my life and you would not be in my life either if I had not chosen the United States Air Force as my career.

It was October 1946, and the Texas state fair was on at Fair Park where I was inducted into the army ten months earlier. I revisited the old site as well as all of the people I could find whom I knew when I left for the service. I had a great visit with Shorty and Mrs. Cox, the school custodian at Plano. Shorty had retired from the school system. His birthday was in August, and I sent a check to him each year for his birthday until he died several years later. It was as difficult for me to leave for Washington when my furlough was over as it was when I left the induction station ten months earlier.

CHAPTER TWENTY-THREE

Kenneth's First Duty Station

It was late in October 1946 when I arrived at Union Station in Washington DC. I was surprised to find a military office there in the terminal. I thought this may be the best place to find out how to get to Andrews Field as it was known then, named after Lieutenant General Andrews. A corporal was on duty, and he told me he would be relieved shortly, and I could ride to Andrews with him. What a break!

I wondered around the terminal until he was relieved and rode in a military Jeep with him. I asked questions all the way during the ten miles out of Washington DC. He told me that it had been a pretty good base but that SAC just moved in and took over, so he didn't know what the future would hold. My heart dropped because my basic training had been at the San Antonio Aviation Cadet Center which was also called SACC, pronounced the same as the Strategic Air Command (SAC). There are major differences, but I thought I was coming to a basic training center. I recall that as we arrived at Andrews, there was a raised mound of dirt, and the word Andrews spelled out. That mound of dirt is no longer there, and the main gate is in a different location in 2015. I had no idea that my bride-to-be was also moving from Bolling Air Base, DC, to Andrews Air Force Base about the same time. She worked in the civilian personnel office of Continental Air Command which was being renamed as the Strategic Air Command under General George C. Kenny.

The corporal knew how to find my orderly room when I signed in Saturday afternoon, but I was not due in until Sunday. My barracks was just three buildings down the road, and it is still there in 2015 though it is no longer used as a barracks. It has long since been converted to an office building. When my granddaughter Wendy graduated from high school, I took her by to see my old barracks years ago.

The non-commissioned officers club was just across the way. I could smell steak cooking, but I had to wait until I made corporal to go. The month I made corporal, the club moved across the base, and the club became a library.

Finally, I had a duty station, so for the first time, I could empty out my duffle bag and put everything away. When I poured out the contents on my bed, the little New Testament, Psalms, and Proverbs given to me by the smiling Gideon some eleven months earlier was right on top of the pile. It was Saturday afternoon, and none of my fellow students had arrived, so I walked up to a church that I had seen next to the orderly room. It was a little old church that had been converted to a chapel when Andrews AFB was established during the war. There was a small graveyard inside the fence, and service times were posted. It served for both Protestant and Catholic services at different times.

The chapel is still active along with several others on Andrews Air Force Base. There were some civilians who lived off the base who continued to come. This may have been their church before it was annexed by the base. I had the privilege of delivering a Gideon message there in 1991, some forty-five years later when I was a Gideon in Prince George's County, Maryland.

As my buddies began to arrive, I was the old hand on the base, having preceded them by twenty-four hours. I could show them the dining hall and where a few other things were located. I had located the finance office. It was next to the fire station and flagpole across from the personnel office. I went to personnel on Monday morning, and my records had come in. Each of us were given an incoming clearance sheet. The purpose was to clear the base when arriving or departing. We had to go to more than a dozen places to have the sheet initialed. That is when we learned how big Andrews was. We had to ride a bus to the SAC side of the base. I recall that is was seventeen miles around the perimeter road. We were assigned to a flight where we had a morning formation to be sure everyone was there, and then we marched to work.

Two of us, I believe it was Kretsinger and myself, decided to walk over to the finance office and introduce ourselves. The finance officer was Captain J. B. Regan, and the deputy was Chief Warrant Officer (CWO) G. J. Ross. Captain Regan was dressed in what we called the Class A uniform. He had two gold diamonds, one on each side of his lapel, which is the finance insignia. They were not really diamonds or gold but little metal objects that looked like gold and shaped like a diamond. I still have my old nameplate with the finance insignia carved in the middle. I had it hand carved in the Philippines for $2.50. The officers were glad to see us, and they looked forward to seeing us come to work on Tuesday morning. This was on either late October or early November 1946.

When we reported in the next morning, we were greeted by all of the civilian employees. They were more than glad to see us. There was only one other military enlisted man there. He was Master Sergeant McKim, and he was called the chief clerk. He now had a crew. He was a great guy, nothing like the other sergeants we had been associated with during training. I still remember a few of the names. Mr. Ed Cunningham ran the travel section. Mrs. Gertrude Kapplinger typed travel vouchers, Mrs. Adeline Triband ran the commercial accounts section, Miss Kitty Brown ran the officer's pay section, and Mrs. Smith ran the enlisted pay section. There were a few more I cannot remember.

It was a small number compared to the offices I served in later days. Everyone was assigned to a different section except me. My records still had "Limited Service" stamped all over them. The personnel office had called Mr. Ross (warrant officers were addressed as Mr.) and said to him, "Let's see if this man is going to be adapted to your office. He may not have what it takes to be a finance man, so don't assign him to a specific section. Just use him as a gofer or detail man until you decide if he will work out or not, and then we will either reassign him to some lesser duty that he can handle, or he can stay in your office."

I thought this may be my chance to get out, so I looked into what was required to get a hardship discharge. I thought I may qualify since I was the only one with a dependent mother and had a Class F allotment that cost the government an extra $12.50 a month.

In the meantime, Mr. Ross began to send me over to the base adjutant's office with certificates to be signed. As best I remember, officers who were not living on base had to have the adjutant's approval on some certificate in order to receive basic allowance for quarters. I made a lot of trips over there, kept the potbelly stoves fired all day, and did any other chores that had to be done. I convinced the other four not to worry about me. I expected to be getting out just any day.

Days passed. Personnel told me I did not qualify for a hardship discharge. In the meantime, we got a new finance officer, Major H. N. Elkins, Jr. He had me doing military change list for each of the payrolls. We paid in cash during those days, and the total payroll had to be broken down into the exact change needed for the agent to pay all of the troops. The total of each denomination plus the change had to equal the total of the payroll. He had me help him count out the payroll money for each squadron. I went with him to the bank at Upper Marlboro, Maryland. He, Mr. Ross, and I counted the money before we left the bank. He had me prepare all of the Class A agent forms for those who come to pick up the money. Agents paid the troops and then returned the money for those who were not paid for some reason. Some commanders would redline a soldier if he did not sign the payroll properly or signed outside the prescribed lines. The payroll forms were WD AGO Forms 336 (War Department, Adjutant General Office). I also counted out the returned money, made up the receipts, and briefed the payrolls—that is, charging the correct amount for pay, quarters, and subsistence and charging the collections to laundry, old soldiers home, courts martial fines, and government property loss or damage (GPLD) that had been charged to the soldiers. Each item had an account number.

Major Elkins was a big gruff man, and everybody knew he was a major and therefore concluded that there was nothing wrong with me. He sent a letter to personnel directing that "Limited Service" be deleted from all of my records. I never knew what he said, but when the endorsement (that is, an endorsement to the basic letter) came back, it included a set of orders promoting me to corporal. I was embarrassed to put the new stripes on for a while because I was the first of the five to be promoted, and I didn't even have an assigned job. Their promotion orders came a day or so later. I did not put my new stripes on until their promotion orders came. We all put the stripes on at the same time. Pay for a PFC was $54, and corporals made $66. We were paid in cash on the last day of each month.

Base movies were fifteen cents. Jack Hargons and I went every time the movie changed. A new movie theater opened up in the SAC building across the base about that time, and this permitted us to go just about every day. Popcorn and soda cost a nickel; we could have a nice evening for a quarter. I was the only one of the five who had a Class F allotment, so my pay was $22 less each month. Interestingly enough, some borrowed money from me before the end of the month, and when they paid me back, I had as much money as they did.

Mrs. Adeline Triband ran the commercial accounts section all by herself. Mr. Ross thought I should be assigned to her, so when she took off a day or went on leave, her section would be covered. She was a retired school teacher who was also the sole support of her mother. We had a lot in common. She was a great teacher. In what seemed like nothing flat, I knew all there was to know about commercial accounts. (That's paying for all of the bills the base accumulates for various services.) After a few months, Major Elkins moved me to another section, and I was to continue to be a backup for commercial accounts. Ed Cunningham made the strongest pitch for me to come to the travel section. Ed had been doing travel vouchers for years, and he knew all of the regulations well. I learned a lot from him in a hurry.

As soon as I was proficient, I was moved to enlisted pay. I knew how to do that. It was just a matter of sitting there with an adding machine, reading the remarks put on by the personnel office, and filling in the blanks. I was teamed up with Mrs. Greasy. We became longtime friends. The procedure was fairly simple. Personnel office clerks typed up the payrolls. They sent the forms to the finance office in original and two copies around the twentieth of the month. We each worked a copy, then compared the copies or proofread them, made any corrections necessary, and then copied the correct figures to the originals and prepared the change list. This was all to be competed a day or two before we went to the bank to get the money and put up the payroll.

I was only a corporal for four months before being promoted to buck sergeant, a three-striper. My pay jumped to $78 a month. I had accumulated thirty days' leave, so it was time for a nice long furlough.

CHAPTER TWENTY-FOUR

Kenneth's First Furlough

I had accumulated thirty days' annual leave in the summer of 1947. I rode a train to Texas and back to Washington DC. Flying was expensive. I don't remember what the fare was for the train, but I went coach, the least expensive way.

Once again, Ray Woods gave me a car to drive, but I refused to drive it all the way to South Texas to see my sister Corda. That would have been OK with Ray. I just did not feel comfortable putting all those miles on a free gift. I rode the bus to Uvalde, Texas. That was as close as the bus came to Crystal City. I do not remember if I waited until I got back to Dallas to get the car or if I had it in advance and turned it back in. J. D. Hardaway and my sister Corda met me at the bus station, and we returned to the Spinach Capital of the World, Crystal City, Texas. Helen, their daughter, was married by now to Henry Etter, and she lived in Weslaco, Texas, down in the valley. Popeye the Sailor Man's statue is near the town square in Crystal City, Texas.

J. D. let me drive his car. Corda and I drove to Weslaco to visit Helen. There was a lot of nothing between these two cities, and Corda talked my ear off all the way down and back. Later, I learned that she, like Shirley, didn't want me to fall asleep at the wheel as we traveled through sagebrush and mesquite trees on a road that was straight as an arrow for mile after mile. I am so glad I made the effort to go because this was the last time I got to visit with Corda before she died.

Helen was ironing when we arrived. She was pregnant with Janice who became my first great-niece. It was hot, and I remember that she had to stand back from the ironing board because Janice was kicking it over. We had a great visit. I do not remember how long we stayed. I met her husband, Henry Etter. He was a water meter repairman for the city of Weslaco. The only other time I saw him was when Shirley and I were in San Antonio in 1962. We joined them at the Garner State Park several miles out of San Antonio when I was at Lackland Air Force Base to write the proficiency tests for accounting and finance in 1962. I remember Janice and Jimmy playing with Linda and Larry in the Garner State Park.

Anne was Corda and J. D.'s youngest daughter. She was several years younger than Helen. She must have been about five. She stuck to me like glue. She sat on my lap every chance she got and talked a blue streak. She loved to untie my shoes. We had a great time and still do every chance we get to visit. Anne married Bill Winterhalter, and they made their home in Ohio where Will, Holly, and my namesake, Kenneth Deal Winterhalter, were born. Bill passed away. Years later, Anne married Walter Doughty, a dairy farmer. They still live in Coshocton, Ohio, in 2015. Anne's life is surrounded by her children and grandchildren as well as Walter's children and grandchildren.

Back in Dallas, I made the usual rounds. Jack fixed me up with a blind date who was a sister of a friend of his. He and Velma had divorced now, and Mama was living with Jack and helping to raise John Arlee, Jack's son. I took Arlee to the movie. He was about six, and we did a lot of things together. I think there was a fishing trip involved, but we must not have caught many because I can't remember. I think Ray Woods had given up on the idea of me coming back anytime soon, but he continued his desire as well as offered a car to drive anytime I was home.

CHAPTER TWENTY-FIVE

Kenneth's Last Years at Andrews AFB

O ur finance office moved from the east side to a new office on the west side of Andrews. We moved in the new Strategic Air Command (SAC) building that was commonly referred to as the Baby Pentagon. It had five wings. They were not all filled in like they are in 2015. The wings are no longer discernable. It is one large building. We who lived in the barracks had already moved twice. Now we were moving again to the west side of the base where we would be close enough to walk to work. We had a separate building for the latrine, and it was used by boys in several different barracks. I recall coming home from Washington one night and finding a washing machine running with a cat inside. It was a front load with a window in front. I opened the door while it was running, and water spilled out on the floor. That was the first time I had seen a drunk cat. I finally helped him find his way out. He probably never visited another washroom after that! We had one afternoon a week called ground training. A golf course was to be built, so our ground training was clearing out the underbrush for the new course. The finance group was moved from base to SAC headquarters, and our organization changed to Squadron A, Sixtieth Air Base Group. We were now under the Strategic Air Command instead of the wing on the base. General George C. Kenney was the commanding general. He was a very short man. When I met him in the hall, I had to look down at the four stars on each shoulder.

He was replaced by General Curtis E. LeMay, and things began to pop at the headquarters. During the war, he commanded the low- level bombing in Germany then the firebombing of Japan and the final push that convinced Japan to surrender. He began to build up the command like an old supply sergeant may have done. He set up several wings with squadrons in each wing. These were skeleton units with one officer and one enlisted man. I was the first sergeant, and a first lieutenant was the commander. We did a morning report each morning. He had dozens more doing the same thing. Then when funding became available for all of those wings, he began to fill them up and expand the command at record speed. He brought in officers and enlisted men from all over the world. He knew them from the war days and made them wing commanders and sent them out to SAC bases all over the world. More often than not, I would not get their travel card filed before they were on their way to another base following his orientation.

I recall talking to his aide and secretary about his travel orders. He, General Clarence S. Irvine, more often than not went to bases that were not in his orders which required amended orders in order to pay their travel pay. I suggested that they either wait until the generals returned and then cut what was called a VOCO (verbal order of the commanding officer). I developed a phrase that could be used in the orders. CIPAP (Change itinerary and proceed to additional places is authorized) in the orders became standard for them, so orders did not have to be amended. I had a good relationship with the general's aide and secretary as well as most all of the command and staff officers. We found a way to use a group travel voucher to pay the enlisted flight crews. This cut down on paperwork and sped up the payment. I found that I had a lot of flexibility because if something wasn't covered in regulations, the general told us to write a SAC regulation to cover it. No one up the line had the courage to challenge it.

CHAPTER TWENTY-SIX

Kenneth Deal Meets Shirley Taylor

J ust like the second coming of Christ, you knew that it had to happen sometime. If you have read Shirley's bio, you have the first version. There are always two versions, and you may as well have them both.

It was in the spring of 1948 at the Baby Pentagon on Andrews Air Force Base in the SAC building, where Shirley was the command instructor for military correspondence. She was teaching a specialized class on how to cut stencils. Better explain stencils. Some readers even today in 2015 may not have this word in their vocabulary, much less those who may read this in 2050 or later. Stencils were bluish wax-type instruments that a typist used instead of paper in order to have a product that could be used to make multiple copies. By placing the stencil on a drum with an ink supply, a clerk could turn the crank handle to make as many copies as needed. The typewriter keys made an impression in the wax of a good blank stencil. Orders, brochures, pamphlets, and the like were produced without having to use a printing press.

SAC's deputy commander, Major General Montgomery, had ordered a document to be produced, and when the stencil was cut, it was either too dry to properly take the impression of the typewriter keys, or the keys on the typewriter were not properly adjusted so impressions would be neat and clear. I never did see the document in question, but it did not suit the general.

He ordered that every person in the headquarters who could type take a course so they would know if a stencil was good or if it was being properly cut so as to avoid publishing an illegible document.

Shirley drew the job of teaching every person in the headquarters during a one-hour class. She was scheduled every hour during the day. We never cut stencils at the base finance office, but we could type, so we fit into the category of being scheduled to attend the class. I thought it was a waste of time, but to comply, I gathered up all of my crew who could type—which was all of them—and we signed on a roster outside the classroom. By the time we finished signing in, Shirley had started the hour-long class. She politely asked us to come back in another session as she already begun the class.

I made a quick check of the roster, assuring myself that everyone had properly signed in, and announced to my crew.

"You have just attended the class on cutting stencils. It will appear in your records as such." We never returned to the class. Shirley says we still don't know how to cut stencils, and the keyboard on a computer will not cut a stencil anyway. I like to give the story a Texas embellishment by saying that the first time I met Shirley, "she ran me out of the classroom." Now, don't you think that sounds a lot better?

It occurred to me that if this book lasts into enough generations, today's computer may be just as obsolete as the stencils have become. I can visualize publishing a book such as this without ever touching a keyboard.

In addition to teaching typists how to cut stencils, her job extended to secretaries throughout the headquarters. Every letter leaving the headquarters had to go through a section that checked the borders, the proper heading procedures, and perhaps a few other things. It was not easy to get a letter out of the command headquarters, but when it went out, it was perfect. Shirley had to be pretty strict with her students for them to qualify as secretaries.

I had one other occasion to meet Shirley while we were still at Andrews. My check-writing machine went out of order at the base finance office. I put out an SOS to civilian personnel. I needed all of the available typist to write checks in order to meet the civilian payday. She was among that group, but she did not like my instructions any better than I liked hers. "No mistakes, ladies.

If you make one mistake, void the check as they must be error free." This made her and other nervous, so we had a lot of voided checks. If you have read Shirley's bio, you will recall that when the command moved from Andrews AFB, Maryland, to Offutt AFB, Nebraska, she did not move immediately as her dad was recovering from eye surgery. I went with the command in late October, and she joined the command in January. I never miss the opportunity for a second Texas embellishment. It is so easy to say that she chased me all the way from Maryland to Nebraska before she caught me!

CHAPTER TWENTY-SEVEN

SAC Headquarters Moves to Omaha, Nebraska

On October 25, 1948, exactly two years from my reporting to Andrews AFB, I was promoted to staff sergeant (E-5). The orders came out one afternoon, and there was a dance at the service club that evening. I quickly purchased some new stripes; there was not enough time to sew them on my jacket. I glued them on my olive drab Ike jacket because I wanted to go to the dance that night as a new staff sergeant.

There was a facility in Virginia that housed up to six thousand girls at one time who worked for the government in Washington DC during the war. A busload of girls would be brought out to various bases around the metro area where there was a service club. These were not hookers as you may have read about during the Civil War. I remember that a girl I was dancing with was cold, and I think she was hinting for me to loan her my jacket. I would have, except for the fact I still had buck sergeant stripes on my shirt underneath the jacket. So I just let her freeze rather than expose two different sets of stripes. My pay was pushing a hundred dollars a month; it was actually $96.00 base pay, but this grade brought with it a provision that entitled me to $37.50 allowance for Mama. This meant that my Class F allotment of $37.50 had to be stopped, and a new Class E allotment had to be started. I started it in the amount of $50.00, so Mama got a raise also, and it only cost me $12.50 a month to give her $50.00.

Orders came a few days later for the transfer to Offutt Air Force Base in Fort Crook, Nebraska. Offutt AFB was located on the old Fort Crook army post. A bomber plant built during World War II was located on the base. The headquarters now occupied the bomber plant, and conditions were not nearly as good as in the new headquarters building back at Andrews. The Defense Department— maybe it was General LeMay, I'll never know—thought that a command who was going to watch the entire USA and later the entire world should be centrally located.

Jack Hargons and a few others from our finance office were soon on our way to Nebraska in a C-47 aircraft, so there was no travel pay. I remember helping Jack find an apartment in Washington when he married Beth and again in Omaha when Beth joined him there. I was a brand-new twenty-one-year-old staff sergeant. That was rare in those days. When I hung my overcoat up in the closet, it still had corporal stripes on it from last winter. This was a shock to the men in the barracks.

Captain L. C. Mulvaney was the base finance officer at Offutt AFB. I was on the first general order that established the air force as a separate branch of the service, but Captain Mulvaney elected to stay with the army. I knew him later in our careers when he was a lieutenant colonel at Fort Lewis, Washington, while I was at McChord AFB in Tacoma, Washington. We visited a few times and often rehashed old finance stories by phone.

When he found that I was experienced in all phases of finance, he established a new position. It was called vouchering division. I supervised everything in the entire office except the cashier and accounting department. I began to select the chiefs of various sections. Miss Kitty Brown was made the chief of officer's pay, and Jack Hargons worked with her. SSgt. Harold Duffy was placed in charge of travel. Sergeant Delbert Owen was placed in charge of the enlisted pay Branch, and commercial accounts was headed up by a civilian lady whose name I cannot remember. The chief clerk was Technical Sergeant John Disarro who was later promoted to master sergeant and then replaced by Master Sergeant Ickes. Sergeant Ickes had previously been an officer and after the war was reverted to master sergeant. Later, during the Korean War, he was called to active duty as a lieutenant colonel, and he became comptroller of Tactical Air Command (TAC) at Langley AFB, Virginia. When Captain Mulvaney went back to the army, he was replaced by Captain Vincent J. Buckley. Captain Buckley was a bachelor. He was one of the kindest officers I had known up to that point. I really had to be careful because whatever I said went regarding most all decisions. I later knew him as a lieutenant colonel at Hamilton AFB, California, when he introduced me as the instructor of a new pay system being installed by the air force in the early 1960s. He had since married and had five children by then.

Before Captain Mulvaney left for the army, he taught me the basics of how to research entitlement questions and solve problems. I learned how to trace an entitlement all the way back to the United States code that picked it up from Congress and onto the US comptroller general and the General Accountability Office, down to the war department (later called Department of Defense), into the various military service branch regulations, and down to the various commands. I may have had an inkling of the impact of this knowledge, but I am sure I had no idea of the value this would be to me in later years when I had responsibilities that far exceeded what I thought I had as a young staff sergeant. Captain Mulvaney had worked in army finance through all of the ranks up to captain and attended every finance course the Army offered.

One February morning in 1949, a young airman reported to me, "Private Brown reporting for duty, sir." Robert Brown, fresh out of basic training, had been assigned to the base finance office. I learned that he preferred to be called Bob, so I'll use that term to include a long and interesting relationship. It is one that is still s current and fresh in 2015 as it was in 1949. I was not accustomed to having a finance clerk assigned who had not been to the finance technical school. I had no idea what to do with this young airman as he had no experience.

I assigned him to our travel pay section which was located near my office as the chief of military, travel, and civilian pay and commercial accounts. My thoughts were that I would use him as I had been used when I first reported for duty at Andrews Air Force Base, Maryland. He began to learn the joint travel regulations so fast and fit in with the other airmen that he soon became the chief of travel pay for SAC headquarters. I could not find anything he was not willing to do, so I gave him outstanding efficiency reports resulting in grade advancements.

Bob is the only person we know and with whom we communicate who attended our wedding at the chapel at Offutt Air Force Base, Nebraska. Following his tour of duty, Bob had some accounting jobs that eventually resulted in him being the treasurer of the Episcopal Church headquarters in New York from which he retired. We visited back and forth with him and his lovely wife, Anne, and their two boys all of these years. Bob and Anne also live in a retirement facility where they volunteer their talents. Bob is currently the president of the council.

Every February, early in the month, I get an e-mail that merely states, "Private Brown reporting for duty, sir." Our relationship has been priceless.

CHAPTER TWENTY-EIGHT

Kenneth's First Car While in the Service

I purchased a two-tone green four-door 1946 Chevy sometime early in 1949. It was a nice car, but the shocks were so worn that it bounced along. We still laugh about it now. I paid a thousand dollars for it, making monthly payments throughout the year until it was paid off. Sergeant Delbert Owen had a 1947 Chevy that looked extra good as he kept it in top condition. Delbert and I were roommates in the barracks.

It was a cold day in January 1949 when Shirley Taylor brought her travel voucher into the finance office. I was in the back of the office approving all types of vouchers for payment, but I saw her at the counter. She inquired about a place to stay, and my officer's pay section chief, Kitty Brown, had just lost her roommate who got married. She needed a roommate to share the cost of the rent at the Logan Hotel in downtown Omaha. They both jumped at the chance, and Shirley moved in with Kitty in room 514 of the Logan Hotel. Shirley thinks that they moved to a larger room; however, I remember it as a small efficiency apartment with a bed that folded up into the wall, making it one room including a small kitchen.

Kitty invited Delbert Owen and Clifton Turner up to the apartment for dinner. Clifton worked for Delbert in enlisted pay. Kitty also invited a few others to come up to the apartment after dinner. I was in the other group who was to come later.

We had a nice party as I recall, but I had no girl in particular. In fact, I was the boss of most all of the guys plus Kitty, so I was very noncommittal. Just along for the ride based on the invitation.

A lady in Shirley's office, Ann German, was married to Warrant Officer Donald German. His name was on most of the orders that we processed for payment as he was known as the adjutant who signed on behalf of the commanding officer. Ann invited Shirley to go with her and Don to a bowling alley. I guess she asked Shirley if she knew anyone she may invite to come along. Shirley called me to see if I was available, so I joined them for the evening. I wondered why she didn't call Clifton, her dinner date. Clifton married Skippy, a girl in Shirley's office. Clifton died years ago, and Skippy has died also.

Delbert and Kitty matched up, so we double dated often; Kitty and Shirley invited us up to the apartment at the Logan Hotel for dinner as often as they could get away with it. These were cheap dates for Delbert and me because more often than not, we did not go anywhere. It was months before Shirley and I ever went out alone. We went to a big band dance in a huge building with hundreds of people. I don't know which band was playing, but it was a place where one could order dinner. Shirley was full of questions, and the more she learned about me, the more she could associate me with her dad. She learned that I had plans to leave the air force at the end of my enlistment and return to Dallas and that my lifelong desire was to become a farm animal veterinarian, if I could get the school I wanted at Texas A&M under the GI Bill. If not, I would go back to Ray Woods Tire Company or go to Frito Lay Corporation who had made an offer as they knew my enlistment was coming to an end. I kept tires on their trucks all during the war years.

On one of our trips where John Disarro and his wife accompanied us as chaperones, we were at Lake Okeebogie in Iowa. Delbert proposed to Kitty. That really shook me up. I had no idea they were that serious. I was best man at their wedding on September 2, 1949, and Shirley was the bridesmaid. Shirley decided to take a vacation and go home to Maryland. It got kind of lonesome with Delbert gone and Shirley gone so long. I decided to extend my enlistment for six months and give some serious thought about both Shirley and the air force. I visited the Bradys who owned the house at 2526 Van Buren, Bellevue, Nebraska, where Kitty and Shirley moved from the Logan Hotel. Shirley needed a roommate, or she would have to move to something smaller that she could afford. They worked on me to marry Shirley and move into their basement apartment. I remember that Paul Brady made his own homebrew, and he filled me up on it while he took a pencil and paper and asked me about our finances. Shirley was as GS-5; she earned more than I did as a staff sergeant. My base pay was $154. If I married, there would be $77.10 for quarters allowance and $31.50 for subsistence. I would still have the $50 a month allotment from my pay for Mama. Paul added it all up and convinced me that we could get married and pay the $80-a-month rent and could probably save enough to buy a new car.

When Shirley came back, I realized how much I missed her and how hard it would be to run off to Texas. Shortly after she came back, we became engaged. It was a short engagement. Shirley knew the headquarters staff chaplain, Lt. Col. John S. Bennett, and she wanted him to marry us. He did at the base chapel on Friday, December 2, 1949. This was exactly three months after Kitty and Delbert were married. They were our best man and matron of honor. Shirley's big boss at civilian personnel, Mr. Bob Groover, a GS-15, gave her away. My twenty-third birthday was December 5, and it came while we were on our honeymoon. I still kid about aging a whole year in three days!

Paul Brady was right; we bought a new 1950 streamlined silver-streak Pontiac early in 1950. We drove the 1946 Chevy to Plattsmouth, Nebraska. There was a long wooden bridge over the Platte River, and the Chevy bounced all the way over the bridge. When we returned, the new Pontiac was steady as a rock all the way across that bridge. We both still remember crossing that bridge both ways. It was the first new car for both of us. I remember that it cost $2,060. We received a trade in allowance of $900. We pooled our money and paid cash for the balance as we did for every other new car we have bought over the last sixty-five years. We have never had a car payment in our married life, and we have had many cars. That was the first of five Pontiacs, then we had a couple of Fords, a Dodge, a couple of Oldsmobile's, a Fleetwood Brougham Cadillac, and four Subaru's.

CHAPTER TWENTY-NINE

Kenneth and Shirley's Life Together

There will be some duplication between my and Shirley's autobiography. I will attempt to cover the balance of my two careers while she covered our travels, family life, and other events in the section of her writings that begin with "1949 and Counting."

We discussed what the future may hold for us in both a civilian and a military career. Shirley said that if I wanted to stay in the air force, she would cheer me on to master sergeant. That was the top enlisted grade in those days. If I wanted to become a civilian and go back to Texas, she would be most happy to go there and help me pursue a civilian career. While we were thinking about all of this, orders came to report to Camp Stoneman, California, and to wait for further orders to a base in the Pacific. Jack Hargons was on the same set of orders. This was the clincher as to which career I would pursue. It was fortunate because when the Korean War came along, I would have been called to active duty just as I was getting settled in to do something in Texas.

We took a delay en route that enabled us to introduce our new spouse to each other's family. Shirley covered this trip and the visits. I left her with her parents in Maryland and with the new Pontiac. She transferred into a job at Andrews AFB, Maryland, waiting for orders to join me, not knowing where I would be going in the Far East.

Jack Hargons and I arrived at Camp Stoneman the same day. We were there three weeks attending formations every day where orders were called out for various assignments. Finally, our names were called. We were both on the same orders to go to Clark Air Force Base in the Philippines, and we were happy to be on the same orders as we had been from Lowry AFB to Andrews AFB to Offutt AFB to Camp Stoneman and now to Clark AFB.

We left Stoneman by ferry that took us to the port where we boarded the General William O. Darby, a big two-stacker troopship. We sailed for twenty-one days with a stop at Guam to pick up about one hundred fifty sailors. We arrived at Manila Bay among half-sunken ships still there from the war. We were transported by military carryall trucks the approximately sixty miles to Clark Air Base, arriving late in June, two days before the Korean War broke out. We were still in the processing center when it was announced, so we worked day and night shipping out pay records. The Forty- Fourth Fighter Squadron was dispatched immediately. We were assigned to the Eighteenth Fighter-Bomber Wing which operated from Clark. Although Jack and I never went to Korea, we were in the wing that did participate in the war. The Eighteenth had a powerful war record, and we were included on the orders for the awards. Personnel never removed us from those because they said all of us in that wing contributed to the success the eighteenth had.

I'll skip over most of the assignment there as it is covered by Shirley. Due to the war, dependent travel was restricted for a full year before Shirley and Beth joined us. I was promoted to Technical Sergeant on December 14, 1951, a grade I held for nine long years. Finance became what was known in those days as a frozen career field. That meant there were no promotions to master sergeant because the spaces were all full.

I was also under the Thirteenth Air Force and was awarded the Outstanding Technical Sergeant of the Command award.

This resulted in a trip to the Fifth Air Force headquarters in Japan to compete for the outstanding Technical Sergeant for all of the Pacific Command. There were eleven from all over the Pacific in this competition. I came in third. That was the only way a person in a frozen career field could be promoted to master sergeant, so I missed that opportunity as only one Master Sergeant was made. I thought that I may very well retire as a Technical Sergeant with twenty years of service.

We worked for Captain C. S. Wolf, the finance officer at Clark. Later, I worked for him when he was a Lieutenant Colonel at the Accounting and Finance Center in the early 1960s. It was here in the finance office that I detected a fraud case. We had a Technical Sergeant in our office who arranged to be paid without having the payments posted to his pay record. He had a good thing going for him until I caught up with him. The entire finance group was made to attend his court-martial, for the training of it and to know that crime does not pay. The sergeant, with about fifteen years of service, was sentenced to a dishonorable discharge, reduced to airman basic, and given seven years at Fort Leavenworth, Kansas.

While in the Philippines, I won a recreational trip to Hong Kong. Henry Kirby also won that trip, and we had a few days there to shop. Do not remember how we won the trip, but Henry and I were the only ones in the finance office to win. I recall taking a thirty-six image roll of color slides and learned at the end that the film never advanced through the camera. Fortunately, I did have my 8mm movie camera and came home with some good coverage which has been converted to VHS tape and later to a DVD.

We were the servicing finance office for Formosa (since named Taipei). First Lieutenant Virgil Carson and I flew in a C-47 up to Formosa to pay the troops. There were four different locations. We lost a piece of housing off the motor about midway in the flight. The pilot ordered everyone to put on parachutes just as a safety measure. He was concerned that a piece may come off and lodge in the engine, and we could be in for trouble. Nothing else came off, but I recall looking down and seeing nothing but water. Many thoughts ran through my head.

When we arrived in Formosa, I saw where all of the P-47 and P-51 fighter planes were stored after the war. They were stored there on the airstrip. Mechanics took a motor housing off one of them and hammered it into shape to fit the housing on the C-47. While they did that, I rode a Chinese train then a staff car to four different sites to pay the personnel. I believe it was Taipei, Tinan, Hsinchu, and I can't remember the fourth one. Names may all be misspelled, but that is the way they are pronounced. I had a .45 caliber pistol and pistol belt, but I took it off and put it in the bag of money while I was on the train. Train attendants kept trying to feed me and give me tea, but I took nothing for fear of being drugged as I had about $45,000 in military payment certificates. MPC was known as script. We did not use American money because of the black market value of US dollars.

Two significant things happened while I was on that trip. My sister Corda Mae Hardaway died, and I did not know that until much later, when I returned to the Philippines. The second thing was that Mainland China had decided to invade Formosa. The airplanes were detected by the crews we had stationed there, and the invasion was called off. When we departed Formosa, I saw the weather operator get a call on a crank-type phone. He would go look out the window to see what he could see regarding the weather and come back and respond on the phone.

We sold our 1950 Pontiac to some Filipinos from Manila for 6,500 pesos, which was $3,250. That was about $1,250 more than we paid for it new. The only problem was we needed all of those pesos to be converted before we came home, so we had to sell the car early in order to do that. I purchased an old 1941 Nash Rambler for six hundred pesos and exchanged currency for friends who needed pesos to shop on the local market.

The Rambler must have been there most of its life. It was a real challenge. It had a shimmy in the front end that began at twenty- eight miles an hour. It had a warped axle on the right rear side. I had to remove the wheel and grease it every weekend. A piece of the brake lining fell off once while I was doing that. I put some manila hemp in the place of the brake lining. Worked fine when it was dry, but when it rained, it would turn the car around on a dime, so it was really dangerous. When the engine got hot, it would vapor lock and would not start. Shirley left it all over the base for me to rescue after it had cooled down. We used the money we saved and ordered a new 1952 Pontiac Chieftain to be picked up at the factory in Pontiac, Michigan, on our return to the US.

We came home on the troopship General Altman. It was a one stacker, much smaller than the Darby we came over on or the Buckner that Shirley came on. It took twenty-one days with stops in Guam and Hawaii. My assignment was Larson Air Force Base in Moses Lake, Washington, right out in the desert. We were only there three weeks. My unit had moved out in advance of my arrival. We waited on orders which took us to McChord Air Force Base, Tacoma, Washington. Shirley has covered our leave time between stations and our arrival at McChord AFB. We were there from the summer of 1952 until March 1956. These were some good years for us. Our first child, Linda Lee, my permanent doll, and Larry Kenneth, our only son, were born at the base hospital. Linda was born on February 19, 1953, and Larry on August 14, 1955.

I was operating a one-man finance sub-office at the military airlift transport command (MATS). Airmen and soldiers from the army were being returned from Korea and Alaska, arriving in big C-124 Globemaster planes. The day Linda was born, I had disbursed over $7,500 in travel pay. I was too busy to check and see what was going on at the hospital where I had deposited Shirley early that morning. When I shut down my office at 5:00 p.m., I went to the hospital. They were so busy I could not get anyone to wait on me or give me any information. I went back to the office and called them on the phone and learned that we had a baby girl. They arranged for me to come over after visiting hours and see her and visit with Shirley.

Our favorite candy was made in Tacoma. It was called Almond Roca. I bought a couple of tins of that candy. It came in nice round cans and was individually wrapped in gold paper. It was celebration time at the main office with candy and cigars.

We were friends with several air force couples. Some of them had children born there around the same time. This is the group with whom we have a reunion every couple of years called the McChordites. We began those reunions in 1992 with the first one on a farm in Indiana. We went back to the same farm in 2010. We had been to all seven couples' homes in seven different states now and starting over. Each couple has been married to the same spouse over fifty years. We are the oldest at sixty-six years now in 2015. We act as coordinators to keep the group together even now, although we no longer meet together as we did for many years. Shirley and I hosted the last reunion in Grand Junction, Colorado, in 2012.

While at McChord, we traded our 1952 Pontiac Chieftain for a new 1955 Pontiac. It was the first year that Pontiac made a V8. It was an all-new car from the ground up, "built to last 100,000 miles," as the slogan said. We kept that car for ten years, took it to Okinawa, and brought it back, putting over that one hundred thousand miles on it before purchasing a 1965 Pontiac Safari station wagon when we were in Denver, Colorado.

I really got a lot of experience meeting the promotion board while at McChord. I met the board twenty-two times and never was promoted. I was well versed on the current events, and I gained much knowledge of the air force from all of this experience. I was a fairly young technical sergeant in a career field with extremely limited quotas for stripes. TSgt. Richard Houk finally transferred to the Office of Special Investigation (OSI) and managed to get promoted to master sergeant then to warrant officer by moving from the air force to the army.

I had my first real on-hand experience with the Air Force Accounting and Finance Center headquarters while I was at McChord. Our office received twenty-one notices of audit discrepancies (NOAD) at one time on various payments we had made. I was the chief of the audit section at the time, and it was obvious that these were issued in error. Much to my surprise, my finance officer, Captain T. M. Medina, asked me if I wanted to go to AFAFC at Denver and explain our position. I jumped at the chance, gathered up all of my regulations, and flew to Denver. This was about 1954, and the finance center was staffed with civilians and several officers as section chiefs. There were no enlisted personnel assigned there at that time.

I was able to prove my point and left all twenty-one of the NOADs there with them. They were surprised at my knowledge of the regulations and the fact that I brought them with me. It was apparent to me that I was far more knowledgeable of their own regulations than they were. There was a Lt. Col. S. A. Fulcher there who was so pleased that I came. We had a long chat; I asked him if they ever planned to have enlisted personnel assigned to the center. I had seen his name as a finance officer ever since he was a captain. It was a pleasure to know him personally. He did not know if the policy of having enlisted personnel at the center would ever change but said that he sure would support the policy if it is ever considered. I did not know at that time that I would be assigned to the Air Force Accounting and Finance Center twelve years later.

It was very early in the morning of August 14, 1955, when

I took Shirley to the base hospital. There was another lady there at the same time to have a baby. Her last name was Rose. Both babies were coming about the same time. The nurse was scurrying around, and when the first one was born, she announced to us in the waiting room that the Rose-Deal baby was born. Sergeant Rose looked at me, and I looked at him; neither knew which baby was born to whom, and they were too busy for us to find out. We decided to keep Larry Kenneth, and Sergeant Rose got the other one. I was happy that we now had a boy and a girl.

Linda was now walking and talking and was noticed by everyone as one of the prettiest blue-eyed little girls around. I was impressed that she talked so clearly and understandably from the very beginning. She talked on the phone to her Grandma Taylor and to all of my sisters about her new baby brother. It appeared at first that Larry had red hair; we even called him Rusty. I believe we will have to be satisfied that his daughter Wendy has the closest thing to red hair.

When my enlistment was up in March 1956, we decided to take a discharge instead of reenlisting and to travel back east to see if I could find an opening at a base in the Washington DC area. I had ten years of service now, and it was too much to let go down the drain because I could retire with just ten more years.

When we packed up, and the movers took Linda's bed, she wanted to know where she was going to sleep that night. We had a long drive to Texas, then on to Washington DC with two small kids. Linda had made the trip once before she began to crawl. We took a thirty-day leave and drove 7,600 miles. We had a metal platform that had straps that fit across the front seat so we could put a baby-size mattress in the back seat. There were no seat belts in those days. I remember looking back once, and she was nowhere to be found. We stopped the car, and I found that she had slipped between the mattress and the front seat and was laying on the floorboard under the mattress. She looked up at me with those big blue eyes just like that was where she was supposed to be.

On this second trip, we stopped somewhere in Oregon the first night. When we were having breakfast, the waitress said to Linda that she kept all kids there who did not eat all of their breakfast. Linda had no idea that she was kidding, so she kept her eye on that waitress as she crammed every morsel of food in her mouth. We thought for sure that she would be sick when we were back on the road, but she made out real well on that long trip. We had an apparatus that plugged into the cigarette lighter that heated food for Larry. It blew up once when it got to hot. We enjoyed the travel through parts of the country we had not been before and did a lot of visiting along the way.

CHAPTER THIRTY

The Deal Family at Grandma and Grandpa Taylors

We arrived in Maryland on April 1, 1956, and Pauline and Reggie were glad to see their grandkids. I went out to the finance office at Andrews AFB and met Mr. Neal Hesselton, the deputy finance officer, to see if he could use a technical sergeant in his office. He learned some of my background and was delighted to do what he could to get me assigned there. He called the recruiting office at Alexandra, Virginia, and arranged for me to reenlist, provided they would send me back to him. They were delighted also, and I began a new three-year enlistment on April 4, 1956. I had the only short break in service from March 13 until April 4. I was paid for more days of accrued leave than the break in service.

Mr. Hesselton soon learned that I was experienced in all phases of finance and asked me if I would train several civilian employees in the accounting department who were merging to become accounting and finance employees. It was a pleasure to train them. They were able to retain their ratings and merge into a new series of government specialty ratings. I was awarded my first Air Force Commendation for taking on that project. Interestingly enough, twenty years later, Mr. Hesselton worked for me following his retirement from government service. We remained friends until he died in his early nineties.

Shirley has covered the time we spent building our first new house on the Taylor farm. Actually, we had it built on a twenty-five- acre tract that belonged to Shirley since she was ten years old. Linda and Larry got to break ground for our new house. Fifty-nine years later, that home is still on Old Fort Road in Friendly, Maryland. It has been one of our greatest assets over the years. It was fairly obvious that my next assignment would be overseas. It did come on March 1958 for a tour in Okinawa. I was hoping for Europe, having been in the Far East on my first overseas assignment.

I enjoyed my time in Maryland using Reggie's 1952 Ford tractor and his old Dodge and international trucks and helping with the pigs, cattle, chickens, and garden. Shirley and I were on a very strict budget. I recall that every now and then, Pauline would insist on keeping the kids and encouraging us to go out to a movie or to dinner.

Shirley and I were keeping records of every penny we spent. She knew Mr. Wedding who worked at Andrews and came by our house, so I paid him $3 a week to ride with him. Years earlier, Shirley had ridden with him when she worked at Andrews AFB while I was in the Philippines.

Two of my sisters, Beatrice and Tony, and their husbands, Jake Moore and Berle Poteete, visited us. They drove Jimmy Moore's new 1958 Chevy from Texas to Maryland. They enjoyed our new house and visited the Washington DC area for the first time.

CHAPTER THIRTY-ONE

The Deal Family at Grandma and Grandpa Taylors

Orders came early in 1958 for Kadena Air Base, Okinawa. Larry was just over two, and Linda was just over five. This was one of the hardest family separations we had to experience. When we see one deployment after another take place, we have compassion for the families. It must be much harder these days than when we experienced it under generally peaceful conditions. We were thankful that we had built our house earlier and that Shirley and the kids had a nice place to stay near the grandparents. I had no idea how long it may take to have them join me.

Shirley has covered this time which was about a year before she and the children could join me at Kadena. We did enjoy the assignment, weathered a few typhoons, and traveled the length, sixty-four miles, and width, eight miles, at the longest and widest part of the island. This was one of the hot spots during World War II, and we witnessed some of the aftermath.

TSgt. James W. Valk arrived shortly after I had reported in. He came from George Air Force Base, and his family was back in California. I learned that he too had previously been assigned to McChord AFB and had left for an assignment in England before we arrived at McChord. Jim was a travel pay expert, and he was pleased to know that I was also. It was the first time that either of us had someone we could talk to who understood the travel regulations. I had been assigned to the audit branch with some cashier duties, and Jim went straight to the travel branch. The finance officer was Lt. Col. H. N. Nichols who was soon replaced by Major W. M. Armor. The Deputy was Captain E. J. Meggison who had a nickname, Wild Bill, for the new Accounting and Finance Officer. We enjoyed our relationships with the local civilians.

Jim Valk has also written his memories and shared a few pages with me. He researched and included some interesting history of Okinawa. Jim has given me permission, I am going to quote from his personal book some facts that I think will be of interest in the years to come.

"The battle of Okinawa was to be the last land battle of World War II and the most costly of the war in the Pacific in terms of lives and material lost. Control of Okinawa was important because it was scheduled to become the staging ground for the final assault of the war—the Japanese homeland. The battle began in March 1945 and continued through June 1945. The battle involved approximately 548,000 US military personnel of whom 12,513 were killed in combat and 38,916 were wounded. Of the 1,300 US Navy ships that took part, 79 were sunk or later scrapped. Most of the Navy loses were as a result of Kamikaze attacks. We lost 763 aircraft but the Japanese lost 7,830. It is estimated that the Japanese had 66,000 killed or missing, 17,100 wounded and 7,455 captured. Probably the most terrible statistic is that it is estimated that there were as many as 150,000 Okinawan civilians killed. The Japanese used them as human shields and had convinced them that the Americans would murder them if they surrendered so there were a huge number of murder/suicides among the population. (Depending upon the source used to obtain the above numbers they may vary quite a bit.)"

My former Accounting and Finance Officer at Andrews AFB, Major E. F. Ogozaleck, had recommended me for the Air Force Commendation Medal. It caught up with me at Kadena. Promotions in our career field were still frozen However, I was pronounced as the Outstanding Technical Sergeant for the Third Air Division and competed at Headquarters Fifth Air Force in Japan, along with others in frozen career fields when the air force decided to make one promotion from the group. I came in third place, so I had to wait until the freeze was lifted to be promoted to Master Sergeant on December 1, 1960, just a few days short of nine years in grade as a Technical Sergeant.

The Air Force Accounting and Finance Center finally began to take enlisted personnel, and I knew MSgt. Henry M. Kirby who had been assigned there. I was with Henry in the Philippines during the Korean War. We were roommates until our wives arrived, and we grew up about twelve miles apart in Texas. I applied for an assignment there and was accepted. I think Henry may have had something to do with me being accepted. My assignment came through just as our rotation time came up in early summer of 1961.

We shipped our 1955 Pontiac back early so it would be at the port in California when we arrived. We flew from Kadena in a four-engine prop Constellation, stopping at Wake Island to refuel. It was a thirty-three-hour flight. Larry did not get airsick until after we landed in California. We spent the night in transient quarters at Travis AFB, and I picked up the car and loaded up for the trip to Texas and Maryland.

The speed limit on Okinawa was thirty miles per hour for the entire island. It took us several hours to get up to the speed limit after being restricted so long. We began to meet funny-looking vehicles. They were pickup trucks with campers. Something new took place while we were out of the country. Cars were passing us with their windows all rolled up. We learned that new cars were now being equipped with air conditioning. We stopped somewhere along the way at a root beer stand where we enjoyed a frosted glass filled with root beer as a highlight of the trip. Once again, we had many visits in Texas and Maryland before arriving in Denver.

CHAPTER THIRTY-TWO

Kenneth's Assignment at AFAFC, Denver, Colorado

My assignment at the Air Force Accounting and Finance Center (AFAFC) headquarters from June 1961 until June 1966 was the longest and probably the most productive assignment I had in the Air Force. Shirley has covered our living arrangements and travels during that time.

I will try to limit my coverage to the military assignment. I was the sixteenth enlisted man to be assigned to AFAFC. There were about thirty officers and approximately 1,800 civil service employees when I arrived. We were housed in two very long former warehouse-type buildings with a wide space in the middle. The headquarters staff occupied a big brick building at the north end of the two office buildings. One of the buildings also served as the Air Force Reserve Personnel Center headquarters for the Air Force, and two new RCA 301 computers were in the process of being installed. One was for the Reserve Center, and one was for AFAFC. Each computer occupied an enclosed office space with a raised floor which contained all kinds of wires under the floor, and these two rooms were air conditioned unlike the rest of the buildings. I suppose that the computer I am using today, produced by Lenovo (formerly IBM) that has Microsoft Windows 10 operating system and a thousand gigabytes of hard drive capacity, may very well have equal the capacity of those old RCA 301 computers. I strongly suspect that it can be just as frustrating. I lost two chapters this morning. Have no idea where they went. It takes a little patience to do a project such as recording a history such as this book. My computer will no doubt be obsolete as this book is read in only a few later years.

This will be a longer segment because I want to include some detail here that shaped the balance of my Air Force career. It resulted in two promotions leading me to the top of the enlisted grades. I had the opportunity to serve in that top grade for over four years after I left the Accounting and Finance Center at three additional installations.

As I write this chapter, Shirley and I are at the close of a long July 4 weekend. It is Monday, July 5, 2010, two days after what would have been my dad's 133rd birthday and a day prior to my sister Ruth's. She would have been ninety-nine on July 6, and Jack would have been ninety-four on July 10. Today's devotional Our Daily Bread, published by RBC Ministries, contains a scripture from Matthew 14:23 as he speaks about Jesus, "When He had sent the multitudes away, He went up on the mountain by Himself to pray. Now when evening came, He was alone there." Alone in the presence of the Father.

That is where we are, alone in the presence of the Father, up on a mountain in New Mexico. I pray that some of the teachings of this chapter of our book will be used by future generations in the business world and perhaps even in military service. If it appears to the reader that I am calling to much attention to myself, that is probably why I have waited so long to put these memories on record. I am only doing it because of the prodding from both our children and grandchildren. (It is now early 2016, and the delay in finishing this project is partially the same reason. It seems we are calling attention to ourselves which is not normal for us.)

My first assignment at the AFAFC was in the adjudicating branch for military pay. For short, it was called AJP. I was the first enlisted person assigned to that branch. This may have been at the recommendation of MSgt. Kirby who alerted both the chief and assistant chief that they may want to request me. It was headed up by Major Harris as chief. His assistant was a GS-13, Paul J. Harrington, whom everyone called Pappy. The assignment was right down my alley as its purpose was to rule on questions regarding military pay. There were twelve GS-11s and two secretaries.

I took an altogether different approach than the other fifteen enlisted personnel assigned to other areas. They felt that these civilians were earning twice the pay and only knew half as much as they did. Well, that was true in some cases, but these guys spent a lot of time griping, drinking coffee in the cafeteria, and what I called goofing off. They were reluctant to share knowledge with these civilian employees, most of whom had never been on a military base, and some did not know one rank from another or the difference between enlisted and officers.

I decided to fit in with the employees right from the beginning. They were really nice people, hard workers who had over the years advanced in grade from just auditing the figures on pay records that had been sent to the center from all of the bases around the world. As a result, they were promoted from those jobs to higher grades. They were now in a job requiring knowledge of how and why those figures were authorized by law and regulations.

This section received all of the inquiries that came in from the various major commands, and in some cases, from air force bases around the world. Some of the major commands required their bases to send the questions to them first. If they could not answer them, they would forward the question on with an endorsement as to what they thought the answer may be for AJP to rule on it. So the questions were not just routine questions, but they demanded some knowledge and background experience. As a result, the majority of these inquiries were sent on down to the judge advocate general (JAG). Based on the response from JAG, the technician would then answer by letter. Each incoming request would have a suspense ticket on it for seven days, and Pappy would assign it out to one of the GS-11s for processing. If they or the JAG office needed more time, the suspense ticket would be extended and a letter sent explaining that a response would be forthcoming.

Pappy Harrington began to notice that I was responding seven to ten days faster than most of the technicians. Each of my responses also included a memo for record that was to be typed on the file copy only. In my MR, I quoted the authority for the response. In some cases, it would be an air force regulation or a reference to a finance tech digest or to a comptroller general decision. In some cases, it would be the US codification of the law or even the public law. Whatever it took to support my answer would be included in the MR in case the answer was challenged. I never sent a request to the SJA; as a result, my response was much faster.

Major Harris suggested to Pappy that he assign more cases to me. It didn't matter how many he assigned to me, he could not bog me down. Major Harris confided in me that was his decision to see where my breaking point was. He had never found an enlisted person in his career whose breaking point he could not find. I had my own footlocker full of regulations of all sorts that I gathered over the years, so research was often just to my three by five card file.

The other enlisted personnel thought I was dumb to provide answers to the civilian employees. They came as master sergeants with the idea of retirement, and most of them did in fact retire as a master sergeant. A newly assigned Master Sergeant Harold Renneberg reported in for duty in the systems branch, and I detected his skill right away. I suggested to Hal what I was doing, and since he was just as knowledgeable as I was, he picked up on my methods and used them in his branch.

To make a long story short, we both left the Accounting and Finance Center for an assignment in Europe. I left first as a chief master sergeant, and Hal left a year after he made chief master sergeant and joined me at the headquarters of United States Air Force in Europe at Lindsay Air Station in Wiesbaden, Germany, after I had spent a year at Ramstein Air Base, also in Germany.

The first crisis we experienced at the finance center was the Cuban missile build-up by the Soviet Union. There was a Department of Defense order to recall thousands of reserve officers to active duty. The air force records center was a part of the complex at AFAFC. This process required orders to be issued, clothing allowances to be paid, and travel authorizations to be issued—all with haste. Most of all the sections at both AFAFC and AFRRC panicked. The commander, Brigadier General Paul W. Scheidecker, had a fit when he surmised that no one seemed to know what to do. As he was browbeating his staff, my division boss, Colonel Loomis, said to him, "General, I have a couple of Master Sergeants who can put this show on the road pronto, but they would need the authority necessary to do so." Apparently Colonel Loomis had been briefed by Major Harris and Pappy Harrington on our ability to do the job.

General Scheidecker put out an urgent memo that all sections were to follow our lead and respond to whatever request we made to get the job done. To make a long story short, the process worked as smoothly as silk. Hal and I never exceeded the authority given to us and reverted back to our respective sections without any fanfare. Hal's assignment was in the systems division, also under Colonel Loomis, because the air force planned to install a new pay system using the National Cash Register (NCR) 390 computer system. Next came a call for an NCO to go to Lackland Air Force Base to participate in writing proficiency tests for the accounting and finance career field. I was selected to go for six weeks of temporary duty (TDY). I took Shirley, Linda, and Larry with me, and we found a motel with a swimming pool. It was August, and all the way to San Antonio, we met cars heading for Colorado to escape the heat. I enjoyed the duty. It was in an air-conditioned building. It was one of the hottest summers on record in Texas. I believe it was August 1962. We had twenty-three straight days where the temperature never was under a hundred day and night. Shirley and the kids rode a bus back home to Colorado to escape the heat. When I returned to AFAFC, I learned that once again, the staff judge advocate section was getting all of those field questions again and that Major Harris had been replaced by Major Aldridge. So I had a new boss. Major Harris had been signing my letters going back to the field, but Major Aldridge asked me to sign my own letters just as the civilian employees signed theirs. I suggested he think about that because it may not be a good idea for a master sergeant to sign a letter going back to a major air command or a base. He called a few finance officers he knew and asked them what they thought. Most of them thought it a good idea if I signed the letters going to the base finance offices and he signed those going to one of the major air commands.

Major Aldridge and Pappy Harrington were asked by the adjudication branch for travel pay (AJT) what they thought about using me for travel questions instead of using SJA. I had no objections, so I was no longer assigned incoming letters. I just responded to both the pay and travel sections as a helper. This expanded my territory across two sections, both of which were under Colonel Loomis who was suffering from cancer. His deputy, Mr. Bert Francis, a GS-15, primarily ran the division, taking all the pressure possible off Colonel Loomis.

The air force was gearing up for the new pay system that would use the NCR 390 to post to pay records by the use of magnetic stripes imbedded in the pay record. A paper tape punch machine would create the input to the computer, and all of the accounting function would be accumulated in the computer which would print out all of the required accounting data in the detail necessary to account for the dollars being spent for various items of pay. There was a tremendous amount of controversy regarding this system. One major item was how this would work in a combat zone like Vietnam. It was decided to test a manual system that could be used in a combat zone. We did not have a manual system.

The Royal Canadian Air Force (RCAF) sent one of their squadron leaders (equivalent rank of major) to AFAFC to be trained on our pay system. His name was Stewart Simpson. His wife, Gwen, and his son and daughter plus triplets—two girls and a boy—came with him from Ottawa. He was paired up with a lieutenant colonel for training. This did not work as the colonel was an administrative officer with little interest about the pay system. He was reassigned to a civilian employee who was one of those that had been put out to pasture waiting retirement. He was a special projects officer for things such as this. Right away, Stewart knew this was not going to satisfy the requirement.

He asked if he could be paired up with a non-com as he called it, a non-commissioned officer. I was selected, and we became lifelong friends until he died years later. We are still in touch with his wife, and we have visited them in Ottawa as well as having them visit us in Maryland. He asked me to call him Stew or Stu, and he considered me the equivalent of a Canadian warrant officer. We developed a manual pay system, just the two of us and the use of a secretary. We gave it the name of AMPS or Accrued Military Pay System. In briefings, he chuckled when I referred to it as Apes, Monkeys, Pests, and Snakes. I tested it at Lowry Air Force Base, and he tested it in Vietnam as he wanted to make that trip. Together, we debugged the system so it would work stateside or overseas with or without electricity and under combat conditions.

In the meantime, the air force purchased 175 NCR 390 computers to be installed at air force bases around the world. I was given two civilian employees from the quality examination (QE) division, and three airmen were brought in from bases out in the field to test the system. Once again, questions from the field had to be referred back to the JAG for both pay and travel.

There was a disgruntled GS-14 who did not get his promotion to GS-15 who said there was no way that a manual system would work and would produce the same reports as the mechanized system. The General Accounting Office in Washington DC had a subdivision at AFAFC. This disgruntled civilian managed to get a team from the GAO at AFAFC to give me a surprise audit to prove his point. Three auditors spent three weeks on site at Lowry Air Force Base only to disprove his point. This didn't satisfy him, so he drew up papers that he thought would result in a court-martial for me. Colonel Loomis got word of this, and when he put a stop to it, the employee who thought he was indispensable threatened to resign. Colonel Loomis accepted his threat and processed termination papers, and he was out of there in less than ten days. (It really can happen even for government service employees, especially if they threaten to quit in writing.)

Another shock to all of us was when General Paul W. Scheidecker was killed in an automobile accident. He was driving out to the skeet range, and he passed up his turn. As he turned in the middle of the road to go back, he was hit broadside and was killed instantly. He always enjoyed commander's call. There were only about fifty of us officers and NCOs, and he was a stickler for everything that was military. He was one of the most safety-minded commanders, except for General Curtis E. LeMay, under whom I served. That is why his accident was such a shock to all of us.

The general was replaced by Colonel Tom Corwin who soon became a brigadier general. Staff officers must have briefed him on Master Sergeant Renneberg and me. He ordered immunization shots for both of us because he wanted us ready on a moment's notice to travel to any part of the world where there may be a crisis relating to accounting and finance. We had to take all of the boosters and keep them up to date. General Corwin had been a corporate tax lawyer who was called back to active duty during the Korean War. He knew that if he had to make a trip, he would need some expertise at hand. He was interesting to travel with because he wanted his NCOs to eat with him in the officer's club and stay at the bachelor officer quarters. And when he specified wheels-up departure time, anyone not on the plane was left behind. It was a joy to serve with him. Later, he visited the base where I was assigned, Ramstein Air Force Base in Germany. I was also called back to AFAFC on special projects from two different bases in Europe and another time from the Data Systems Design Center headquarters in Washington DC, when it was located in the Forrestal Building on Independence Avenue.

On the exact date of my minimum time in grade, I was promoted to Senior Master Sergeant (SMSgt). This was on April 1, 1963. Then, exactly three years later on April 1, 1966, I was one of only sixteen in the air force in my career field to be promoted to Chief Master Sergeant (E-9). This is the top enlisted grade where only 1 percent of the total strength of the enlisted force can serve. I believe that is still the case today over forty years later. This did not set well with some of the old guys who came there as Master Sergeants and stayed as such, so they began to peel off into retirement. This is not uncommon among general officers and corporate executives who are passed over for promotion.

I was still based at AFAFC when the Department of Defense (DOD) initiated a program to centralize military pay for all branches of the Defense Department. It was called Joint Uniform Military Pay System (JUMPS). I was selected to spend time at the navy finance center in Cleveland, Ohio, to study some of the idiosyncrasies peculiar to the navy and marine corps. I spent a lot of time at the Army Finance Center at Fort Benjamin Harrison, Indianapolis, Indiana. There was a First Lieutenant Sharp from the marine corps who was asked to do the same thing regarding the army and air force pay. He worked his way up through all of the enlisted grades, and his name reflected his character and knowledge. I had not worked with an officer more knowledgeable of the details of finance since I worked with army captain L. C. Mulvaney in the late 1940s at Offutt AFB, Omaha, Nebraska. Most entitlements were the same for all services. However, the procedures were not all the same, and there were a few entitlements the navy had that were unique to their service. Following the development of the Air Force Manual Pay System, I had spent some time training the army finance center personnel on what to expect when they were paying air force personnel on an army installation. The mechanized system was not practical to pay a few airmen or officers who were on duty with the army. I had also taught the manual system to those at the navy finance center for the same reason.

The army had been given the job of developing a Joint Uniform Military Pay manual, and the group who drew the detail was the same type group the air force used to audit the military pay records sent in from various installations around the world. Colonel Kittle, an army finance officer, had been given the job. He knew me from previously teaching his team how to handle the Air Force Manual Pay System when they had only a few air force personnel to pay on army installations.

Colonel Kittle really did not want that job because he was confident his crew did not have the expertise. At this particular time, my immediate boss was Mrs. Jane McCall, a GS-14. She really wanted the Air Force to write the manual, so she arranged for me to come to the Army Finance Center and review what the army team was doing. Colonel Kittle asked me point blank what I thought about his team writing the joint services manual, and I told him they do very well for the army, but limited knowledge of the Navy, Marine Corps, and Air Force was showing up all through the pages they were writing.

Based on my report, he requested the job be given to the air force, so it was transferred back to Denver. A new division was created, called MP for military pay. The manual, with changes, is still in effect today for all of the uniformed services. General Corwin was delighted at these turn of events, and I was moved into that directorate along with many others and had a major role in the development of what is today called the Joint Services Military Pay and Allowance manual.

I may have been the first enlisted person who was recommended for the Air Force Commendation Medal by both the army and the navy. I had already been awarded that medal by the air force on a previous assignment. So the air force awarded an Oak Leaf Cluster, denoting that this was a second award. In later assignment, the United States Air Force in Europe and the Air Force Data Systems Command made similar awards adding another Oak Leaf Cluster.

It was now March of 1966, and I had just completed twenty years of active duty. In the months just prior to this, I had spent two months at the factory of National Cash Register in Dayton, Ohio, as the liaison between the air force and the company who had sold 175 computers to the air force. During this time, I accompanied the vice president of NCR, Mr. Paul W. Lappito, to many bases in the United States where NCR 390s had been installed. His mission was to report to the base commander and the base comptroller, advising them of the change in the pay system and offering support for any problems that may arise.

Some interesting developments surfaced here. A GS-15 division chief, Joe Throckmorton, and my immediate boss, a

GS-14, Jane McCall, and Lt. Col. C. S. Wolf whom I worked for in the Philippines when he was a Captain were all seeking the opportunity to accompany Mr. Lappito and one of his systems men, Charlie, a young guy, on this around the USA trip. The directorate chief, Colonel John J. Driver, called them all in and quizzed them about their knowledge of the system being installed. He ruled them all out and sent me on the trip. He explained that it would be hundreds of dollars cheaper to send me since we were just about out of travel money, and enlisted men were paid far less per diem rates than officers and civilian employees. I was not even competing for the trip, so fortunately they all just laughed and took it in good stride.

Colonel Driver was not much of a talker, but he was a driver. There was a saying in the directorate that he could drive a wet noodle up the rear end of a leopard with a red-hot ice pick. (They did not say the leopard would have to like it.)

Following this trip, I filled out my application for retirement. During the trip, NCR had offered me a position with the company when I retired. I had spent enough time in Dayton that I was not interested in going there, but I was told that NCR was everywhere and that openings came up almost every day. There was a beautiful training facility in Dayton that all employees must attend before being assigned in the field much like the requirements that IBM (International Business Machines) has for their employees.

The command chief master sergeant in personnel was not a finance man, but he knew that my records had been sent to the Air Force Personnel Center, Randolph Air Force Base in Texas to be considered for promotion. He also knew that Colonel Driver had sent Lt. Col. Joseph J. Vanya from AFAFC to Randolph to sit on the promotion board. I did not work for Lieutenant Colonel Vanya, but I knew him very well. He was the local accounting and finance officer for AFAFC. He was also the master of my Masonic Lodge, Revelation 180 in Aurora, Colorado. When

Lieutenant Colonel Vanya returned from Randolph, he avoided me completely. The only person he told of my promotion was the Commanding General and the command Chief Master Sergeant. He did this so that my retirement papers would not be processed. Those selected to chief had to elect to stay in the air force one year following the acceptance of the promotion.

The effective date of my promotion would be April 1, 1966. So that it would not appear to be an April Fool's joke, General Thomas P. Corwin called me, Colonel Driver, and my immediate boss, GS- 14 Jane McCall, up to his office to announce the promotion to Chief. This was several days before the effective date. I recall General Corwin stating that there were only sixteen chiefs made, and my orders reflected that. And since I had been in grade as a senior master sergeant (E-8) since April 1, 1963, I was just barely eligible. A senior master sergeant had to be in grade three years or more to be considered for chief.

The big decision was that I accepted the promotion, withdrew my retirement papers, and agreed to stay one more year in the air force. General Corwin made this announcement to me several days before April 1. I had time to purchase a new uniform with the new chevrons before the effective date of the promotion. Somehow, I managed to keep this a secret from Shirley. I could never have done it on an air force base, but we were the only military family living in Sunset Ridge, Westminster, Colorado. Shirley had very little contact with the military world other than taking our kids to the hospital at Fitzsimmons Army Hospital and stopping in the commissary and Base Exchange.

At breakfast time on April 1, I came into the kitchen with a new uniform and with Chief stripes on. Well, my bacon was burned, the eggs were hard, and the juice glasses run over, etc. She was excited to say the least. Then I told her it was just an April Fool's joke, but she didn't believe me. I wanted to see what she thought about another year in the air force. I recalled that when we got married, she said she would cheer me on to master sergeant. That was as high as the enlisted grades went back in 1949. Two super grades, E-8 and E-9, were added in the 1950s. Time in grade for each of these was a minimum of three years. I was fortunate to advance to both grades with the minimum time in grade. The one year obligation turned into some major events that lasted another four and half years that are covered in the next chapters.

CHAPTER THIRTY-THREE

Kenneth's Last Overseas Assignment

T he Air Force Personnel Center at Randolph AFB, San Antonio, Texas still had my records. When they sent them back, they attached another set of orders assigning me to Chateauroux Air Base in France. So I had an assignment which would close out five years at the Accounting and Finance Center, the longest assignment I had at one installation while in the air force.

This was one more decision we had to make. The tour in Europe was for three years. In order to take this assignment, there was now a three-year commitment instead of one year. I discussed it with Shirley who was about three months pregnant with Vikki Kay. Since she could still travel, we decided to take the assignment rather than retire from the air force.

I believe she has covered in her bio about us selling the house, making the trip, having changing orders in Paris to England, then going on to Ramstein Air Base in Germany. So I will skip all of that and get right to the first days at our new overseas base.

This was a new experience for me, reporting in as a chief master sergeant at a base where no one knew I was coming. My last real air force base was at Kadena Air Base, Okinawa, where I was a fairly new master sergeant when we left in the early 1960s.

The Chief Master Sergeant at the personnel office at Ramstein Air Force Base, Cal Golden, greeted me warmly. He was also the square dance caller of a group we later joined at Ramstein Air Base. He knew by my Air Force Specialty Code (AFSC 62790) that I would be assigned to the base finance office. I explained my change in orders, and no one knew in advance that I was coming. He told me that I would no doubt be the chief of pay, travel, and civilian pay as he glanced at my records. I arranged with him to review the records of all the military personnel assigned to those sections. He gave me a desk and had the records pulled for thirty-six NCOs and airmen. I spent one day reviewing records and making notes before I ever reported in to the finance office. Chief Master Sergeant Cal told me that if there was anything I wanted to do with any of the personnel, I should let him know, and he would arrange it. I told him that I planned to have the best operating office in Europe, and that meant some of the personnel who don't pan out may have to go.

I was surprised to hear him say, "Give me their names, and I will have them on orders the same day. We will either send them home or find a place in the command for them."

I had never had that kind of authority before. We were at Seventeenth Air Force Headquarters which had jurisdiction of a large part of Europe.

My first day at the office was a bit of a shock to the finance officer, Captain Nolan C. Alcock. He later retired as a major and worked for me at F. L. Jenkins, Realtor in Maryland. I sold him a home in Clinton, Maryland, and hired him as a realtor around 1973 when I was managing a subdivision in Clinton.

The chief of pay and travel at USAFE headquarters at Lindsay Air Station in Wiesbaden was Lt. Col. John J. Guili. He wanted to move me immediately from Ramstein to his office. He knew me when he was the chairman of the Perdiem,

Travel, Transportation Committee (PDTAC) at the Pentagon, Washington DC, and I was in the adjudication sections of pay and travel at AFAFC. We spoke often on the phone and used some of the very first FAX experimental machines with handwritten notes answering each other's questions. Next to Army Capt. L. C. Mulvany, Lieutenant Colonel Guili was the first air force officer I knew who was knowledgeable with all of the laws and regulations pertaining to both military pay and travel.

The rule was when you signed in at a base in those days, you were not eligible to be moved for at least one year. This was to avoid a lot of travel expense among other things. Well, he kept tabs on that, and exactly one year later, I moved to his office as the chief of pay and travel for all of Europe. The centralized pay system process was heating up, and Europe was to be the test command to see how well checks out of Denver would work for some eighty- four thousand military personnel. Lieutenant Colonel Guili became anxious and brought me up to the headquarters on temporary duty in advance of the one-year limitation. I kept the family at Ramstein and rode a staff car back and forth on weekends for a few months prior to the official transfer.

My first few days at Ramstein Air Base near Landstuhl, Germany, were spent interviewing all of the enlisted personnel in military pay, travel pay, and civilian pay sections of the base finance office. I recall one SSgt. Joan Bullock, who went out and told others that she felt like the "woman at the well. He knew all that I ever did, and he has only been here one day."

I had some authority I never had before; I laid down some high expectations. A few who did not measure up were out of there the first week based on the combination of their records and my interview. It made a big impression on the rest including my accounting and finance officer who knew that I had just come from the Accounting and Finance Center headquarters in Denver, Colorado. USAFE headquarters tried to grab me before

I was settled in.

Captain Alcock asked Lieutenant Colonel Guili how he knew me, and the response he got kind of chilled him, "Chief Deal and I have been in more trouble in more cities than you can imagine." This was a wild exaggeration, but it served its purpose. What Lieutenant Colonel Guili was referring to was that he and I conferred on inquiries from bases in many cities by phone or fax without ever going to those bases. However, when I later worked for him at USAFE headquarters, we did in fact visit many bases.

There were three good section chiefs Master Sergeants. Paul J. Krisik was chief of military pay. I replaced the chief of civilian pay when we moved all of pay for civilians in Europe to Ramstein. I replaced the chief with MSgt. Donald Younts. TSgt. John J. Wittner was travel section chief. I made Staff Sergeant Strasbourg sub-chief of allotments because I learned from AFAFC this was a weak spot, and the errors reported in checkpoints needed to come down. So I began to sign off on all outgoing documentation on allotments.

I had a standing five-minute staff meeting every morning at 0800 with the section chiefs. I recall on the second day, no one was there on time, but I started the meeting as though they were all there. As they came wandering in, I was half through, and the meeting was terminated by the time the last one arrived. The next day, and days forward, they were there waiting on me at 0800. Later, I learned that they had a communicating system with each other to make sure they were there. We worked as a team. If one section had a problem or was under the gun for meeting deadlines, I moved personnel on temporary basis for an hour, day, or week to balance out the effort. This concept was new to them. Even today, years later, when I visit with Paul Krisik who retired from the air force and went to work for army finance at Aberdeen Proving Grounds as a civilian pay chief, he used as many of my systems as he could remember. Paul was a little high strung, and I had to sit on him a few times, but he became a superior section chief and managed to get his airmen and NCOs involved in things other than finance duties.

During the one year I was at Ramstein, twenty-two of the thirty-six received promotions. We had the Airman of the Month and the NCO of the Month awards for the squadron, eight out of the twelve months. I had meetings to teach them how to meet various boards and what they needed to do to become qualified to be recommended. Air Force Commendation Medals were awarded to three NCOs. We had the best softball team on the base and had some real fine parties. MSgt Paul Krisik was a real leader.

Captain Kathleen Wilkowskie reported in and became deputy Accounting and Finance Officer. This was her second assignment to Europe, but she was still a young captain. There seemed to be some friction between her and Captain Alcock who shortly became a major. She asked if we could meet daily at 1:00 p.m. for a few minutes so that she could be updated on what was going on. I detected in these meetings that she was under some stress. Some of her stress was overflowing to me, so I spent some time with her and explained that if she was going to remain in the service, she may as well make up her mind to retire as a colonel.

I explained the pattern she needed to follow through the Armed Forces Staff College, etc. I also advised her that she needed to know how to deal with majors because later, when she moved to USAFE headquarters, she had another one to deal with. Years later, she retired as a colonel. Shirley and I visited with her when she was in school at Fort McNair in Washington DC and again after she retired in Montgomery, Alabama. She still gives me credit for taking her under my wing when she was a young captain, showing her how to make colonel. Even today, we are e-mail friends as we share many of the same political views. She shares the same date of birth, not the year, as Shirley, and they exchange cards and notes. I will have more coverage on her later as she progressed through the ranks and became the commanding officer of the Air Force Data Systems Design Center headquarters after it moved from Washington to, Alabama. We also became friends with her mother and visited her once as we were passing through Minnesota. She also visited in our home when we were in Maryland.

There was an amusing event at Ramstein when an airman from an off-base unit that we serviced showed up for his pay. Apparently, he was not available for payday at this unit, and his funds were turned in, so he came to the office to pick up his pay. I don't remember his name, but Sergeant Krisik brought him back to my office because he had the bushiest hair I had ever seen on a military person. I told him we would pay him as soon as he got a haircut. He was kind of feisty and had no intentions of getting a haircut. I took him to the base commander and explained that he was from a certain off-base unit but reported for his pay, and I did not plan to authorize his payment until he got a haircut. The base commander Colonel McDonald was a big full colonel, and he told the young airman to take two dollars that he pulled out of his pocket and go get a haircut and report back to him. So I took him to the barber shop, and they sheared off a bucket full of hair. I paid him his pay and took him back to the base commander to return the two dollars.

This made base news, including the base commander's staff meeting. Our base comptroller, a lieutenant colonel, heard the base commander tell his staff, "We need more NCOs like Chief Deal in the base finance office."

I overheard a staff sergeant in our office announce, "I'm not ever going to need a haircut!" Word really got around fast.

A few days later, I walked in the personnel office for some purpose. There was a WAF (Women's Air Force) Captain who jumped up out of her chair and did a check on everyone's hair. I placed a few of the airman in my office on base restriction until they updated their shoes, hats, etc. (Word had spread all over the base.)

Shirley and I joined the Order of the Eastern Star while we were at Ramstein so we could be of assistance to Linda who was a Rainbow girl in the Masonic Fraternity. TSgt. John Whitner was a Mason, and Captain Kathleen Wilkowskie was also a member of the Eastern Star. I served in the local lodge as the junior warden because they were doing Colorado work, and I was qualified for all positions. If we had not moved after one year to Wiesbaden, I could have become master as the staff finance officer; seventeenth air force wanted to recommend me as he was the outgoing master. I had been alerted of my pending transfer.

One would think that the crew at the base finance office would be happy to see this crusty old chief leave and consider it good riddance. Instead, they gave a gala going-away party for Shirley and me. There were a lot of gag gifts, and they took this opportunity to roast me pretty good. I had no idea of all the things they picked up and brought up at that party. There was an abundance of thanks for making them walk the chalk line and for all of the promotions and awards. It was also their first experience of having someone who had a direct line to the Air Force Accounting and Finance Center headquarters, as well as to the command headquarters at USAFE.

Ramstein Air Base was the first base where I had the opportunity to operate in the capacity as a Chief. My two later assignments were both at headquarters. However, my boss at the Data Systems Design Center, Colonel Woodrow W. Jenkins, put me in charge of the enlisted force for the one year I served there.

Vikki Kay was born on October 1, 1966. Shirley has covered that portion of our stay. This made her a German citizen as she was born in the hospital at Landstuhl just off the base. This is the same hospital where the wounded from Iraq were brought first before being sent to other US hospitals like Walter Reed in Washington DC.

Larry became a Boy Scout while we were at Ramstein and was able to do a few neat things. This was a major growing period for him as his legs kept growing out of his pants. One of his friends was Bart McDonald, the son of the base commander, Colonel McDonald, who was promoted to brigadier general while we were there. I never knew how that friendship developed. Bart was often a daily visitor, and I never knew of the things they did, but I figured I would be able to get him out of whatever he got into with Bart. I learned later that Bart would talk the general's driver into taking them places in the staff car. I guess it was well that neither the general nor I knew about all of the things they did together. There was a store off base that they referred to as the old lady's store. They always had some funny items from that store. Larry was introduced to gummy bears. Prior to my departure from Ramstein, I learned that Colonel Elmer D. Coon, recently promoted to full colonel, was being reassigned from a base in England. I knew him as a lieutenant colonel at AFAFC where he was in charge of the retired pay division. I had been detailed over to the section within retired pay that paid the reserves and Air National Guard personnel who were not otherwise assigned to a local base. This short detail became invaluable to me which will be covered in more detail in the chapter that covers my assignment at the headquarters of the Air Force Data Systems Design Center. I offered to sponsor him and his wife, Gerry, since I also knew them through my lodge at Aurora, Colorado, and at the finance center.

I met them at the airport on Frankfurt, Germany, and we drove back with their entire luggage packed into my 1965 Pontiac station wagon. It was a huge spacious car, and they were so pleased that everything fit. I broke the news to him that I was being transferred to the headquarters soon since I was already shuttling back and forth between Ramstein and Lindsay Air Station. He had mixed emotions about me leaving but decided that I may be of more help to him by being up there than at the base, so he did not object. I gave them a general briefing of the base and how to obtain the special license plates that were issued to all full colonels (O-6) and chiefs (E-9) and explained where various facilities were located on the base.

Colonel Coon was later assigned to USAFE headquarters as the director of accounting and finance. He was my, Captain Wilkowskie, Lieutenant Colonel Guili, and others' boss. We had assignments at three different bases together. He was later assigned to the Air Defense Command in Colorado Springs where he retired. Shirley and I visited them a few times. The last visit was just a few days before he died. We were Masonic brothers; Gerry had been one of the Eastern Star state officers for Colorado, and Dee as she called him was her chauffer around the state. I had a prayer for him; I saluted him for his last salute just days before he died in 1997. Gerry moved to her home in Columbus, Missouri where we have visited her, and she came to Colorado for an Eastern Star Conference and visited us. She commented how good it was to be back with air force people who spoke her language. Their daughter, Norma Jean, was in the Rainbow Girls with Linda.

Europe was the first of the seventeen major air commands in the air force to have centralized military pay. We were the test command with about eighty-four thousand military pay records to be converted and paid out of the office at Denver, Colorado.

Colonel Charles J. Pratt, the director of accounting and finance at USAFE, made the final arrangements for me to come up to Lindsay Air Station. Lindsay had no airstrips or runways; it was located in part of Wiesbaden, Germany, and it operated as the headquarters for all of Europe. I will always believe that they selected Europe as the test command because I was there and had been through the development stages of the system back in Denver. I think that had something to do with Colonel Coon's promotion and moves to both Ramstein and Wiesbaden.

The next two years was a major challenge. My days were packed with phone calls all over Europe and also to Denver. I was fortunate to have one of the very best secretaries I had ever been associated with at Lindsay, Mrs. Anne Wust. Anne was a German girl. She had worked for a time in California at a law firm when she was married to her first husband. She had a good command of the English language. She spoke German to phone operators which gave me the priority I needed to speed up communications. When she heard me talking to offices in Turkey, Spain, Libya, England, France, and others, if she heard me make a commitment to call Denver, she would have my party in Denver on the line by the time I hung up.

Mr. Paul Doyle, who I worked with at AFAFC, was in charge of the operation at Denver. Paul, Stewart Simpson, the Canadian, and I had gone hunting together in the mountains near Colorado Springs. I think our group was hunting for grouse. Stewart and I became lost. We finally acknowledged to each other that we were lost. Stewart fired a shot in the air, and Paul fired a shot in the air. We continued in the direction of the shot, occasionally firing another shot to which Paul responded until we made contact with our hunting party. That was the only time I ever become lost while hunting.

Paul had a regular greeting every morning, "Ken, it sure is morning, isn't it?" More than once, I called Paul in Denver to get him out of bed at 0400 in the morning to meet one crisis or another. The time change made it difficult for us because it was 3:00 p.m. our time before they came to work. When Paul answered, I said, "Paul, it sure is morning, isn't it?"

Once, I remember that the checks scheduled in on TWA's

flight were not on board. I made one of those 4:00 a.m. calls to him, and he made sure they were on the next flight. It was absolutely essential that we did not miss a payday during the test period. Paul's widow told me that he often spoke of our experiences both at the AFAFC and of the test in Europe.

Adding to the challenge of centralized military pay in Europe, we had just centralized all of Europe's pay for civilian employees at Ramstein during my year there. Getting the civilian time cards in from all over Europe was a major problem. I coordinated with Lieutenant Colonel Guili that I was going to send a priority TWX (a message transmitted by wire used long before e-mail or whatever may be used to communicate when this is read years later) to the commander at every installation with a list of missing or late time cards. Information copies of each of these would also be transmitted to USAFE headquarters. Seventeen messages went out at one time, and that was the end of that problem.

The comptroller of USAFE was Colonel Lloyd J. Martin. He had been in grade as a full colonel for seventeen years. He was one bitter colonel who just could not make general. He gave my director, Colonel Pratt, a hard time all the time. I suggested to Colonel Pratt that he let me send up a daily activity report with a brief of all that was going on. He got one every day and began to initial it and return it to our division. Occasionally, he would put a note on it or ask a question that would be answered the next day or by phone to his secretary. That worked beautifully and kept him off Colonel Pratt's case. Colonel Pratt thought I was a genius. Funny thing is that the report was not an air force directed report, but if it was late or if it did not show up one day, you would think that a crisis was underway. That is something I learned in my civilian career that worked quite well, and I even use it occasionally in prison ministry with the chaplain and with Good News prison ministry and my jail ministry team in Colorado.

As my tour in Europe came to the end of my three years, there was one more big decision to be made. I could elect to be retired at the port on returning to the United States, or as a chief, I could select where I wanted to go; if there was an opening, I could go, provided I committed to one year service at that installation. We really needed to be close to Shirley's aging parents. Like us now, they were in their late eighties, and they needed help. I felt my best chance of finding an opening would be at a recently formed command located at the old Census building in Suitland, Maryland, just outside of Washington DC. It was called the Air Force Data Systems Design Center (AFDSDC). I did not know anyone there, but they jumped at the chance to have me assigned to that command. (Very few ever asked to be assigned to the Washington DC area if they have been there before).

As a chief, I had the option of flying or coming home on the SS United States ocean liner. Since my previous trips on the ocean on a troopship as a troop-class passenger were not very comfortable or exciting, I elected to come home first class in a luxury ocean liner. We thought a few times that may have been a mistake, as we were traveling with Vikki Kay who was now a little less than three years old.

We had cleared our government quarters at 23A Washington Street where I had been the building commander for two years. This was an eight-unit building with two sets of maids quarters compared to a twenty-four-unit that I had at Ramstein. We had a great group of families there except for one young couple. They finally got into a squabble one night, and I heard all of this noise and threats. I called the air police to come, but in the meantime, I had dressed in full uniform and entered the apartment only to find the young airman holding a knife to his wife's throat. I disarmed him from the knife just as the air police arrived and arranged to have her returned to the States. I recall one of the young air police airmen looking at me and shaking his head, saying, "Chief, you have one hell of a lot of nerve to just walk up to an angry man with a knife in his hand."

We checked into transient quarters for one night then left to drive to the port at Bremerhaven. It was an exciting time in Wiesbaden for the Germans as well as for the Americans. Apollo 11 had just touched down on the moon on July 16, 1969, and there were reports back from Neil Armstrong, Buzz Aldrin, and Michael Collins that it was "One small step for man and one giant leap for mankind" or something similar to that. I think that in 2016, you can still hear that historic statement by going to the Internet at history. nasa.gov and search for "one small step."

With today's leadership progressing in the direction it is going, you may not be able to even find that statement in the history books of tomorrow much less the Internet. It was such a pleasure to drive downtown, and when the German people recognized you to be Americans, they pointed to the moon with big thumbs-up. It was great to be an American and to be going home! I thought many times about what I would have missed if I had taken my retirement back at AFAFC. Our accomplishments were no comparison to placing a man on the moon, but we had served our country well. The new pay system test also had a thumbs-up, and the next step would be to implement it for all services just as we did the Joint Uniformed Services Pay manual earlier.

Shirley has covered our trip home in her bio, so I will just mention that Vikki Kay and I spent a lot of time in the nursery on the ship playing with toys. She had some cute sayings that cracked us up. Whobody was one of them. Whobody took my blanket ... whobody did it ... Grandma and Grandpa Taylor had a lot of fun watching her grow up, and when we traveled to Texas, my brother and sisters were so pleased that we had another little girl.

CHAPTER THIRTY-FOUR

Kenneth's Last Duty Station in the Air Force

I believe it was August 1, 1969, when we passed by the Statue of Liberty in New York, debarked from SS United States, rented a car, loaded our bags, and drove to Bolling AFB, Washington DC. That is where my records would be kept during my assignment at the AFDSDC. The duty station was temporarily located in one of the old Census buildings at Suitland, Maryland, pending the completion of the space allotted for it in the James Forrestal Building, 1000 Independence Avenue, Washington DC. My section chief was Major Gerald Von Bargen. The division chief was Lt. Col. W. C. Handle, and Colonel Woodrow W. Jenkins was the director. The commander was Colonel Jack McGregor. I remember Lieutenant Colonel Handle smiling and saying, "Now that I have a good Deal, we will both have a Handle on things."

My sponsor was MSgt. Dave Clark who had arranged housing for us on Bolling until we could move into the home we built on Old Fort Road, Friendly, Maryland, back in 1956. Dave was the only military man who directly worked for me. He was a top-notch systems analyst. Before the end of August, Colonel Jenkins made me the command chief of his directorate. He asked me to attend all of his staff meetings, and immediately, I had sixty-four of the highest trained computer specialists, programmers, and systems analysts in the air force.

Although I was not called a first sergeant, I had the equivalent responsibility. They ranked from airman first class to senior master sergeants. Fortunately, these all worked for officers and civilian bosses, and my responsibility to them was primarily from a military point of view as opposed to being their direct supervisor.

Sitting in the staff meetings, I was current on all that was going on and the problems associated with various projects that were underway. Most of these projects were over my head and out of my area of knowledge since other than accounting and finance operations were also being developed. There was one section within my directorate that had the responsibility of developing a computerized system for the pay of reserves and National Guard personnel. These are sometimes called weekend warriors because some of them worked weekends and had one or two days' pay coming. Others were called to active duty for fifteen or thirty days a year to maintain their reserve status.

I was in the staff meeting when the Major in charge of a group of civilian GS-9 to 11 technicians and two secretaries had been working on this project for four months, and they had come to the conclusion that it was impossible to develop a mechanized system for this group who had such weird pay requirements. They recommended that the project be closed down and let it continue to be handled manually. I could see the disappointment on the faces of Lieutenant Colonel Handle and Colonel Jenkins. This major in charge of the project was also against having me sit in on the staff meetings. He had in glare in his eyes each time he looked at me.

Following the staff meeting, Colonel Jenkins had some efficiency reports of enlisted personnel to discuss with me. I volunteered to take a look at the system that was about to be ditched to see if I had any recommendations for the Colonel. Then I discussed it with Lieutenant Colonel Handle and Major

Von Bargan. Major Von Bargan and I carpooled together along with another major as we all lived in the same general area. As a Chief with twenty-four years of service, I qualified with more points than any of them, so we had good underground parking space for free. They really hated to see me retire because they lost their good parking space.

I knew that this reserve pay system had been developed on a local level several years earlier at the Accounting and Finance Center. The Reserve Records Center was there, and I had been detailed as an advisor on the system in the development stages five years earlier. I made a few phone calls; sure enough, it had been running locally for five years, and all of the bugs were worked out of the system. AFAFC had the responsibility for paying people in this category who were not attached to a facility with paying capability. My contacts at AFAFC shipped the system and the manuals to me. This is one of the few times in the air force when I cheated by not revealing this source to the officers in charge. I discussed with Colonel Jenkins the possibility of letting me have a programmer, a systems analyst, and a secretary to take a few days to look at the project before it was ditched.

He said to me, "Take your pick." I asked if he had any in that category who were eligible for promotion that he would like to see promoted. If so, I would like to have them for the project. I could see a twinkle in his eye; he was excited. "Give me a couple of days, and I'll have them for you."

I asked that we set up shop in an area away from the team that had been working on the project because I didn't want it sabotaged, and I put a security classification of Secret on the project which eliminated the staff from discussing it. I had the systems analyst take the local manual and make it an air force regulation and the technical sergeant programmer adapt the program to AFDSDC specifications. The secretary put all of this on paper, and we took it to the section that run the test on both the program and the documentation. It came back error free. I declassified everything and handed the complete package to Colonel Jenkins in two weeks as a fully tested complete package with the air force regulation to support it. He was flabbergasted. I told him promotions were in order for the crew, and I would dismiss them back to their various sections. Along with the project, I gave him recommendations for the Air Force Commendation Medal for the military and superior sustained service award for the secretary. I suggested that he give the Major a second chance. He thought I was nothing short of genius. I will explain in another chapter that I revealed my secret and confessed my sin to Colonel Jenkins some five years later after he retired and was the Treasurer of the Credit Union at Andrews Air Force Base in Maryland.

Shortly after AFDSDC moved into the Forrestal Building in Washington DC, the announcement to move to Gunter Air Force Base in Montgomery, Alabama, was made. My year of commitment was coming to a close, so I decided this was a good time to close out my air force career. We were settled back in our own home at 10,000 Old Fort Road in Friendly, Maryland. The kids had a year of school behind them, and Shirley's parents, Reggie and Pauline Taylor, really needed us more than ever.

My retirement date was set for September 1, 1970. Colonel Jenkins had a problem processing my retirement papers, but he recommended me, and I was awarded for the highest award the AFDSDC was authorized to issue. There were several retirement parties for us. One big party was at the Andrews Air Force Base NCO club and another luncheon at Suitland, Maryland. During that luncheon at Suitland, Major Von Bargen told Shirley that I was the first and only chief he knew who was good at everything. He said all chiefs had to be good at something, or they never reached that level, but that in the year that he knew me, he learned that I was good at everything. However, he was disappointed that Colonel Jenkins sort of pulled me away from his section most of the time for other duties.

I guess one should not look back, but we all do. When I worked with inmates later in the county jails, I noticed that they are often reminded by Satan of their past. I suggest that they remind Satan of his future, and he will leave them alone. When I saw the number of Master Sergeants who retired at AFAFC in that rank, I am glad I took the approach I did when I was assigned there in 1961. The difference in retired pay for these retirement years has been one of the rewards.

My message to my kids, grandkids, their grandkids and great-grandkids and the relatives of my nephews and niece and their children is to make a special effort to uphold the Slight Edge Principle. That is, "In everything you do, let your performance be just slightly better than most of your competitors." I have always believed that setting goals should be like shooting skunks. It's better to aim high and miss than shoot low and hit that stinker and have to put up with the results.

There is a rule that I like to use when establishing a goal. I like to split the word goal down the middle. (Go al). Then I place a d in the middle and add another l at the end. This places God first and then all things will fall in place. But seek ye first the kingdom of God and his righteousness; and all these things shall be added unto you (Matthew 6:33, KJV).

I answered my draft call on January 29, 1946, and spent a few days as a draftee in the US army before reenlisting in the Army Air Force on February 7. I was on the first general order establishing the United States Air Force in 1947. My retirement date, the date I was transferred into the status of reserve, was September 1, 1970. I remained in the United States Air Force Reserve until February 1976 when I was officially retired from the United States Air Force after thirty years of active and reserve duty.

CHAPTER THIRTY-FIVE

Kenneth's Post Military Service Career

On September 1, 1970, I woke up as a retired chief master sergeant from the United States Air Force. On that day, I would be moved to the reserve status until a total of thirty years' service was completed, which happened on February 7, 1976. I would then be moved to a fully retired status. I looked in the mirror and said to myself, "Chief, you are looking at your staff."

It was an adjustment. The day before retirement, as the command chief of the Air Force Data Systems Design Center in Washington DC, I had sixty-four of the best airmen and non- commissioned officers in highly trained areas such as military, civilian, and Air National Guard pay and allowances. I had computer programmers, finance systems analysts, and computer operators ranging in rank from airman first class to senior master sergeants.

I have often wondered what it would have been like if I would have had a dozen of these in a startup software computer company. In addition to my retirement certificate, Colonel Jack McGregor presented me with the Command Meritorious Award plaque, the highest award given by his command. General Jack D. Ryan, Air Force Chief of Staff as of September 1, 1970, signed my certificate. I can still get into my Air Force uniform forty-five years later. I reaped one benefit by retiring on September

1. There was a small pay raise effective that day for military personnel, and my pay was based on the new rate although I only served one day in September. Just prior to retirement, I had a standard form (SF 171) prepared. This form is similar to a civilian resume. I paced the streets of Washington DC, leaving a copy at just about every department head in the government. The Department of Agriculture had a need for my services in a job that would be a GS-11. (Government series with a rating of 11 would have been at a salary range just above my military active duty pay.) The department head who wanted to hire me had two problems. Although I had a lot of experience, my formal training in computers was missing. Also, there was a hiring freeze, and nothing he could do would permit me to be eligible. The freeze on hiring extended into most all government agencies. Several of the agencies advised me that they would keep my application on file until the freeze on hiring was removed.

My old friend Richard C. "Jack" Hargons, now a CMSGT, came in as my replacement. Jack planned to stay for thirty years before retiring. We served together the first six years at three different bases, and now he was replacing me at retirement.

I knew the area well and was taking him and his wife, Beth, around to find a place to live. Jack and Beth had two sons, Rick and Michael. They had to find a house to rent rather than buy because the design center was in the process of moving to Alabama. We were settled in our home, and Shirley's parents needed our help more than any other time in our married life. Shirley's bio covered our family life, so my coverage of that area will be limited.

I made the rounds with Jack and Beth, stopping at several real estate companies trying to find one that handled rental properties. We found a nice place for them to live in Clinton, Maryland, about eight miles from our home. In our pursuit, one of the realtors asked me what I would be doing now that I had finished my military career. He invited me to come back on

Saturday morning and talk to the broker about becoming a real estate agent.

I learned from the broker that if I could obtain a license, there would be no problem in getting a job in real estate. The procedure at that time was altogether different from today. One had to study on his own and apply to be tested. If they passed the test, they worked for a year in real estate, during which time they attended a formal class offered at a university or a community college. If they passed the formal class, they become eligible to renew their license.

The real estate company was a new startup company. They opened an office in a house on Allentown Road in Camp Springs, Maryland. It was located just a few houses east of Branch Avenue intersection of Allentown Road on the left side of the road toward Andrews AFB. The upstairs was vacant; they hoped to fill it with agents like me. I went up there every day to study for my test. I found that I could listen to people coming in asking about real estate. I could hear half the conversation of incoming phone calls. I could also listen to those agents who had returned with clients after having looked at homes as they discussed financing and procedures for writing an offer. It was also convenient for me to ask questions and have items in the real estate book explained to me.

Real estate, much like the air force, had many terms. I recorded these from the real estate book on a reel-to-reel tape recorder. I spent several hours lying on the floor with headphones, trying to beat myself to the answers. It proved to be one of the best methods for learning real estate terms I would need to know to pass the test and use in the business.

I recall that when our daughter, Linda, changed jobs and went to work for the air force, I gave her my old JANAP 169, a joint Army- Air Force-Navy publication, with most of the symbols she would be using. By the time she retired, she could spew out new terms and symbols that came along which were all new to me.

Near the end of October 1970, I applied to take the real estate exam. It was administered in Baltimore, Maryland. The results were to be mailed in about three weeks. The longer I waited and continued to shop for a job, the more apprehensive I became about whether I passed the exam. I spent a lot of time in the real estate office of the two men who had started the new company, Webster and Grasso. They only had four agents. I picked up what I considered many boo-boos the agents were making. I could sense those losing customers even before they lost them, both in person and on the phone. I was in the upstairs of the real estate office, but I could overhear conversations.

My license notification came by mail, and I passed the test. My temporary real estate license was effective on November 30, 1970, three months following my retirement from the air force. My new career began as I went to the real estate office with enthusiasm and announced that I passed the test.

Mr. Lou Grasso, one of the owners, called me into his office and announced the company was closing. The owners had a disagreement and decided to disband the company. He suggested Larry Eul Realtors as his first choice for me to apply to a new company.

A licensed sales agent had to have a broker to sponsor them. Larry found that I was a retired chief. He was a retired technical sergeant, so he hired me on the spot. His top sales person was a retired master sergeant, and he had a chief working part time, awaiting retirement from the air force. Larry had two sales managers. His staff of about twenty were broken in to about ten each. Merle Ballard had one group, and Francis "F. L." Jenkins had the other group. He assigned me to Ballard's group.

I learned that the sales managers presented any contracts the agents wrote and that Larry's wife, Roberta (Bert), took it from there, set up the interviews for mortgage, and followed through until settlement. The sales managers did not do anything else except participate in sales meetings. They each were also listing and selling agents.

It was December, and it had not been a good year for real estate. Fortunately, I did not know that, or I probably would never have chosen real estate as a career. All of the good sales people were just resting in December. I had no customers, but I did have a list of names and phone numbers that had contacted the old, now defunct office, so I began working them until I could get some customers.

On December 2, 1970, Shirley and I celebrated our twenty-first anniversary. I was employed again. This time I was self-employed, as I was considered an independent contractor. I had many reservations about selling real estate. I had not sold anything since I left Ray Woods Tire Company back in Dallas in the 1940s. Shirley said that she would cheer me on, knowing that there would be night and weekend duty and that I would not have as much family time as I had in the air force.

I sold my first house on my forty-fourth birthday, December 5, 1970, to a couple who had walked in earlier to the Webster-Grasso office. I remember giving them a cup of coffee in the old office while they waited for an agent. I called them to see if they had been successful in finding a home. They had not been, and the agent had not made any contact with them since going out of business. These folks had no idea that this was my first sale until Shirley sponsored her into the Eastern Star several years later. Sometime later, I listed and sold their home again. Just took two days, and the home they purchased for $34,000 I sold for $44,950.

Before Christmas, I had sold three homes and listed my former boss's home, Lieutenant Colonel Handle, from the design center. Larry Eul made a big to-do out of this at the last sales meeting of the year. In one month, I had exceeded some of his part-time salesperson's accomplishments for the entire year. No one told me it was a bad time for real estate.

I began 1971 with a bang, selling my first property, a vacant lot, on New Year's Day for the first sale of the year. Larry approached me about being office manager. I was not interested because it seemed to me that his wife, Bert, ran things in the office. He was just interested in me organizing the front desk and all of the property listings, etc. I did this as a favor, but he paid me $300 anyway.

I was not fond of waiting for the managers to present my contracts. In some cases, another company sold the house before my contracts was presented. I sold three homes one weekend, and since the manager was out selling, I went ahead and presented the contracts. I had all three ratified by Monday morning. I was not pleased at how my customers were being serviced. I had difficulty finding the status and progress made after the sale.

A big surprise to me was the opposition I was getting from the sales force. I learned later as a manager, this was routine. If a new person became successful, it was OK as long as they were less successful than the old hands were. I think I handled that as a manager better than most because of the experience I had early in my real estate career.

I had been with Larry Eul's office about seven months when I lost three sales in a row. All were lost due to bad processing. I knew that I could have saved every one of them by just giving ordinary customer service, and I confirmed this with the customers. F. L. Jenkins had some similar experiences that were costly for him also. He decided to open up his own company. Since he was an associate broker, it would just be a matter of converting his sales license to a broker's license.

He hired me away from Larry Eul and opened his company

on July 1, 1971, around the corner at 6413 Old Branch Avenue, Clinton, Maryland. I was his only agent.

There was a parade in Clinton on July 4. He entered me in the parade with my father-in-law's 1966 Ford F250 pickup truck. We had signs printed for each side of the truck with the name of the new company. Larry rode in the truck with me, and we won a trophy for whatever category we were in. He had a small airplane circling the parade carrying a new sign streamer of the company. That evening, we sponsored the fireworks display at Clinton Park. F. L. was a retired fireman. He had a license to put on a fireworks display. We dug holes in the ground for the mortars to fit in and lined up all the fireworks with a canvas top to keep sparks from igniting our inventory. What a job! I have great respect for fireworks displays. Clinton, Maryland, residents knew we were in business the very first week.

F. L. purchased a used construction trailer in Virginia and had it transported to a new subdivision he had just listed in Westchester Estates. Bob Farger was building some new style homes there. We sold them from $32,950 to $34,500. The price was a shade higher than most homes were selling for, and most sales were contingent on the owner's home selling. Therefore, we listed those homes for sale as well. (I later resold some of those customers who bought new homes for $59,000 when they were ready to sell.)

We rented a power generator for the construction trailer until electricity was available from the subdivision. We had a phone in the trailer and one in the office with the same number. It was a little awkward, but we managed. F. L and his wife, Jane, were in the office, and I was in the trailer. As we sold homes, we began to recruit agents. Some of the people to whom we sold homes also became our agents. It was a slow process, but as we sold a subdivision, we would move the trailer to a new subdivision. Our next one was in Chris Mar Manor. Stan Ridgeway Realtors had a bigger subdivision of nice homes just a couple thousand dollars less than Bob Farger's homes, but they were not near as nice as Bob's homes. Stan did not have anyone sitting on his development except on weekends. We had the best of both worlds. I sold more of Ridgeway's homes than his agents sold. I was there every day. I knew the homes, the builder, and the construction people. I had many long days that went well into the evenings. The toughest part of the job was missing so much of the kids' growing up time.

I recall telling the kids that if I sold a home in December, we would purchase a new color television. I did, and we devoted the commission to a big—at that time—twenty-one-inch consoled color TV). The cost was $550; the commission just barely covered the cost. New home commission was only 4 percent. When we sold a co-op, which is another realtor's listing, the two brokers split the commission. Then the selling broker's portion of the commission was divided with the sales person.

Our 1965 Pontiac was showing major problems from the gas we used in Germany, which did not contain additives necessary to keep the engine clean. All we could afford was a little 1970 Ford Maverick when we traded the wagon. It was a big comedown from the big station wagon, but we made the new Maverick do for a few years.

Real estate began to come out of its period of recession in 1972. Prices were increasing, demand was up, and it was a problem to keep up without working many extra hours. In September of 1972, I became a million-dollar salesman for the year. (That is, the total sales value of all homes that settled hit or exceeded a million dollars.) In those days, rarely a sale in our area exceeded $50,000. It took a lot of activity to hit a million before the end of the year.

I celebrated by trading in the little Ford Maverick for a blue four-door 1973 Ford Galaxy purchased from Clinton Ford. The company no longer exists today. The new car proved to be a great real estate and family car. Seats were vinyl. This helped the spills by kids traveling with parents while we were looking at homes. It had a lot of trunk room to accommodate real estate signs, which the Maverick did not have. Larry was walking home from Friendly High School. I stopped to pick him up in the new car. He was impressed when the wheels spun as we took off. Larry and a friend had driven the Maverick to Florida during spring break. Linda was at college in Frostburg, Maryland. I drove up around Thanksgiving to pick her and a couple of girls up. I asked Linda if she wanted to drive the new car home, and she did. She had been looking for the little white Maverick and was impressed that she got to drive the Galaxy with only four hundred miles on it all the way back to Friendly, Maryland.

As we entered into 1973 and on in to 1974, offers continued to come in from government agencies who could now hire again. I was so ingrained in real estate that I did not consider any of them. F. L. Jenkins wanted me to be sales manager as new agents' questions were beginning to affect my time and sales. I did not want to get away from sales. Managing would also result in a pay cut which I could not afford.

Much of my time was spent serving on the Prince George's County Board of Realtors Ethics Committee. Total time was one year as a member, one year as deputy chair, and one year as the chair. I had the opportunity to see firsthand the kind of violations being committed, the penalties, and who the offenders were, both sales persons and brokers, which was important to know. This took a lot of time away from sales activity, but it was excellent experience for the days and years ahead.

Larry Eul, my former broker, sent a secretary over to our office with a check for $3,000 representing the commissions lost due to inefficiency of processing. I sent it back with a note of thanks. I knew that was his way of recruiting me back to his company.

I had tested this new occupation well enough to have

confidence that I could make a living in real estate. I took a few actions to increase my knowledge in both the real estate industry and in the business world. I began to take courses in real estate during the various break in regular classes at Towson State College, Baltimore, Maryland. Towson is now a university. Real estate was taught for a week at a time in between regular classes. The designation for a completed course was certified real estate broker (CRB). This certification entitled a real estate agent to become a real estate broker. I also needed to learn more about the business world, so I became a member of the Christian Business Men's Committee (CBMC). I served in all of the positions of a local committee. This voluntary organization provided the principles that contributed to my success. In addition to becoming chairman of the local committee, I was appointed the regional chairman in the metropolitan Washington area which included five separate committees. I became a lifetime member. I was also chairman of a summer Family Time Out week that included CBMC families from five states that met for a week during the summer. Our director during those three years was Paul Lantz. I learned a lot working with Paul and his wife, Dixie.

CBMC focused on Biblical business principles. I took advantage of business by the book workshops, business leadership forums, forums groups, and wisdom groups. I learned that the profits one makes and the profits one is planning to make need to be honest in the eyes of God. I learned that those who reject making a profit by fraud, who stay far away from bribes, and who refuse to listen to those who plot enticement to do wrong may have to make tough decisions in both business and management (Isaiah 33:15–16).

In November 1974, I became a member of the Oxon Hill Lions (Liberty Intelligence Our Nation's Safety) Club that met in Friendly, Maryland. I was appointed and elected to all of the positions in the local club. I became the editor of the local

Lions Club Growler. At the district level, I became the editor of District 22 C News. I was designated as the Lion of the Year by four different club presidents. Shirley joined me first as member of the Lioness Club and later in the Oxon Hill Friendly Lions Club. When ladies Lioness Club became Lions, I was appointed by Lions Clubs International as the Guiding Lion for a year. I was the only male in the club. Later, both Shirley and I were awarded Melvin Jones Fellows by Lions Clubs International. I have included both CBMC and Lions activity because these two organizations included an education in business principles and community involvement that shaped the balance of my career. The Lions district we were a part of had a program called Roaring Lions. This was a speech development class. Following graduation, I taught the class four times. This experience became invaluable to both my career in real estate and in community events. Later, it assisted me greatly in my membership in the Gideon International.

Routh Robbins Realtors, with seventeen offices, was the largest firm in the area. They were building a new office building directly across from Andrews AFB. I sold many of their properties because they were a big listing company and had the inventory my customers wanted. They sent a letter of thanks to me for selling their properties. They also advised me that according to the records of the multiple listing service, I sold more of their listings than from my own broker's listings. Then they dropped the bombshell, telling me that if I had been working for them at their commission rates, my earnings from their listings alone would have been over $3,000 more than my current commission rate. Wow!

I did not sleep much that night. The next day, I decided to check them out. I found they had a sliding commission scale. Anyone who earned as much as $30,000 a year moved into the top bracket for both listings and sales. They offered to bring me aboard at the top bracket. I began the process of transferring my license. It was tough for me to do. I just decided if I was going to stay in the real estate business, I may as well look out for myself and family as well as my customers. Therefore, I faced the situation and made the move on November 1975.

Shirley's bio covers our family life, but I will just mention briefly that I became the Lion of the Year under four different Club presidents and eventually became a Melvin Jones Fellow, the highest award given by Lions Clubs International as well as club president and lifetime member of the organization.

The executive director of Prince George's County Board of Realtors, Paul W. Fowler, selected me as the first realtor associate to sit on the Prince George's Board of Directors, along with eight brokers as the governing body of the real estate board. This was a newly established position. As a non-broker, I represented just over 2,300 sales agents in the county. Routh Robbins Company was pleased to have their man representing the sales force. At this time, there was not a single staff member of the company on the board of realtors. I made information available from each of the meetings to management. So for the first time, they knew what was going on as well as what was planned for the future.

My first appearance on the board at the regular meeting drew stares and a cold shoulder. I expected that, so it came as no surprise. I decided to just sit tight, be calm, and play the game of respect as the only non-broker although I was eligible to be a broker. By the third meeting, I was one of them. Each in his own way were doing backhand sorts of recruiting. This made me smile with tongue in cheek. This job was very time consuming. However, the experience paid dividends in the years ahead.

My new manager was recently retired air force colonel, J. Loren Peck. He had been a B-17 and then a B-52 pilot. He was overjoyed to have a crusty old retired air force chief on board that could talk and understand his language. He authorized me to skip a two-week fast start class they required for all new agents. He suggested that I go for the first day just to see what it was all about. I did and decided to stay for the full two weeks. I could see that the knowledge of how the company worked would be advantageous to me. It was in the years to come, so it was a good decision. I obtained three listings from past customers, and one of them sold while I was in the two-week course. It was a shock to the new agents in the class.

The third week I was with the new company, we were called together for an early Christmas party. It was a decoy to get us all together to announce that the Routh Robbins Company (owner Routh, pronounced "Ruth," was in a wheelchair) had been sold to a West Coast firm, Coldwell Banker. None of us ever heard of them. I began to watch the old-timers in the company like a couple, Dick and Barbara Wood, and others to see their reaction to this surprise. I wondered if I had made a major mistake moving to this powerhouse of a company with seventeen offices in Maryland and Virginia.

I began to listen to the president of Coldwell Banker as he outlined their background and history. When he announced that our company would continue to be called Routh Robbins Realtors for a number of years, a big commotion and noise of approval went up from approximately three hundred agents and managers. The more I heard, the more I liked them, and the old-timers seemed to be taking it in stride. Routh Robbins's multiple sclerosis had taken its toll on her health, and Don McNary, her partner, was primarily in charge and would become our president. I decided to hang in there and see what would happen next.

CHAPTER THIRTY-SIX

Kenneth's First Job with Coldwell Banker

The only changes we could see in the beginning was that no real estate signs were being ordered until a decision could be made on what would go on the new signs. The old-timers began to hoard the existing signs. New people like me had no signs to put on their listings. Listing properties was my game.

As I obtained new listings, I explained to my homeowners, and most of them were just as happy not to have a sign anyway. I began to get appraisals in, and the results back before putting properties on the market. Then, I had a policy of putting the home on the market at $50 below the appraised value. This gave me the most saleable inventory in the office. As a result, I got very few offers below the listed price.

When I did get a lower offer, I was not embarrassed to recommend to the owner that they counter the offer right up to the listed price. The market was hot, and I had the inventory. While not having a sign bugged me no end, it proved to be an advantage. Our company agents knew of the homes and our salespeople, which meant we had both sides of the transaction, and it sold my listings. I proved that a good property, properly listed, would sell generally within the first thirty days, sign or no sign.

Our agents wanted to put their sign they had been hoarding

on the property with a sold panel on it. I picked up a few signs as a result. Awards began to come; I became the top listing agent in my office then in our region, and by the end of 1976, I was the top listing agent in the company of seventeen offices with about four hundred salespeople.

I closed out the year with fifty-one (settled) transactions. This was one short of a settled case each week of 1976. I achieved a million-dollar sales status by the middle of the year and two- million-dollar status by the end of the year. These were in addition to awards from the Prince George's Board of Realtors and a Community Service from the county.

Agents began to ask me how I managed to get to the office so early in the morning. Before going to the office, I had already been over to the farm and had fed the cows, and I was still the first one to arrive at the office. Shirley began to help me with the paperwork I was busy for the most part in 1977. I managed to carry those records into the year and was president of the company's president's club. I became the realtor associate of the year for Prince George's Board of Realtors in 1977. I was the fifth top listing agent in the state of Maryland.

I also had a life-changing experience while working real estate in 1977.

CHAPTER THIRTY-SEVEN

Kenneth's First job with Coldwell Banker

Before I include this testimony, I will explain an event that I hope will be of interest, especially to those who spend time on the keyboard of any electronic device.

I was up a couple hours earlier than usual on one of those cool Colorado mornings. I decided to review previous chapters and make corrections with a fresh mind. This took a couple of hours. Before I finished typing in the title to this chapter, I must have hit some keys on the keyboard that I have not hit before. My computer screen switched formats, the toolbar I was using disappeared, and something I have never seen before appeared in its place; no matter what I seem to do, the original toolbar would not reappear. I was afraid to save the changes I made into this new format. I just stopped and left everything alone.

The next couple of hours, I fed birds, had breakfast, read all of my devotions. I have several from church, Gideons, CBMC, plus the Word of God. I did all of the bathroom chores and prayed. Before returning to the keyboard, I was wrestling with a comment in one of the devotions. "When Satan reminds you of your past sins, remind him of his future."

The next thought came to mind reminded me that the evening before, I had put everything on a separate flash drive.

Therefore, I closed out everything that was totally distorted and copied the saved data. Yes, I lost my corrections and a few hours' work, but I also lost those distortions. Satan despises Christian testimonies, but he cannot overcome the power of God, so I will let him tremble while including this life-changing experience.

You may recall in an early chapter that I made a decision for Christ around age fourteen during a revival meeting and that baptism was in a muddy pond full of crawfish near Lucas, Texas. This would have been 1939/40 time frame.

By early April 1977, my years accumulated to age fifty-one, my first career was behind me, and I was into my second career of real estate. I was so busy with new priorities that I teamed up with a buddy. Mrs. Janice Owen was also busy, and we agreed to look after each other's business when one of us was not available. This gave us freedom to take a day, a weekend, or a short vacation with confidence our customers would not suffer from our absence.

Jan and I often met for prayer. We briefed each other on the status of our listings and pending transactions. I met Jan before either of us joined Coldwell Banker. Real estate agents hold a listed property open often. The day many use for holding an open house is Sunday. My policy was to attend a church near the listed property I planned to hold open so I could go to the property immediately following the worship service. I attended local church, and Jan was there. They introduced me as a first-time visitor, Jan knew of me, and like her, I was a real estate agent. She made a special point of calling me on Monday, thanking me for coming, and inviting me back. (Years later in 1999, Janice and her husband, Wayland, became members of the Gideons International.)

Sometime during early 1977, I was on duty Sunday afternoon in the real estate office. I was on the phone when a giant of a man walked into the office. In his hand was an open Homes

Magazine. He pointed to a listed property, and while I was still on the phone, he announced to me, "I want to buy that home." He stood towering over me as I finished my phone conversation and then repeated his announcement.

The real estate market was hot but not this hot. I introduced myself to George Hubler and began to ask a few questions. "Have you seen that property, perhaps with another agent?"

"No."

"Would you like to see the property?" "No."

"Do you know where it is located?"

"No." George would not sit down to be qualified; he wanted to sign a contract to buy that particular property. I finally insisted that we look at the property, and then I would be glad to assist him with the purchase. Never before or after did I have this kind of an experience with a customer.

As we viewed the property, I could see that George had to bend over while we were in the basement. His height prohibited him from standing erect. I suggested we look at some other properties in the area where he could stand erect in the basement. As we looked at other properties, I learned that George was a GS-15 government employee in the Department of Housing and Urban Development (HUD) in Washington DC. Although he was well qualified to buy the property, the mystery heightened even more.

George signed a contract on the property at the end of Lime Street in Temple Hills, Maryland, full price. It was settled within thirty days with no contingencies or unusual conditions. The lending company, knowing that he worked at HUD, must have approved his loan almost immediately. Settlement would probably be less than thirty days. There were no snags in the paperwork.

Settlement day came; George was very quiet as he signed all

of the documents. He was not interested in walking through the property, and he had nothing at all to say to the owners. He had no interest in what they offered to tell him about the property.

As we left the office of the settlement attorney to return to my office for his car, George asked me if we could stop for a drink. We stopped in a bar, and he wanted a martini. I bought two. I wondered what they were like as I had never had one. George killed the first one; I pushed mine over to him. He killed it and asked for another one. I tried to start a conversation with George.

"Are you OK? Is there anything wrong?"

George calmly replied, "I am going to kill myself tonight."
"George, you just bought a beauty of a home."

"Yes, I know. I'm not moving into it. This is the last day of my life."

The seriousness of this situation began to engulf me from head to toe. I offered to buy him another drink, but I went to the payphone and called Shirley instead. I asked her to call our pastor and have him meet us at my office. I had a situation I did not know how to handle. It had all of the makings of a suicide. I picked up another drink for George from the bar and excused myself while I called Shirley again. The pastor was not available. He had gone to a meeting with four other pastors in preparation of a meeting scheduled at our church the following week called Five Nights for God. Each pastor took a turn at bringing the message in a revival meeting. I asked her to call a neighbor who was also a pastor and ask him to come. Reverend Edmonds arrived at my office just as we pulled in.

The pastor joined us in my car, and we talked until dark. George had a friend who told him that if he bought that home, she would marry him. She changed her mind, and this is what set George off. We had some assurance that George would go home and sleep off this idea of taking his life. As he drove off in his car, we watched as he stopped at a liquor store in the shopping center and emerged with a package. We looked at each other and prayed.

George called me early the next morning, and all I could do was thank God that he was still alive. "Could you and the pastor come over this evening?" I told him I would call the pastor and call him back. Pastor Edmonds agreed to come if George would stay off the bottle all day.

George responded, "You don't understand. I cannot do that."

I told George that was the only way I could get the pastor to come. George hung up.

At about three in the afternoon, George called me again. "I've made it this far. If you and the pastor can come, I will make it until you get here."

I called Reverend Edmonds, and he agreed. Not knowing what to expect, we went. I made my friend Janice Owen aware of the situation. She and Shirley prayed for us as we went to George's apartment. I later learned that Jan solicited her church and also her prayer warriors of the urgency.

George greeted us, and we began to pray immediately. After some time, George sprawled out on the floor. A long lingering noise came out of his mouth that I never heard before. We continued to pray, and finally, George relaxed and went to sleep. Reverend Edmonds and I quietly got up and left him there on the floor sound asleep.

On the way home that evening, I had a vision of a scripture, Romans 2:4. As soon as I entered the house, I picked up the first Bible I could find. It was the Living Bible which I seldom ever used except for cross reference or explanation purposes. There it was. "Don't you realize how patient he is being with you? Or don't you care? Can't you see that he has been waiting all this time without punishing you; to give you time to turn from your sin? His kindness is meant to lead you to repentance."

As a friend of the King James Version most of my life, that verse now had a new meaning that I never discovered before. The next morning, as I explained the events to Jan, she continued to nod her head. "Yes, I know." She seemed to know the whole process in advance of my explanation. This was another mystery to me—that she was not even surprised at my explanations.

George called me around noon asking if he could attend a breakfast meeting with me at the Christian Business Men's Committee in Hillcrest Heights, Maryland. We went the following morning, and as George gave his life to Christ, he asked for all the literature we could furnish him on how to be a Christian. I put his newly acquired home on the market. We sold it, and he came within a thousand dollars of breaking even after all the charges for settlement fees. George began a new life with Christ, a life that was exempt from alcohol. Exempt from many of his old friends as well. The first of our Five Nights with God was on Monday. Ellen Culp was the first pastor to deliver the message. She preached on the Holy Spirit. Shirley and I both went forward, and as she placed her hands on my shoulders, I felt what seemed like an electric current from head to feet.

Yes, it was a life-changing experience. It was interesting how God used a sinner to route me into this situation. I have been working with inmates for over thirty-five years. Yes, I have witnessed many life-changing experiences with them. It is especially interesting when one of them leads another inmate to the Lord.

CHAPTER THIRTY-EIGHT

Kenneth's Management Experience with Coldwell Banker Real Estate

I n early 1978, Coldwell Banker began to expand the number of offices. Our numbers rose from seventeen to thirty-three by the end of the year. My manager, J. Peck, began to work on me to become his assistant manager.

The Prince George's County Board of Realtors had a rule that one could not have the designation of a manager unless he or she had three or more continuous years of full-time real estate experience. When J. Peck took the job with the newly built Andrews office, his status as manager was questioned because he had not been licensed three full years. He had joined Routh Robbins office on St. Barnabas Road in Oxon Hill, Maryland, following retirement from the Air Force. By J's own admission, he was not a good salesperson. He did like to manage, and he was a good manager.

Executive Vice President Leonard Whittaker asked me if I would consider having my name placed on the official records as the manager of the Andrews office. J. Peck could be my assistant manager, and the agreement would be just among us. I would not have the capacity of manager except on paper, and the sales agents never had to know the arrangement. Therefore, I had a leading and growing office incognito status only the president, Don McNary, Leonard Whittaker, and I knew of the arrangement.

During the three previous summers, I took real estate courses at Towson State College in Baltimore. These three classes resulted in my Graduate, REALTOR Institute (GRI) designation in real estate, which also gave me the eligibility to be a real estate broker. Therefore, I was qualified to hold the title and also to become a real estate broker.

J. Peck began to work on me to be the assistant manager of the Andrews office. I resisted because I had my hands full just taking care of my business. I had been listing and selling about seven years, and many of my former customers were ready to sell again. They also kept me in customers they referred to me. I had no desire to get in management. One of the reasons I left F. L. Jenkins Realtors was due to the same pressure, and I was often used as a manager when I was not holding that position.

General Manager Bob Culbertson contacted me and told me that J. Peck had put my name in as a prospective manager at a recent meeting. Coldwell Banker had sent Mr. Robert Rathburn from the headquarters of Coldwell Banker headquarters in Irvine, California, to be our new vice president. He had instructions to grow the number of offices in the metro area of Washington DC. Our company was the first acquisition by Coldwell Banker on the entire East Coast. There were no Coldwell Banker offices between California and Maryland at that time.

It is very necessary that I pause here and explain that Coldwell Banker, as a company, was very good to me. That was not always the case for some of the personnel who worked for Coldwell Banker. There were instances I detected that the company's interest was not protected through lack of either knowledge and experience or self- interest and sometimes just pure stubbornness. My experience at two separate headquarters in the Air Force and the extended time spent with corporate personnel with large companies gave me a distinct advantage or perhaps a sixth sense of when things were not as they should be. Seems like a long explanation. I will try not to repeat it as I give examples in various situations that arose over the years.

A luncheon appointment for me to meet with Bob Culbertson and Robert Rathburn, the newly appointed vice president was scheduled. I kept the appointment as a favor to J. Peck. We met at a Steak and Ale restaurant in Alexandria, Virginia. It was an interesting meeting for me because I did not intend to accept an appointment in management. I was completely relaxed, and I made no effort to impress either one of them. The funny part was that they were not relaxed at all. They were doing a selling job. In addition to being the regional chairman of the Washington DC Metro Christian Business Men's Committees, I had joined the Gideons' ministry in May of that year. I could not identify either of them as businessmen of the character that I was being trained in at that time. I learned about the company expansion plans and new office buildings in the process of procurement, had been procured, or planned to be procured. I left the meeting making no commitment other than I appreciated their offer and would keep in mind. I made sure to leave the impression that I had not aspired to get into management.

A couple of months passed, and all of a sudden, a set of orders came appointing me assistant manager and making J. Peck the branch manager. I did not think much of it as J. Peck completed his three years. He was now eligible to be the branch manager. However, that was not all that it meant. I was to be his assistant. That was in March 1978, and all of a sudden, my status changed, which permitted me to continue to list properties but took me out of sales completely. The salary income as assistant manager was to offset my sales income; however, I could keep all of my pending sales through settlement. No one said anything to me about being an assistant manager, and all of a sudden, like Pogo, I was one.

I told J. Peck that I would play the game for a while to see if I wanted to keep that status or revert to being just a sales associate. The office staff and all of the sales associates encouraged me to keep the position. I found that my concentration on listings without sales activity was increasing my listing inventory faster than before. I decided to let the status stand. I no longer had what we call floor duty. My customer contact became purely referral and repeat business.

On August 1, 1978, J. Peck received a promotion to regional manager. The company established two regions. J. Peck took one region, and Fred Hauser took the other region. Both were retired colonels from the Air Force. All of a sudden, I was the branch manager of the Andrews office at Camp Springs, Maryland. This changed my status one more notch. I could no longer list or sell properties. My salary as an assistant terminated, and my income was on a commission override, a percentage of what the office produced.

J. Peck did his best to convince me that this move would be in my best interest in the end. He was confident of my ability; his only concern was that there was one thing I would not understand but would have to deal with. He said that I had fifty-one listings and nineteen sales the year before, and not one homeowner or purchaser ever called or came into the office to complain about some element of service. J. Peck told me that would no longer be the case, and he was concerned about me adjusting to that phase of managing.

J. Peck left the office on Friday evening with no goodbyes to anyone. He left a memo posted on the bulletin board that he was assuming a new role and that I was the new manager. I could not believe it; I had six homeowner and/or purchaser complaints before the Tuesday morning sales meeting.

I suppose that was a great way to break in to management. It gave me the ammunition I needed to train and train and hire correctly. He did not warn me about one other problem.

It probably had not been one his major problems. No matter to whom I turned a customer over, the job would not be accomplished to my satisfaction, and my former customers would not be as pleased. When I look back on all the problems that a real estate manager has in a thriving office, I consider that is the one thing that is the hardest to deal with. It haunted me the balance of my real estate career.

I had income from personal real estate settlements right on up through the balance of the year in addition to my newly acquired commission overrides from the agents. On November 1978, I had twelve settlements scheduled. These were my listings I had before the appointment to branch manager. I decided early in the month that the income from these settlements would purchase something I always wanted. I walked into Lindsay Cadillac in Alexandria, Virginia, and drove out a 1978 Fleetwood Brougham, fully equipped. I traded in my 1973 Ford and paid cash for the balance. I bought the car on my fifty-second birthday, which was December 5. My commission came to $14,200. My trade in allowance plus $12,000 cash bought the car. I kept that car in top shape until December 1996. I gave the car away to good friends Charles and Cora Crist. I met them when I joined the Gideons' ministry on May of 1978, and they had need of a car at that time. They loved the car as much as I did, so it was a joy to present it to them. They kept it well into the next century.

I will mention here in case Shirley did not cover it in her bio. I purchased and paid cash for a new 1977 Oldsmobile Cutlass Supreme. Janice and Wayland Owen let me park it at their home until Christmas Eve. Larry and Linda picked it up and parked it in our driveway. While we were in church on Christmas Eve, they tied a ribbon around it as her Christmas present in December 1976. She loved that car and kept it until we replaced it with a 1989 Oldsmobile Delta 88.

Our company awards ceremony for the calendar year 1978 was on February 1979 at a downtown hotel in Washington DC.

My sales activity terminated in March, and my listing activity terminated in August. I still walked away with the Top Company Listings Sold Award and a President's Award for the year with only three months in sales and seven months in listing activity for the year. The company now had thirty-three offices and 450 sales associates. Those became my last awards as a salesperson, but they just began as a manager.

Bob Rathburn, the company's vice president, was at the awards function. He got into some kind of a scrap with his wife and left before the evening event was over. One of the managers at their table had to take her home. In addition to his domestic problems, a rift grew between him and President Don McNary, causing the headquarters to be divided down the middle. There were problems between Bob Rathburn and the two regional managers. By year-end, it included me as well. Bob Culbertson had been given a five-year contract. There was a rift between him and Don McNary, so there was a three-way rift. Bob Culbertson would not leave the company, so Don McNary paid his salary for balance of his contract to get him out of the company. It became difficult to get a decision that would hold up under three leaders. The best description I can compare it to is the relationship among the Democrats, Republicans, and the president in the 1990s and again in 2000s.

Family members need to know that large companies are not immune to internal friction. This happens more often than the public knows. Fortunately Coldwell Banker is a solid company and does not tolerate the same problems over and over.

CHAPTER THIRTY-NINE

Kenneth Used His Own Judgment in 1979

The Andrews office closed out 1978 as the top office in both regions in these areas; one of my sales agents, Tom Pauling, became the top listing agent. I was the top listings sold agent. Our office was the top listing office for the thirty- three offices. The Springfield, Virginia, and Alexandria, Virginia, offices were number one and two in gross dollar sales and gross profit, and our office was number three. The sales prices in the two Virginia offices were consistently from $10,000 to $20,000 higher for comparable properties. The sales price of homes made the difference.

I appointed Tom Pauling as my assistant. The time we spent together was merely teaching him how to manage so I could recommend him as a branch manager after he completed the necessary three years as a sales agent. Tom was a former math teacher in one of the local high schools. He was young and was recently married when he came to our office. J. Peck had hired him during summer school break to see if real estate would work for him or he should return to teaching. I was able to give him a choice between the Annapolis, and Gaithersburg, Maryland offices. He chose the Gaithersburg office. Later on, Tom replaced J. Peck as one of the two regional managers.

I previously served three years on the ethics committee and was currently serving as a director on the County Board of Realtors. It was important that both my office staff and I operate within all the guidelines of both county and state. In addition to being on the county board, I was now the liaison director between the State of Maryland Realtors Association and the County Board of Realtors. This took more time than I liked, but it permitted me to be on the tip-top of everything and provided excellent material for me to pass on to and train my sales associates with. I was always so surprised how the Virginia managers insisted on listening and knowing what was going on since they were under a different set of rules for both counties and state. I offered to excuse them from spending time listening, but since they had no such representation in their board or state association, they were all ears.

Coldwell Banker had a number of lawsuits pending in Virginia. Our seventeen offices in Maryland did not have one for the entire year of 1978. The Virginia regional manager estimated that we saved three thousand hours that they had to spend. I thought it was of interest that some of the Virginia managers told me they spent more time before the board and in defending from lawsuits than I spent in my role with the county and state associations. I concluded that preventive maintenance and correct hiring and training were all worthwhile.

Most of our offices were profitable in 1979, but the rift at the headquarters was draining the company's finances faster than we could pump the money in to the accounting department. The rift grew to a point where the fourth floor of the Skyline Terrace office building in Virginia was divided into three sections. There were no yellow ribbons marking these, but the regional managers explained that each of the three had now hired their own staff. The new staff members were instructed not to work with or cooperate with of the other two. It became necessary for each of the two regional managers to hire secretaries. Expenses of the headquarters now reached a higher level. This meant that each office portion of a general administrator fund had exorbitant monthly fees to support the headquarters. My office share went from $3,600 a month in 1978 to $7,900 a month in 1979. I could only get $20 a month for coffee, $20 for stamps (one roll of a hundred), and $20 a month for film. My advertising budget was cut in half.

I took a different approach from all of the other managers in Washington DC, Maryland, and Virginia. They began to charge for coffee and only providing it free for customers. They quit providing postage to agents for correspondence, appraisal requests, etc. Most discontinued their picture boards that show current listed properties. Agents who wanted to advertise in the Homes Magazine could do so by paying $75 for a page that showed their listed properties. It had an adverse effect on the sales agents.

My approach was different, and I did not get anyone's permission. Reflecting back to what I did as a sales person, I devoted one full commission each year to a fund that I used to settle little problems along the way. One example sticks in my mind. I had a transaction that became so meticulous that the settlement depending on whether or not a clothesline in the backyard remained with the house. I purchased a new clothesline for $3.29. I took the old line down and gave it to the sellers. Sometimes there were yards to mow; Larry did some of that for me. Once there was a set of storm windows replaced that cost $439. These are just two examples where I took care of the cost to settle and move on.

On average, these little problems took most of the one commission I reserved each year. Routinely, I ordered four cases of Benson's three-pound fruitcakes through the Lions Club each year and visited my customers just before Thanksgiving. I wonder if any of those are still in the freezer. I ordered writing pens, calendars, door hangers, and plastic trash bags for cars (Shirley and I are still using some of those). Looking back at my old business account checkbook and income tax forms, I spent $3,870 of my own money in 1979 in order to provide free postage, coffee, and adequate advertising and to maintain the only picture board in the entire company.

Did it pay off? I think it did. First, I kept the morale of my agents up. Next, I noticed that the agents from the Oxon Hill office bringing customers to my office so they could look at the listings on the picture board. Then they sold our listings, there was a bonus for selling in-house listings. Others brought customers in to our office so they could give them coffee while the agent used our computer to search listings.

I never told the top headquarters staff what I was doing. My regional manager knew because when I filed my voucher, I itemized the expense. For example, I may have spent $60 for postage. I attached receipts and claimed only the $20 allowed. I may have spent $100 for film and processing but claimed only $20. Advertising took a bigger bite than anything else, around $300. I took the agents to Thanksgiving breakfast every year.

I just could not solve some problems. My income for 1979 exceeded the net income of Vice President Bob Rathburn. He had a set salary, and my income was on the override percentage of the production. The policy at that time was that each manager would be paid an annual bonus of 6 percent of the net income his or her office generated for the year. As an old accounting and finance man, I kept my own records and compared them each month with the accounting department with whom I had an excellent rapport. My office net income for the year was $103,500. This would have generated a bonus in excess of $6,000. Unfortunately, twenty- six of our offices either broke even or went in the hole. Only five were significantly profitable. They were Vienna, Springfield, Woodbridge, and Alexandria in Virginia and my Andrews office in Maryland.

Bob Rathburn could not accept the fact that some branch manager's income exceeded his income. He decided to take the excess from the winners and apply it to the losers so the company would show an overall profit for the year instead of a loss for some offices. (Does this sound familiar in 2010–2016?) Fortunately, I had reported correctly including all of my expenses with my request for reimbursement of allowed expenses. My regional manager made sure that my bonus covered my out-of-pocket expenses, but that was all.

In order to cut expenses, assistant sales managers were eliminated. Fortunately, Tom Pauling, an assistant, had been trained and was eligible to be a branch manager. He was moved to the Gaithersburg, Maryland, office. My secretary, Terry Nye, took on additional responsibilities of scheduling floor time and some administrative duties previously handled by the assistant manager.

Coldwell Banker had now gained the necessary license to become a mortgage company in Maryland and Virginia. They were not yet authorized to process Veterans administration (VA) or Federal Housing Authority (FHA) mortgages. They were weak in this area because most loans processed in California where the headquarters was located were conventional loans, that is, they were not guaranteed by the government.

Bob Rathburn put on a big push to have loans generated through the home company. We cooperated to the extent that it served our customers well. I learned later the reason for him pushing for loans. He was collecting part of the premium and received payment for signing the loan papers as a trustee.

Sales associates like to work with purchasers and sellers in selecting lenders because they soon learn who has the combination of best rates and best discount points and who are most dependable. Loan officers make it a point to visit as many offices as they can and attract as much business as they can. I had my share of both good and bad experiences with mortgage companies. It was my policy that if a loan officer wanted to do business with my sales associates, they had to see me first. If I approved, he or she did not have to see me again. Greed is the downfall of mortgage companies. Their profit level is so high they remind me of gold miners. They may do well for a while, but more mortgage companies come and go under than most enterprises related to real estate. The more time a sales agent has to deal with loan officers, the less time they have for listing and selling properties.

Bob Rathburn put the pressure on for us to use Coldwell Banker Mortgage to the extent of filing a report that showed what mortgage company we used if it was not Coldwell Banker. Most of the loans from my office were VA, FHA, or an assumption of the original loan. I asked for an exception of reporting these transactions since Coldwell Banker did not process them anyway. This made him mad. He not only refused the request but also demanded that I, as a manager, make an effort to convert the request for VA and FHA to a conventional loan so they could be processed by Coldwell Banker. The service my agents were getting from Coldwell Banker on the conventional loans being processed began to consume my time as a manager. I began to trace the process and talked to several people in the California office, including the vice president of the mortgage company. I recorded my phone conversations and learned that Bob Rathburn was the trustee on all of the deeds of trust where Coldwell Banker was the loan originator. He was paid a fee for this service, and this made my hair red. I generated enough fuss that resulted in the California office calling Bob Rathburn. This made him about as mad as I had become.

The manager in the Alexandria office, Tom Roberts, was more outspoken than me. His bonus was one of those that vanished, and he became a thorn in Rathburn's bonnet. Rathburn took the positions of cutting out Robert's override and mine and paying us a salary; this had the effect of reducing our income by $40,000 a year. Tom quit immediately. Rathburn told the regional manager that he could hire a manager off the street corner. He did not have to know anything about real estate, and he would be glad to work for $20,000 a year. His lack of knowledge and inexperience reminds me of some of today's country leaders. The results were similar to what we see in Washington DC.

I stewed for a few days. I was very active in both the Gideons and Christian Business Men's Committee and Lions Clubs International as well as our church at the time. I spent a lot of time trying to be a peacemaker. Using the beatitude in Matthew 5:9, I tried to retain Tom Roberts. He was one of the best of our managers. It was obvious this move was going to have a major effect on the sales force in Tom's office and my office. Don McNary, president of the company, was having problems of his own plus health problems. I am only revealing situations such as this in this book because its design is for generations of family members as opposed to a book one finds on the bookshelf of a bookstore. Family members need to know and be alert in the days ahead that no matter how good a reputation a company has, it is the people and leadership that make the difference. It will help the reader to know there were two important events in 1980–81. Interest rates on home mortgages skyrocketed. The rates reached a maximum of 21 percent. Qualifying buyers became a major problem. Real estate agents left the business in droves as many did beginning in 2008 when real estate values began to plummet.

The second event was that the home office of Coldwell Banker finally realized that Bob Rathburn was going to bankrupt the Washington company. Bob had been a problem at the headquarters in California. He was made a special projects man instead of terminating his employment. His move to Washington on a special project to get him out of the home office was a mistake. You need to know that both governments and corporations often take this approach. Even church denominations use this approach rather than facing the situation and removing people from responsible positions. It is much like a democracy such as ours in America. We most always do what is right after we have done what is wrong. Coldwell Banker finally removed Bob Rathburn. The last report available is that his wife divorced him. He moved in with his sister and played pool on skid row in San Francisco.

I contacted my regional manager the first week of August 1980 and informed him that my last day as manager would be August 31. The gross profit of my office for August exceeded the next highest office in the company by just over $10,000. I was not with the company at the meeting on early September during reporting. My companion managers gave a standing ovation in my honor, and Bob Rathburn left the room. The monthly gross profit of the Andrews office for August 1980 never was equaled or surpassed as of mid- June 1997 when we moved to Colorado according to my fellow managers.

My office staff and sales force gave Shirley and me a nice luncheon and a picnic table and even gave us the leftover funds collected from the agents as an extra bonus. They also made a poster for us signed with nice messages by all of the agents.

I had retired once from the air force. Now at age 53, I was not ready to retire. My activity picked up with the Lions Club, and I became the club president. Activity with the Christian Business Men's Committee also picked up, as I became a regional chairman of the Maryland CMBC. Gideon functions increased as Shirley was now a member, and I was chaplain. Prince George's County honored me for Community Service Award, and I also activated my broker license and formed a company, Friendly Properties. Many sales agents placed their license with me for referral purposes as they left the mainline companies. Other companies paid my company a referral commission on successfully settled properties. I paid the sales associate who did the referring 75 percent of the commission. No one, including me, became rich; it was a tool to take advantage of personal customers. We did not solicit business. Don McNary's executive vice president Leonard Whittaker got a belly full of Coldwell Banker, and he hung his license with me for a long while until he went to work for Town and Country Realtors.

Dick Caruso came from another company to become president of the now faltering Washington company. My former assistant manager Tom Pauling, manager of the Gaithersburg office, became regional manager. Ernie LaValley, manager of the Oxon Hill office, developed a serious illness and retired. Tom called me and said, "A new breeze was blowing in the company."

CHAPTER FORTY

Kenneth's Second Start in Real Estate

om Pauling sent a beautiful letter to me when I retired from Coldwell Banker on August of 1980. He felt that I had been responsible for the change in his career path. Tom, recently promoted to regional manager on the departure of Bob Rathburn, invited me to talk with the newly appointed president, Mr. Richard "Dick" Caruso, of the Coldwell Banker headquarters. Tom told him about me when Dick asked him how he got into real estate and management in particular. Tom was young and not very popular with several of the older managers. I recall those days back in the 1940s when I was a young service manager in Dallas' largest service station.

Ernest LaValley was branch manager of the Oxon Hill office. We had both been managing sister offices for three years in the 1970s. I filled in for Ernie a few times when he went on vacation and ran both offices. Ernie was in my Lions Club. Illness caught up with him, and it appeared that he would not be coming back to work. In fact, the office had been running by itself, and it gave the appearance that Satan was in charge. Ernie wanted to hold on until the end of the year and declared his retirement date as December 31, 1982. Tom asked me if I would effectively take over as of November and be declared the new manager on January 1.

I took the job and was back in the saddle again. Ernest "Mack" McCready continued to manage my old Andrews office.

We talked often, compared notes, held each other's hand on office problems, etc. Sometimes we toured homes together with both offices and went to regional manager meetings together. Ernie LaValley died a few months later, and I made sure that his wife received all of the commission overrides on transactions that had originated while Ernie was the manager, even though Ernie, for the most part, was not even involved with the sales.

Since I began to fill in unofficially as manager on November 1, 1982, I began to organize a Christmas party for the office early in December. In fact, it was on my fifty-sixth birthday, December 5. Our invitations went out to all of the surrounding real estate companies. I recall putting a footnote on the invitation to Nyman Realtors to the effect, their agents sold thirty-six of our listings during the year; how about bringing your whole office over to our party and let's celebrate? Ed Forman was one of the branch managers for Nyman.

Ed did bring about half of the agents from his branch office over and joined our Christmas party. I have a vivid recollection of the next event. On January 17, 1983, Ed Forman was sitting in a chair in front of my desk asking if he could move his real estate license to my office. I was shocked! Ed explained that his office was the top producing office for Nyman Realty who had five offices. He had just come from the annual awards meeting. There was no mention that his office was the top producing office in all areas of sales, listings, listings sold, and dollar volume. He was disappointed and was ready to make a move.

I hired Ed Forman on the spot and made him my assistant manager. When Ed came to the office the next day, five of Nyman's top sales agents followed him in the door. I hired all five. Then in the days to follow, one by one, sometimes two by two, real estate agents either from his old office on one of the other Nyman offices came migrating to my office.

By the end of the first quarter of 1983, our Oxon Hill office led the other thirty-two of our offices in listings, listings sold, and sales. We never lost that status throughout all of 1983. There were plaques for each of these items that we had to take to each quarterly meeting so they could be inscribed and given to the appropriate office. We brought them back to our office each quarter.

When the end of the year awards were presented, it took both me and Ed on the stage to hold the Top Listing, Top Listings Sold, Top Sales, and Top Gross Commission awards.

Our agents were on their feet applauding. One of our sales associates won a $2,500-worth trip. That was Jules Bloomberg. There were other awards I cannot remember. Our year-end office Christmas parties drew sales associates from many of our Coldwell Banker offices as well as most all of our neighboring real estate offices. Ed suggested that we bring in a seafood guy who shucked oysters and placed them on ice. One of our agents smoked turkeys and hams, and our agents brought in a variety of food items.

The Oxon Hill office was the first prototype office, like those in California where the home office was located. So it is the only earthquake-proof building in the area. It did not have a coat closet because they do not wear coats in Southern California.

Ed had a number of management experiences with Coldwell Banker before becoming president of Watson Real Estate headquartered in Jacksonville, Florida. Shirley and I visited Ed and Evelyn several years ago in their lovely home. At that time, Watson was a forty-five-office company. We are still in contact from time to time as Facebook friends. It was as real treat to meet Mr. Watson and many of the sales associates as Ed enjoyed telling them all that I had been his second boss in real estate.

Bob Eul, the brother of the first broker I worked for, Larry Eul, came to my office looking for a job. He had been working for Larry and Bert. I hired Bob. He was an excellent listing agent and had a good following of past clients. Months later, he became ill. Bob died following a brief illness. His death was rather sudden. Bob had a number of open transactions and several listed properties. Ed volunteered to take over his business and handled every settlement. Ed refused to take any part of Bob's commission. Ed was probably the busiest agent in the office at the time with his own business. Bob's widow was then recipient of over $8,000 in real estate commissions that settled during his illness and following Bob's death.

Larry and Bert Eul learned of our actions and Ed's efforts through Bob's widow. They paid a visit to my office to talk about it. There were tears in Bert Eul's eyes. I think this took its toll on them as Bob told me that he never received a penny for any of the transactions he left behind when he joined my office.

Some changes were taking place in our company in 1984. Sears became our new owner. They purchased Coldwell Banker, and we were now Sears's employees with about all of the benefits Sears offered. Sears owned Coldwell Banker beyond my retirement date before they sold it. So I retired from Sears's employment.

On August 1, 1985, I began a new job as a management consultant for Coldwell Banker Residential Affiliates. Coldwell Banker had been selling franchises to independent real estate companies across the country. Although I was an assistant vice president of the company-owned Washington-based organization, the company needed consultants to work with these newly acquired affiliates in the northeast division. My new office was at 1901 Beauguard Street, Alexandria, Virginia.

A quick review of the next five years is that I was promoted to regional manager on August 1, 1988, and became the senior management consultant on August 1, 1989, for thirteen states from Virginia to Maine, where I had twelve business consultants who serviced 223 independent affiliate Coldwell Banker offices in those states. During the company convention at Las Vegas, Nevada, I received the National Management Consultant award for all four regions in the USA, Canada, and Puerto Rico for the year 1987. Our daughter, Linda, flew in to join me for the presentation.

I turned down the position of management services director for the northeastern division in favor of retirement on December 31, 1990.

It would take another book to cover this part of the details of the five years spent in this role of my real estate career. Traveling four to five days a week, I made many new friends who were company owners, managers, and sales associates. Some continue to contact me some twenty-five years after I retired from Coldwell Banker. Brian Donovan in Pittsford, New York, and J. P. Vaughan in Lynchburg, Virginia, are two examples.

If we ever plan to finish this book, we better just jump to the retirement years.

CHAPTER FORTY-ONE

Kenneth and Shirley's Retirement Years

O n January 1, 1991, I looked in the mirror and said to myself, "Ken, you are looking at your staff." We are writing this chapter in 2015 about twenty-five years following my third retirement.

It has been a great twenty-five years for Shirley and me.

In addition to forty-four videos that capture major trips we have taken, our lives have been filled with voluntary service including our churches in three locations. Also, there were the various organizations we are members of, such as Lions Clubs International, the Gideons International, Christian Business Men's Committee, Masonic Fraternity, etc. Voluntary jail and prison counseling began while I was still working on July 4, 1978, and continued until we departed Colorado in 2013.

We will not be covering all of our travels in detail. This book is primarily written for family and extended family members. Children, grandchildren, great-grandchildren, and those family members to follow may someday choose to view the videos and learn about our travels. The videos serve to settle disagreements about when and where certain events took place. They are also a great aid to our memories.

Our travels during the years 1991–1996 assisted us greatly in helping us decide where we would like to spend part of our retirement. Asbury Solomon's retirement facility was being constructed in southern Maryland during these years, and it opened in 1996. We kept our eyes on this facility as it continued to grow. Several years, later we signed up on the waiting list. We loved the location near Solomon's Island, Maryland.

We visited a few residents there in the early days of operation and kept this United Methodist facility, a branch of Asbury in Gaithersburg, Maryland, in mind for our later years. We were not ready to select a final home as we were only in our early seventies.

Our oldest daughter, Linda, was living in New Mexico. Our youngest daughter, Vikki, was living in Southern California. Linda was a career government employee of the United States Air Force at Kirtland Air Force Base, Albuquerque, New Mexico. Vikki was a registered nurse at Antelope Valley Hospital near Lancaster, and she lived in Palmdale, California. Vikki was married to Robert Powell, and Bernt R. Powell was born in 1993.

I felt a call to move to Grand Junction, Colorado. We did not know a single person there, although we had visited the area when we lived in Denver, Colorado, from 1961–66. Grand Junction was a day's drive from Albuquerque and a day and half from Palmdale. Grand Junction also had an airport, bus and train stations, and a couple of hospitals, and its size seemed to be just right for a city where we were interested in spending a few years. This would place us close enough to visit our daughters and watch our grandson Bernt grow up.

On one of our trips from Maryland to California, Shirley mentioned that she would like to see a big flattop mountain and a monument she had read about. We took a side trip from Interstate 70 and drove part of the way up toward the Grand Mesa, the world's largest flattop mountain. We only went up about halfway to the top because we wanted to have enough time to see the Colorado monument.

We looked for the Colorado monument all the way through the twenty-three-mile road, not realizing that we were in it all the way.

Living in the Washington DC area for thirty years, our view of a monument was along the lines of the Washington Monument or the Lincoln or Jefferson Memorials.

In another one of our cross-country trips in 1995, we stopped by the Coldwell Banker Homeowners real estate company in Grand Junction. We were assigned to realtor Paul Nelson. He gave us a nice tour of all of the area, showing us one home in each of the areas. We explained to Paul that if we selected Grand Junction, it would be the following year before we would purchase a home.

We subscribed to the Sunday edition of the local newspaper to observe over a period of six months, both the news and home listings. We arranged a timeshare for a week at Powderhorn Ski Resort about halfway up on the Grand Mesa. We let Paul know our plans and scheduled an appointment to look at homes. When we arrived at the timeshare unit in April, snow was up to our knees. A path to our unit had been cleared. I called Paul and asked if he showed homes in the snow. He chuckled a little and told me there was no snow there. It was only twenty miles away, I thought, how could there not be snow when it was knee deep where we were just twenty miles away?

During our first day of house hunting, Paul began to see what we were interested in, so he could eliminate and reschedule additional showings. He gave us an opportunity to see one or two homes in each of the major areas. On our way to the timeshare, we were going through the process of eliminating homes, and we passed up our exit to Powderhorn. We learned how important it was not to miss this exit as it was miles through the canyon, tunnels, etc., before we had an opportunity to turn around.

By the end of our second day of house hunting, we had looked at a total of twenty-one homes. We narrowed our selection to three and placed an offer on our first choice. We had decided that if our offer was not accepted, we would place an offer on our second choice, a new home under construction.

The owners of our first choice accepted our offer and invited us out to explain all of the features. The home was in a new subdivision known as Alpine Meadows and was the last home to be built in that development. It had a rock yard. That was a feature I looked forward to after mowing some fifteen acres for several years. The owners explained that it was their retirement home, purchased only six months earlier. Following a number of upgrades to get the home just like they wanted it, both of their children's jobs moved to Fort Collins. They had no reason to stay in Grand Junction, so they put their house on the market. Our timing suited them as they wanted to settle the next month. Settlement was set for May 31, 1997, and we returned home to prepare for the move. Our loan was approved in a very short time, and they asked if we could settle early. We did the settlement by mail on May 16, paying $157,500 for the home at 2688 Amber Way, Grand Junction, Colorado.

We learned from our former neighbors Betty and Harold Brauer that our former pastor and his wife lived in Grand Junction. We contacted Reverend Walter and Pat Boigraine who had also retired in Grand Junction. He was a pastor for most of the five years we lived in Westminster, from 1961–66.

We also learned from our daughter Linda that Evie Smith, a good friend of her husband's, lived in Grand Junction. We met her only briefly at Linda and Gene Stillman's wedding in New Mexico. Evie was a great friend, and we enjoyed her all of the years we spent in Colorado. These were the only two we knew in Colorado when we moved into our almost new home.

That changed fast. We had the greatest number of longtime friends we have ever had in our married life. We had superb neighbors, especially to our immediate left, the Cummings, and to our right, the Partees.

During the next several weeks, we visited several churches. The first visit was to Crossroads United Methodist about six miles from our home. We had stopped there while house hunting as they were sponsoring a health day, and we went through the process. Some of the health findings were to be available in a few weeks, so we took advantage of those various tests, knowing that we would be back for the results. Following a series of visits to local churches, several of them much closer to our home, we selected Crossroads UMC as our home church and moved our membership from Providence United Methodist Church in Friendly, Maryland.

Crossroads UMC at the corner of 30 Road and Patterson Avenue was a good choice for us for the next fifteen years. I became a member of the finance committee, and Shirley joined one of the United Methodist circles. Pastor Doug McKee was not friendly to the Gideon's ministry, but I made a point of being friendly to him. He developed an illness and called on me to sit with him before he died. Our friendship and relationship grew, and he would have asked me to do a Gideon report if he lived longer. His wife was also a minister in nearby Fruita, Colorado. I learned that it was the two of them who turned off the ministers on the Gideons in the other four United Methodist churches in the area. It took five years to restore that relationship in four of the churches. The ministers in the fifth church never agreed to a Gideon report. Following pastors, Dr. Wesley Kendall and Reverend Karen Hurst, were great supporters of the ministry. We had many joint activates, church services, and good times together.

Upon receipt of a change of address, the Gideons automatically updated a member to the Gideon camp serving the area near where a Gideon has moved. Since membership is with the international office, it never changes. We were assigned to the one and only camp in Grand Junction at that time. We were heartily received by the camp members. Grand Junction had been selected as the location for the next Gideon state convention. Irving "Irv" Johnson was the camp president. I announced to Irv that since I had been on the Gideon cabinet for nineteen straight years, I really needed to rest for a year from an appointed position, but I was readily available to help in any area I was needed.

Ed and Elaine Morris had been given the responsibility of chairing the upcoming state convention. They were busy local business owners. They were glad to find someone with knowledge of the ministry, so we had plenty to do in a hurry. The local jail ministry included two Gideons and three ladies.

Clarence McClelland and Paul von Guerard made visits to the Mesa County Correctional Facility. Clarence's wife, Phyllis, graded Bible lessons turned in by inmates Clarence visited. Two Gideon auxiliary ladies, Cynthia Whittier and Glena Barger, visited the female inmates. They were assisted by another lady named Ruth. Clarence learned that I had twenty years of jail and prison ministry that I thought I had retired from before coming to Colorado. He was desperate for help, knowing that his health was beginning to fail.

I applied for the various things that have to take place before one is permitted the clearances necessary to do jail ministry. This took a few months. I began to recruit some additional help when I learned that Clarence was having health problems, and the need was so great that he had only been scratching the surface of what was needed at the local jail. We began to do church services one Sunday a month. We followed up with counseling visits to those who signed up for a visit. We had so many requests that Clarence and I were visiting at least once during every week. Paul Vonguerard was still working, but he did one, sometimes two, of the Sunday church services as we had several areas to cover.

I kept a notebook record of visits and church services for the balance of time we lived in Grand Junction which resulted in filling ten full notebooks. Clarence's health reached the point that he could not find his way out of the correctional facility. There were six areas where inmates were housed. It was going to be hard to convince Clarence to give up making visits, but he recognized that he had to take a lesser role—that of helping his wife grade the Bible studies. These studies were increasing in number as I had now recruited more help. One of the very best helpers recruited was a new Gideon, Ben Mosbey. Another Gideon, Richard Montgomery, transferred into Grand Junction with prior experience in jail ministry. Richard was a great team member for both Sunday church services, morning and evening, and one-on-one counseling.

Our team grew to eight Gideons and three auxiliary ladies. I selected Paul von Guerard to replace me as team leader when we left Colorado. All indications are that the team is active and still growing stronger in service to the Lord.

Dr. Rev. Wes Kendall became our pastor at Crossroads United Methodist Church. His wife, Betty, also became ordained after they arrived. Shirley and I had been members of the evangelism committee headed up by Ben and Sandy Mosbey. Upon completion of their term, the committee was merged with the membership committee as one membership and evangelism committee. Pastor Wes Kendall convinced us to head up the new committee. By now, we were both presidents of our Gideon camp which had been split into two camps. The Grand Mesa camp and the Colorado monument camp became the camps serving Grand Junction. We were in the Colorado monument camp as we lived in the area west of Twelfth Street, the dividing line that connects to Horizon Drive in the north part of the city.

The communications division of the United Methodist Church in Nashville, Tennessee had just kicked off a program encouraging churches to participate as a welcoming congregation church. We decided to participate. Qualifying required the successful completion of a series of specific events and activities that could be measured and documented. Crossroads became the first church in the Rocky Mountain conference to qualify.

We were well into qualifying the second year before the congregation realized this process was bringing in new members, especially those families new to the area who spent time visiting various churches to find a church home.

By the third and fourth year of qualifying, we had an active and vibrant congregation eager to participate as they could see the positive results of being a certified welcoming congregation. It was in the fifth year that we were classified as a Millennium Certified Church. Dr. Rev. Wes Kendall and Pastor Betty Kendall accepted an assignment at a church in Cheyenne, Wyoming. Rev. Karen Hurst became our new pastor. Although we had served four years as chairs of the membership and evangelism committee, we elected to serve one more year to assist Pastor Karen in becoming established. She leaned on us in several different areas for a few years, and we enjoyed assisting her wherever we could. We learned that she was born at the same time we were on our honeymoon, so we knew how old she was, and she always knew how long we had been married. She served the church until her retirement which took place shortly after we left Colorado.

Serving the Lord through the Gideons' ministry during the years we were in Grand Junction, Colorado, resulted in many long- term friends not just in Grand Junction but also all across the state of Colorado. In addition to serving in various offices of the local Gideon camp, we had assignments as zone leaders for a few camps in our area. We also served on the state cabinet as area directors. Our area of responsibility covered one-third of the state of Colorado.

We had areas in Colorado that bordered on New Mexico, Utah, Wyoming, Nebraska, and Kansas, including seventeen Gideon camps. We were chairs of the state convention on two different occasions when it was held in Grand Junction. We also participated in international convention in Denver, Dallas, and Kansas City while living in Grand Junction.

We were blessed by bringing in new members to the Gideons' ministry. Many have become lifetime friends, as well as those who were well established in the camps all across the state of Colorado.

Giving a report in many different churches in the metropolitan area resulted in personal relationships with pastors and members in those churches. Multiple opportunities to speak in many churches over the fifteen years we lived in Colorado were a blessing. I would love to mention all of the names of all of these good friends. Since this is primarily a family history book, we will abstain from doing that.

Our Gideon families from both local camps joined together to give us a going-away party. They invited some special guests from other Gideon camps. Jerry and Donna Swanson in Fort Collins were our Colorado state Gideon presidents. Gary and Lisa Coram, vice presidents who lived in Montrose, were very special friends who wanted to be a part of our last meeting. We were honored by having in excess of two hundred Bibles placed in recognition of our time in Colorado by these faithful friends. Our Gideon Camp Presidents, Lew and Mary Lucas, along with Camp Officers, Mike and Lonnie Kohl, Donna and Lyn St. Peter and others from both local Gideon Camps made us feel very special.

In preparing to return to Maryland, we had placed ourselves on the waiting list with Katie Crane at Asbury Solomon continuing care facility, Solomons, Maryland, some three years earlier. We were informed by Katie Crane in the sales office that we were now eligible to be placed on the ready list.

Paul Nelson of Coldwell Banker Homeowners Realtors was just as ready to assist us in selling our home as he was in assisting us in finding just the right home when we arrived.

This was a time in 2013 when a lot of homes were on the market for months before a sale was consummated. We asked Paul to come tell us what needed to be done to sell our home. Two weeks later, our home went on the market. Buyers were found in three weeks, and they wanted the home within thirty days. Paul brought us a full-price contract from a qualified buyer for the listed price of $219,900. Through the help of many friends and a team headed up by Ben Mosbey, we began the process of emptying out our three-bedroom home with a three-car garage. We selected a one- bedroom apartment with a den and a living room at the retirement community in Solomons, Maryland. None of our children lived close enough to take any of our excess items. Through the masterful skills of Ben Mosbey, an expert yard sale man, skilled in all of the little details of dressing up a house by correcting things I could not even see and expert at packing, we made the deadline settlement date.

Our grandson Bryan Kenneth and his son, Jacob Kenneth, flew in right on time to pick up the truck that he and Ben loaded with the help of Ben's wife, Sandy, his daughter, Pam, and her two children, Noah and Ciera.

Following an overnight stay with our friend Betty Brauer in Westminster, Colorado, we departed for Maryland on Easter Sunday.

CHAPTER FORTY-TWO

The Hardest Move We Ever Made

We made many moves during our twenty-five years in the United States Air Force in our much younger days with the help of the air force. We did not anticipate all that was involved in downsizing from a three-bedroom space to a one-bedroom apartment with a den, a living room and, a kitchen. We had less than thirty days to leave a clean home ready for new occupants. One of our Gideon camp members, Jerry Hooven, a skilled painter, made the house look new.

Fortunately, we had a lot of help. We advertised several items. We sold Shirley's 1997 Buick, some furniture, exercise equipment, outside grill, etc. All items were priced to sell, and sell they did. Three Gideon families, each with a truck, showed up and loaded items and delivered them to purchasers. These were Mike and Lonnie Kohl, Len and Donna St. Peter, and Richard and Linda Long. Our very good friend and former jail minister team member, Ben Mosbey, took items to sell for us in a yard sale at his home. The Mosbey family came to help us pack. They cleaned, repaired nail holes, painted areas where items had been removed, shampooed carpet, and brought along supplies to do everything that needed to be done. Some items required special packing arrangements. Ben seemed to know just what to do.

Our grandson Bryan, who had helped his dad move us from Maryland to Colorado, flew in with his son, Jacob, to move us back to Maryland. The entire Mosbey family assisted in loading the truck. It took the combined skill and knowledge of Ben, assisted by Bryan, to make the contents fit into the truck. Although the Mosbey family did not want us to leave, we know that we would never have been able to leave a clean house and make the scheduled settlement date without them. We will forever be grateful to all of the friends in Colorado who saw us off. We felt like dragging our feet all the way to Maryland.

Bryan and Jake left a day ahead of us. We made one last stop in Westminster, Colorado, to visit Betty Brauer, a former neighbor of ours when we lived there over fifty years ago. We made a few more stops on the way to Maryland as we felt this may be our last trip by car over some of these routes. My nephew David Ross and his wife, Donna, in Valley Falls, Kansas; and my niece Anne Doughty and her husband, Walter, in Ohio were happy that we included them in our stops along the way. Longtime friend Bessie Suckling in Marietta, Ohio, appreciated that we included her in one stop. We spent the night with Paul and Bobbie Drews in Clarksburg, West Virginia, before arriving in Maryland.

Settlement on our new retirement home in Solomons, Maryland was scheduled for April 19, 2013. The truck with our belongings was parked in our grandson's large parking lot. We were fortunate to have the run of Larry and Ginger's home while we visited friends and relatives prior to moving into our apartment at Asbury Solomons in Maryland. We arranged with Rev. Stephen Ricketts for the transfer of our membership back to Providence Fort Washington United Methodist church in Friendly, Maryland.

We were also fortunate to have the help of family members to move items from the truck. Excess boxes were stored in a steel shed on the farm where our son's commercial interior electrical company is located.

The next day was Saturday, and we had loads of help to unpack boxes and set up our bed and other furniture items. Larry and Ginger and their daughter-in-law Angela seem to know where everything should go. Granddaughter Wendy took over the kitchen. Her husband, James Crampton, assisted in shopping for a TV, setting up the stand, and connecting all of the electronic equipment. We just stood by in a daze and watched it all unfold. Dennis Poremski, director of wellness, arranged for the dining room to provide sandwiches, cookies, and water. Other grandparents kept the great-grandchildren.

We had arranged to take the crew to Stoney's, one of the famous seafood restaurants on Solomon Islands a couple of miles away. None of us knew that this was the opening day of the tiki bar on the island. Cars were lined up all over the island. As we circled the island looking for a parking place, our granddaughter Wendy flagged us down and took our car to a parking place. The restaurant was practically empty, enabling us to relax and enjoy what was first of many family gatherings. We enjoyed treating everyone to their favorite seafood dish as we watched the ducks swim by. Our daughter-in-law, Ginger, seemed to know just what was missing in our new apartment. She and her daughter-in-law, Angela, went shopping. They came home with a food pantry and a special coffee maker. Granddaughter Wendy had filled up all of our cabinets and announced there is no place to store your food. This was primarily because we brought some kitchen items we did not need. Now it was time to adjust to a new way of life.

We are part of a complex of over 70 cottages and over 120 apartments in addition to a restaurant, grill and pub, auditorium, assistant living, and health care center. There are many different designs and sizes. We chose an apartment size and design called the Calvert. The facility is located in Calvert County, Maryland. It is in a constant state of being upgraded since it opened in 1996, so we will not try to describe it in detail. You can see it at HYPERLINK "http://www.AsburySolomons.org/" www. HYPERLINK "http://www.AsburySolomons.org/" AsburySolomons.org. We, along with over four hundred others, adjust right along with the improvements.

Quality residents and staff have to be one of the most important values available to us. We enjoy pastoral services, devotions, and weekly vesper services. They make being fifty miles away from our home church bearable. As we grow older, assisted living and health care may become more important to us, along with skilled nursing—all of which are available under one roof. There are many opportunities to volunteer in areas that may be of interest. We enjoy the variety of a restaurant, grill, and pub services and club room, and we participate regularly, enjoying a variety of dining experiences.

Being only fifty miles away from our son, his wife, Ginger, grandson Bryan, his wife, Angela, and granddaughter Wendy, her husband, James, and our four great-grandchildren adds value to our new way of life.

We have accepted responsible positions at both Asbury Solomons and with the Gideons. We do have some limitations, and as those increase in the days ahead, our activity will no doubt decrease accordingly. God has been exceedingly good to us. It has been our pleasure to start a new way of life. We have adjusted well the last six years, and this year of 2019, at ninety-two and ninety-three, with seventy years of marriage behind us, we think the future is bright for the days ahead.

CHAPTER FORTY-THREE

A Letter from Mom and Dad

In many ways, this book is a letter from us to you, our children. It is also for your spouses and children and future generations. Nephews, nieces, great-nephews and great-nieces, as well as for our many friends.

It is the type of book we would have loved to have had from our ancestors on both sides. Through the years, we have often talked about the influence our parents made in our lives. We were taught to take responsibility for our actions. Their strong Christian faith was a model for us. We will try to answer some questions from both our family members and our friends, so our answers may become a little personal.

December 2, 2015, marked our sixty-sixth anniversary. Family and friends have asked us about that, and we will try to respond. During the year before our marriage, we learned there were many things we both liked and enjoyed doing together. Others came about after marriage.

Some things that we jointly did not like also played an important role in our lifestyle. For example, we did not like to be quarrelsome with each other. Paul also points this out in 2 Timothy 2:24. We did not, and still do not, like some commercials that play on stupidity, crime, disobedience, vulgarity, and bad motives and do not reflect Christ-like character.

We both were early church members with a strong sense of

faith that has consistently grown over the years. This contributed to our activity in various churches where we lived and organizations and fraternities such as the Lions Clubs International, the Gideons International, Christian Business Men and Women Committees, Masonic Fraternity, and Eastern Star to name a few. We have most often been active and never passive members in church and in these organizations.

We generally agree on most items such as food, sports, music, radio and TV programs, cars, clothes, and devotional material. We enjoyed travel and visited all fifty states and several oceans and foreign countries. Our children would probably say it was useless to get us to pit one against the other on just about any subject.

The power of the Holy Spirit was conveyed upon us at the same time on April 7, 1977, at the altar of a little country church in Friendly, Maryland. It has been our goal not to quench the Spirit since that time (1 Thessalonians 5:19).

Beginning with Shirley's ninety-fourth birthday on October 14 and my ninety-third birthday on December 5, 2019, we have been asked about the secret of our longevity. A lifestyle of moderation in all things and a desire to follow God's plan (Jeremiah 29:11) for our life have generated many great friends for whom we have a strong compassion for as well as a desire to keep in touch.

If you find that Christianity exhausts you, draining you of your energy, then you are practicing religion rather than enjoying a relationship with Jesus Christ. Your walk with the Lord will not make you weary; it will invigorate you, restore your strength, and energize your life (Matthew 11:28–29).

"If you confess with your mouth the Lord Jesus and believe in your heart that God has raised Him from the dead, you will be saved" (Romans 10:9, NKJV).

We pray that the world will be different for future generations. Today—in a world where role models are entertainers, athletes, and politicians, many of whom lack morals, integrity, and even common decency ... in a world where few seem to stand for anything unless it is to stand for selfish, self-serving rights ... in a world where anything is compromised if it impedes success ... in a world where some care more about public opinion than about what God thinks ... in a world where what is right is what works or what feels good ... in a world where character no longer seems to count—in such a world, the testimony of one life lived for Christ is powerful! One life cleansed through faith in the blood of Jesus. One life that confesses "Jesus is Lord." One life that has the courage to stand for godly convictions in the midst of moral compromise. One life that lives and tells the truth—you can be that one life!

However, do not be deceived into assuming God is more interested in your activity for Him than He is in the condition of your heart. King Saul offered sacrifices, hoping God would overlook his disobedience (1 Samuel 15:22–23). Ananias and Sapphira thought that their generous gift to the church would compensate for their deceitfulness (Acts 5:1–11). Finally, no amount of activity for God will ever take the place of a heart that is right with Him.

"And what does the LORD require of you but to do justly, to love mercy, and to walk humbly with your God?" (Micah 6:8, NKJV)

SECTION FIVE

Photos

Annie Elizabeth (Ruble) & John Newton
Deal, Jr., Wedding (cir. 1898)

Ken's Lucas, Texas Farm

Emma & Millard Dennison
Shirley's Grandparents

Sarah Frances

Shirley's Grandparents, William & Sarah Taylor.

Reggie, Shirley's Father

Edith   Clara   Beulah   Raleigh   Bernice   Calvin

Percy   Sara Ellen   William   Irma   Mae

Grandma & Grandpa Taylor, Linda and Larry

Linda 14, Larry 12 Vikki 3, Shirley & Ken

Ken's Brother Jack, Sisters, Ruth, Tony, Beatrice

Larry & Ginger Deal

Vikki Kay & Rob Powell

Bryan & Angela Deal

Linda & Gene Stillman

Vikki & Mike Murphy

James & Wendy Crampton

Ken & Shirley Deal with our Four Great Grand Kids, Dylan, Wyatt, Taylor & Jake

"Deal family, ages from 4 to 94 at 70th Anniversary, October 26, 2020."

Ken, Shirley, Larry, Ginger, Jake Angela, Bryan, Taylor Deal - Wendy, Wyatt, Dylan, James Crampton

Ken & Shirley's Old Fort Rd. Friendly, MD Home
1956-1997

Linda's Mountain Home, Las Vegas, New Mexico

Daughter Linda Stillman's Mountain House, Linda lives Las Vegas, Nevada

1952 Ford (8N) All kids and grandkids learned to drive on this machine

Cir. 1840 Home of Great Grandfather Capt George W. Deal near Marshall, MO in Saline County, MO

Great-great Grandpa George and Rebecca Deal's Farm, Saline, CO, MO

Ken's only Niece, Anne, with husband Walter Doughty

Ken & Shirley taking Cousins Jean Smith and Carolyn on a ten state tour of the West

Ken's Gideon Bible Dedication Team, Grand Junction, Colorado

Ken & Shirley Deal, Larry & Ginger Deal with Anne & Walter Doughty's Family 2013

45 years following retirement, Ken can still get into his uniform in 2015.

Coldwell Banker Real Estate's National Business Management Consultant Award 1987

George W. Deal (1812-1884)
Ken's Great Grandfather

Ken's great grandmother
Rebecca Coyner Deal (1815-1899)

Front Row: Jacob Kenneth, Shirley, Ken Deal, Bernt Powell
Second Row: Ginger, Vikki, Angela, Wendy, Linda
Back Row: Larry & Bryan Deal, James Crampton

Gideon Friends, Malcolm & Annette Fun with the Deals at Gideons International Convention

322

Shirley Deal at Country Store built by her Father, Reggie Taylor in the 1930's

Larry Kenneth and Bryan Kenneth only trusted us in the parking lot

Linda & Pedro

Larry & Ginger's Mountain Home, Berkley Springs, WVA
Larry's Harley

Chaplain Lt Col Bennet, Delbert & Kitty Owen, Ken & Shirley Deal, Dec 2, 1949

Ken & Shirley Deal following the wedding in the Base Chapel, Offutt Air Force Base, Nebraska

Shenandoah Valley, VA visitors Jean & Carolyn and Stu and Marion Garber

Papa Dennison, Shirley's Grandfather

"Shirley's last visit with her four great grandchildren."

CPSIA information can be obtained
at www.ICGtesting.com
Printed in the USA
LVHW011258150622
721325LV00016B/873